BIG MONEY IN REAL ESTATE FORECLOSURES

BIG MONEY IN REAL ESTATE FORECLOSURES

Ted Thomas

John Wiley & Sons, Inc.

New York   •   Chichester   •   Brisbane   •   Toronto   •   Singapore

Library of Congress Cataloging-in-Publication Data

Thomas, Ted, 1939–
    Big money in real estate foreclosures / by Ted Thomas.
      p.   cm.
    Includes index.
    ISBN 0-471-54859-6 (cloth : alk. paper)—
  ISBN 0-471-54860-X (pbk. : alk. paper)
    1. Real estate investment. 2. Foreclosure. I. Title.
  HD1382.5.T56 1991
  332.63'24—dc20   91–15586

Contents

Preface

Foreclosure property offers profits, opportunity, and financial independence for those willing to learn, innovate, and put to use the rules, procedures, and systems contained in this book.

For whatever reason—financial difficulties, divorce, job transfer, changes in the economic conditions, or bankruptcy—foreclosures continue to rise nationwide.

According to a recent survey conducted by the Department of Housing and Urban Development (HUD), foreclosures within that agency increased from 27,772 in 1983 to 72,000 in 1990.

The Department of Veterans Affairs (VA) recently confirmed that it had more than 30,000 homes in its foreclosure inventory. It also confirmed that its foreclosures were increasing. In 1980, the VA foreclosed on 10,254 properties and the latest figures show an increase to 38,000 in 1990. These properties do not include the thousands of homes foreclosed upon at local Sheriff's and Trustee's Sales.

This book discusses how to locate and purchase these bargain properties—either prior to auction or at the Trustee's Sale. In a special section, the book also describes how to locate the properties that the banks have foreclosed upon and now hold as part of an unproductive inventory, the thousands upon thousands of what the banks and industry professionals call REO (Real Estate Owned).

Chapter by chapter, *Big Money in Real Estate Foreclosures* tells you what you need to know in order to successfully buy and sell real estate in the foreclosure market:

- Finding promising properties
- Using direct mail effectively
- Reading contracts, titles, and deeds
- Understanding inspection reports
- Negotiating with sellers
- Purchasing at a good price
- Obtaining financing and working with bankers
- Rehabilitating the property
- Targeting advertising to attract buyers
- Selling the property for a profit
- Avoiding the pitfalls.

This volume is unlike any other in the foreclosure field. It is a guidebook for anyone who wants to be successful in this area, and is recommended for both beginners and professionals.

To help you further understand the world of foreclosure real estate, each chapter provides actual copies of the contracts, reports, and ads that are the tools of this trade. Case studies from Thomas' own experience bring to life how to locate, buy, and sell foreclosures.

Finally, so nothing is left to chance, he has reproduced the checklists and evaluation forms that will help you carefully plot your moves step by step.

Big Money in Real Estate Foreclosures arms you with all the knowledge and insight that took Ted Thomas years to develop and perfect.

Unlike many who tackle the foreclosure business with uncertainty and confusion, you will approach sellers or enter auctions with proven techniques and methods.

Beyond this wealth of information, however, the book provides guidance for that all-important step—your decision to enter this field.

Buying and selling foreclosures can be a profitable and recession-proof enterprise. Distressed real estate properties are available during good times and bad. Like any worthwhile business, it fulfills a need in the marketplace. It solves people's problems and it makes a profit for the entrepreneur.

But is it for you?

Big Money in Real Estate Foreclosures answers the questions that most people ask when considering a career:

- What type of person is best suited for this business?
- Is sales experience necessary?
- How much working capital will I need?
- Is this making money from someone else's misfortune?
- If it is legal and so profitable, why aren't more people taking advantage of this opportunity?
- How do I get my customers?
- Who will I sell to?
- How about financing?

What must you have to be successful in this field? Common sense, reading ability, and a small amount of cash will get you on your way. No special license or certification is required, and no large investment of time is necessary. You don't need employees or expensive office equipment—just pens, paper, envelopes, and stamps.

You can make money at this even if your resources are limited. I have watched dozens of Ted Thomas' students do it. It will just take a little longer.

Most of all you need patience and persistence—patience to learn how to do it and persistence to carry on until the pay off. There is a direct correlation between what you put into it and what you eventually get in return. With a conscientious effort, you should make between $100,000 and $250,000 a year.

HOWARD RUFF
PUBLISHER, *RUFFTIMES*

1

Problem Solving
for Big Profits

Helping Others Out of Trouble

Making profits from the purchase of distressed property is often a matter of how good you are at helping others out of trouble, understanding the needs and wants of the homeowner. In this chapter, you will learn:

- The reasons for foreclosure
- How to purchase property before the foreclosure auction
- Making a win-win-win transaction
- Pitfalls to avoid—undisclosed taxes
- Understanding priority in the lien process—Who's on first?

Distressed property sales fall into three markets, depending on the particular stage of the foreclosure process: pre-foreclosure, Trustee's Sales, and REO. You can make money in all three markets.

You can buy from the property owner before the foreclosure auction, while the owner is in default. You can buy from the trustee at the Trustee's Sale, which is an auction. You can buy from the lender who has foreclosed and now has the property in his inventory, the REO. This book deals chiefly with the purchase of property during the time that the loan is in default, but before it has been foreclosed. The procedures involved in buying at Trustee's Sales are considered in Chapter 8, and the requirements for buying REO are discussed in Chapter 9.

HISTORY AND REASONS FOR FORECLOSURE

Foreclosures are not new; they go hand-in-hand with property ownership. However, only those few individuals who have the free time, energy, and commitment to research Notices of Default (NOD) and Trustee's Sales notices filed at the County Recorder's offices will know where to find the foreclosed properties, when the Trustee's Sales are scheduled, and how to follow up and whom to contact. (The files and the information are available to the public, but few people know how to take advantage of this fact. Commercial foreclosure/default services offer this access to anyone who wishes to subscribe to their service.) Foreclosures take place everywhere; in good economic times as well as in bad, in wealthy as well as in poor areas. Economic change does not restrict itself to any one category.

Divorce

Divorce is the most common reason for foreclosure. According to statistics, approximately 50 percent of all married women work full time. This extra income is significant, especially if both incomes were needed to purchase the house in which the couple lived. With half of all marriages ending in divorce, it is likely that we will continue to have foreclosure problems. A divorce usually leaves one person with insufficient income to support the same life style and make payments on the house.

The divorce may be clean or messy, often creating resentment and vindictiveness. If cool heads prevail, the home can be sold without too big a loss. When the partners begin to fight, no one makes the house payment. This can mean foreclosure and lost equity.

Unemployment

We all have friends, neighbors, or even relatives who have lost their jobs. Unemployment is no fun, not just because of the loss of income but also because of the loss of self-esteem. As the country changes from a labor economy to a service economy and computers change the ways in which we work, many more people will be displaced and require retraining.

The oil business is a good example of this change. In the 1980s, cities such as Houston and Denver have seen dramatic changes in the workforce. These changes caused widespread foreclosures. It is not uncommon to see half-page advertisements in *The Wall Street Journal* for 100 homes for sale, all foreclosures. Small towns that provide the workforce for major factories often see numerous foreclosures after a layoff or slowdown in the local industry. When major industries such as the automobile, oil, and aerospace industry have changes in policy, direction, or normal business cycles, there will be increased foreclosures.

Medical Problems

Medical bills must be paid or the treatment stops. Hospital and doctors' bills compete with house payments. When you are sick and you have no insurance, the situation can get out of control very quickly. Sickness or disability usually precede the loss of work. This is another of the prime reasons for foreclosure. The homeowner confronted with loss of income and large bills from doctors and hospitals is in deep trouble.

Death

Foreclosures may be a result of death. Without the breadwinner, who will pay the bills? If insurance is not forthcoming and friends and relatives cannot agree to make the payments, foreclosure is inevitable.

Balloon Payments

Balloon payments can trigger a foreclosure when they come due if the owner does not have the ability to refinance the property or pay off the debt. The value of the property may have deteriorated; interest rates might be too high for the owner to qualify for another loan; the owner might not be able to afford it. If the property has not appreciated as expected, the owner must sell or face foreclosure. Most prospective sellers wait until the last possible date and then find themselves facing foreclosure.

MAKING MONEY WHILE HELPING OTHERS OUT OF TROUBLE

Some Basic Questions and Answers

Most foreclosure sales are actually auctions, formally called *Trustee's Sales*. When a property owner has not honored his or her mortgage commitment or agreement, the lender can order the trustee (a third and neutral party between the lender and borrower) to sell the property at a public auction. If you bid at the auction for more than the sum owed on the property, the lender will usually accept your bid. Keep in mind that mortgage lenders are in the finance business, *not* the real estate business. They would sooner recover their financial losses (get the money back so that they can lend it out again) than hold out for a profit on the real estate.

Who are the winners and the losers at the foreclosure sales? Isn't the foreclosure buyer taking advantage of someone else?

If you buy from the owner before the sale or auction, the owner benefits. Although this sum will probably be less than the full market value of the property, it will be more than he or she would get at the auction because the lender will accept whatever bid will give the lender the most money. In order to get rid of the property, the lender may even accept a bid that does not cover the entire amount outstanding on the loan, having decided that he can write off at least part of it as a bad debt. However, the lender will subtract from the purchase price not only the loan, but also interest and penalties. Only then would any of the proceeds accrue to the hapless owner. Your offer benefits the owner directly. Keep in mind that you didn't create the problems of the troubled property seller. Because the seller stands to gain little or nothing from the Trustee's Sale, you are not taking advantage of him or her.

Is it possible to save money at the foreclosure sale?

Yes, foreclosure sales (Trustee's Sales) can save you money. A knowledge of property values is especially important. Properties are sold at discounts from the retail market. But the properties are also sold on an "as is" basis. Pay close attention. The 30 percent to 50 percent you may have saved could easily be spent on repairing a deteriorating roof, crumbling foundation, or termite damage before you can re-sell the property.

What price should I bid?

That is easy! Bid just enough to buy the property but no more than it is worth. Keep in mind you will have holding costs, fix-up and rehabilitation costs, and selling costs before you can recover your investment.

Should I buy from the owner before the sale or would it be less complicated to buy after the foreclosure sale?

Both methods have their advantages. The properties and the circumstances will be different for every sale. If you are buying before the Trustee's Sale, you will be able to visit, inspect, and evaluate the property first. If you are buying at the auction, you will not become involved with the emotions of the sellers, you will need few or no negotiation skills, and there will be very little legal hassle.

Don't banks and savings and loans sell properties?

Yes, these are called *REO* or *Real Estate Owned.* The banks will sell these properties to a qualified buyer; however, you should plan to pay very close attention to market price. The banks rarely feel obligated to just dump the properties at low prices. (See Chapter 9 for more information on REO.)

Do the auction sales require cash?

Most trustees will require that the bidders qualify before the sale. To qualify, you must show your cash or the equivalent up to the amount you intend to bid usually in the form of cashier's checks.

Will all the properties at the Trustee's Sale be sold "as is"?

Yes. Some banks and savings and loans associations will allow you to visit the properties before the sale. Take advantage of this. Ask professional structural engineers, termite contractors, and roofing experts to accompany you on such tours. It will be worth their fees, or they may be willing to do it at no fee on "spec," that is, speculating that you will hire them after you purchase the property.

What are outstanding loans and judgments?

Such debts constitute your biggest risk when buying before the Trustee's Sale. All liens, loans, and judgments against the property will be recorded at the County Recorder's Office of the county in which the property is located. You can research the county records yourself. Most title companies maintain copies of the county records. If you have a close relationship with a title company, it is possible the company will allow you to use its records to research the title and any possible liens or encumbrances.

Can you get rich buying foreclosures?

It is up to you! Like most of the other ways to make a great deal of money, it takes work and talent, lots of education (failures), and a little luck. You need knowledge, dedication, and perseverance. The disappointments will exceed the rewards during the learning period. The profitability is up to you. You can control your destiny through your own efforts.

How soon can I start making money?

It depends on your own motivation and desire. Many people make money after less than one month. However, I suggest you be prepared to wait at least 90 days for your first check.

Can I begin part-time?

It is probably the best way. While you go through the learning process, you can keep your regular job and build up a reserve of funds to use as fixer-upper or purchase money.

How much money will I need?

None, if you want to borrow from partners or very little if you are willing to start out small.

WHAT'S DIFFERENT ABOUT THE FORECLOSURE MARKET?

The Sunday newspaper is a good measure of the real estate market. Thousands of homes and properties are listed for sale each week. These advertisements are so lucrative for the newspaper that editors are specifically assigned to write articles about how great the market is for the developer, the real estate agents and, of course, the buyers. However, they are talking about buyers at retail.

Foreclosure buyers are different. First, you won't get wealthy buying homes or properties at retail prices. A general rule of thumb is that property advertised and listed for sale is priced at 110 percent of its real value. Keep this rule in mind when you read the newspaper, review a broker's Multiple Listing Service (MLS) book, or read any other real estate advertisement. Foreclosure buying is not part of the regular real estate market. You must also understand that only a small percentage of all the properties nationwide will end up in foreclosure. Unless the country is in a deep recession or depression, less than 1 percent of the homes will be in foreclosure. Most buyers check the newspapers and MLS to find properties for sale. Foreclosure buyers check the county records or commercial default listing services to find bargain properties for sale.

Foreclosure sales are outside of the normal market place with the market dominated by investors who are, or should be, knowledgable about values and who understand what they are purchasing. Most savvy investors require substantial profits from the sale of foreclosures. Therefore, they don't bid up the prices. Knowing values and retail sales prices, they won't pay too much at the auction. This is very important to understand. Brokers intentionally whip up a competitive atmosphere around properties, especially in the hot retail markets such as San Francisco, Boston, and Seattle, to create an escalating bidding process that benefits sellers and brokers. Many buyers stop negotiating for their purchases much too early and so pay more than the market values for properties because they feel that they will miss the purchase. Experienced foreclosure buyers are careful not to bid the prices up. The market is not emotional. Typically, foreclosure buyers will start at 70 percent and will usually stop bidding and let the amateur take the property if the bidding goes above 80 percent of market value.

Remember, you're looking for a profit of between 25 and 50 percent. Time, research, and lots of diligent effort are required to buy successfully at the Trustee's Sales. Once you have attended a few sales and understand how the process works, much of the mystery as well as the glamour will be gone. The risks for the intelligent investor are reduced by doing your homework. Knowing values, understanding the market, estimating repair costs, and confirming your figures will make you a tough competitor in the foreclosure market.

You need to learn and be prepared to take the time to understand the foreclosure marketplace. This is not as simple as calling a broker, but it is also not as expensive. Think about buying properties for between 25 percent to 50 percent less than the retail asking price. It only takes one and you'll be transformed into a real estate bargain hunter. Foreclosure properties are worth the effort. Most people are afraid even to consider buying such properties. After all, it is a risk.

The foreclosure buyer is unique in many ways. First, he or she must research many properties to find that one profit-maker or ideal candidate. Second, foreclosure purchases require thorough investigation of the County Recorder's records to seek out any undisclosed liens or encumbrances. Third, negotiations with the seller take place in a different atmosphere in terms of the motivation of the seller and the buyer. Traditional real estate sellers have very little motivation, if any.

The average person wants a bargain property. However, the searching, investigation, and negotiation with the seller often proves to be too much work for the average person. The average foreclosure property is in a state of disrepair and so requires extra diligence on the part of the foreclosure buyer. Because the termite and roof repairs become the buyer's responsibility after the purchase of a foreclosure, the importance of professional inspectors is soon obvious. In summary, foreclosure buyers move rapidly but cautiously as they understand the risks and work to manage those risks.

A CASE STUDY

Helping Others Out of Trouble

The big profits in almost any business are to be made by providing a service—helping people. A property owner whose loan is in default needs help. You may be able to solve the problem.

The following case study, of a pre-foreclosure purchase of property in San Ramon, California, illustrates a typical problem, and a successful solution—for both seller and buyer. The property owner was temporarily out of work and had suffered some difficulties with employment over the past few years. He was realistic about the condition of his home. It was definitely a fixer-upper and the owner, a licensed real estate agent, had already estimated the cost of repair and replacement. These costs were extensive and the foreclosure clock was running.

We had found the property through the usual channels (see Chapter 5 on locating distressed property) and the homeowner had responded to our direct mail solicitation. We set the initial appointment with the owner for the middle of the afternoon. It is usually better to meet with the homeowners during daylight so that you can see the property under the best light conditions. You are more likely to overlook items of importance by doing your walk-through inspection during the evening.

(When your business grows and you are dealing with three or four houses a month, it will be difficult to remember the details of each house you purchase. So use the *Property Evaluation Questionnaire* provided in Chapter 5. This checklist gives you a permanent record of some basic facts about each house—location, condition of the house, loan history, and so forth.)

Where Do We Start?

The seller needed a minimum payment of $7,000 no matter what deductions were provided for in the contract. You will see why as we continue through the transaction.

The *Home Equity Purchase Contract* used for the property in question is dated 3 October 1987 (see Figure 1.1). This contract outlines the agreement between the foreclosed owner and the prospective buyer to transfer the owner's equity to the buyer. In this case, the contract was completed by the seller in his own handwriting as were the modifications to the standard contract in the left-hand margin. The notation reads: "Notwithstanding any payment enumerated herein, such as for encumbrances, termite work, roof work, or escrow fees, buyer guarantees net funds to seller in the amount of seven thousand dollars ($7,000)."

Don't Make This Mistake

The top line of the contract allows space to place the street address, state, and date. The second line allows space for the legal description. This is a critical item. You must determine what you are buying and the legal description is the best means of doing so. The owner had inadvertently used information from the *Notice of Default* (see Figure 1.2) when he completed the contract—thereby giving us the wrong lot and tract number. A property description is not part of the Notice of Default, which consists primarily of loan information and the date, document, book, and page numbers of the Trust Deed (mortgage) record. This information pertains to the loan only, and no mention is made of a legal description.

The Home Equity Purchase Contract reproduced here was not the original. Because the seller was not guaranteed $7,000, he canceled the first contract and asked for a revised contract. We agreed to a revised contract because, after evaluating the property's resale potential and determining that with a reasonably small amount of rehabilitation (paint, carpet, and repairs), we believed that this property would be a profitable purchase, even with a minimum payment to the seller.

The Civil Code in the State of California requires that the seller be given five business days to rescind a foreclosure/equity purchase contract. Therefore, when the seller canceled the first contract, it was necessary to write a new and revised contract rather than modify the old contract.

HOME EQUITY PURCHASE CONTRACT

San Ramon _____ California October 3 , 19 87

Lot 1 ___ 03 ___ Tract 78-455-19161 Book 8923 Page(s) 697

Address 9829 Broadmoor Dr., San Ramon Ca 94583

In consideration of the sum of $___∅___ receipt of which is hereby acknowledged by SELLER, the SELLER agrees to sell and the BUYER agrees to purchase the above decribed property for the sum of $12,000ᵒᵒ ___ NET TO SELLER and to take title subject ONLY to existing encumbrances not in excess of:

ANY PAYMENTS HEREIN, SUCH AS FOR ENCUMBRANCES WORK OR ESCROW FEES NET FUNDS TO SELLER IN (handwritten in left margin)

1st TD $51,262⁶⁵   payable $491⁶⁸   per month 10 % interest incl. TI _____

2nd TD $53,800ᵒᵒ   payable $648¹²   per month 14¼ % interest ____ due date

3rd TD $_____   payable $_____   per month ____ % interest ____ due date

NET AMOUNT
~~FULL PRICE~~ $12,000ᵒᵒ

From the NET amount due SELLER may be deducted all payments on existing encumbrances through the payments due 10-15 19 87 also any taxes, judgements, assessments, bonds and other liens, if any. Impounds, if any are to be assigned without charge to BUYER, in an amount satisfactory to the lending institution. Any impound shortage will be deducted from funds due SELLER. SELLER agrees to execute a Grant

PERSONAL PROPERTY TO BE INCLUDED AS FOLLOWS: KEY____
STOVE w/MICROWAVE
_____

RESCISSION NOTICE ATTACHED YES___ NO___

NOTICE REQUIRED BY CALIFORNIA LAW

UNTIL YOUR RIGHT TO CANCEL THIS CONTRACT HAS ENDED 10-12-87 OR ANYONE WORKING FOR NEW GROWTH CANNOT ASK YOU TO SIGN ANY DEED OR ANY OTHER DOCUMENT.

We hereby agree to sell on the above conditions and terms.

BUYER _____   SELLER_____

BUYER NEW GROWTH FINANCIAL   SELLER Barbara Biddles

ADDRESS 185 Front St. #207   ADDRESS 9829 Broadmoor Dr.

Danville, Ca. PHONE 837.2106   San Ramon PHONE 555-0614

© 1988 New Growth Financial

Figure 1.1   Home Equity Purchase Contract

NOTICE OF DEFAULT AND ELECTION TO SELL
UNDER DEED OF TRUST
PART II

NOTICE IS GIVEN:

That ALPHA SAVINGS AND LOAN ASSOCIATION   is Trustee   under a deed of trust signed by

BERT BIDDLES AND BARBARA BIDDLES, HIS WIFE, AS JOINT TENANTS.

and dated   06/19/78   and recorded   07/14/78 , as Document 78-95519,   Book 8923,   Page 697,   of Official Records of the County Recorder of   CONTRA COSTA   County, California, and given to secure payment of a promissory note for $56,000.00   dated 06/19/78, payable with interest in favor of

ALPHA SAVINGS AND LOAN ASSOCIATION.

A breach of the obligations contained in the deed of trust has occured. The following payments have not been paid and are due:

THE MONTHLY INSTALLMENT OF PRINCIPAL AND INTEREST DUE 05/01/87, AND SUBSEQUENT INSTALLMENTS DUE THEREAFTER, THEREBY DECLARING THE ENTIRE PRINCIPAL BALANCE OF $51,262.65 DUE AND PAYABLE, TOGETHER WITH INTEREST THEREON FROM 04/01/87 AT THE RATE OF 10.000%, AND LATE CHARGES AS SET FORTH IN SAID DEED OF TRUST, AND TOGETHER WITH ANY AND ALL SUMS ADVANCED BY THE BENEFICIARY UNDER THE TERMS AND PROVISIONS OF SAID DEED OF TRUST, AND DELINQUENT TAXES, ASSESSMENTS AND INSURANCE PREMIUMS, IF ANY.

The present beneficiary under the deed of trust has signed and delivered to the Trustee a written declaration of default and demand for sale, and has given to Trustee the deed of trust and all documents evidencing the secured obligations, and declares all secured sums immediately due and payable, and elects to cause the property described in the deed of trust to be sold to satisfy the secured obligations.

Dated 07/07/87   ALPHA SAVINGS AND LOAN ASSN

By:_____

Morris Murphy

Figure 1.2   Notice of Default

In doing so, we neglected to review all of the data that was included at the top. The correct data should have been taken from the Grant Deed which is dated 24 November 1971 (see Figure 1.3), as is the legal description: "Lot 11 of Tract 3478, filed September 19, 1970 in book 132, page 32 of Maps, in the office of the County Recorder of said County."

As the new owner, you should request and review a *Preliminary Title Report*. This report will identify liens or encumbrances that may be attached to the property. The seller will deed the property to you after the five-day right of rescission expires. Although you have legal title at this time, contractually you have an additional five days to rescind the contract. *Rescission* means to return the parties to their original positions. Included in Figure 1.4 are the first four pages of the Preliminary Title Report. Note especially page 1, on which the property description given corresponds with that on the Grant Deed. Official records require mention of the Assessor's Parcel Number (APN), but the Grant Deed in question did not show an APN. On page 1 of the abbreviated Preliminary Title Report we see the Assessor's Parcel Number 212–161–003 for this property. The number was probably omitted by mistake when the Deed was drawn up in 1971.

Making the Contract Binding

After waiting, as required by California law, for the five-day right of rescission to expire, you, as the foreclosure buyer, may have the seller transfer the property to you by Grant Deed. In order for this to be a valid contract, the seller must be paid a consideration. In most circumstances, I pay sellers $25. Yes, $25! I suggest you prepare the buyer as well as the title company for this. The first time you purchase a property for only $25, the title company will struggle with disbelief and so will your friends. The outlay of $25 appears to be the minimum amount required to purchase a parcel of improved real estate. The $25 is only the consideration that passes between the parties at the time the Grant Deed is executed and conveyed to you. Your check in the amount of $25 is acceptable as being enough money given in exchange for the Grant Deed to make the transaction legal and to obligate both parties. The Equity Purchase Contract is a promise to pay in the future larger sums of money when all the stipulations of the contract are fulfilled. In this particular case, the contract required a minimum payment of $7,000 no matter what the roof or termite repairs might require.

I recommend that the sum paid out be no more than is necessary to make the contract binding because you will not know the actual amount of cash—if any—that you will ultimately be able to pay to the owner until you have received the reports of structural condition, the termite and roof inspection reports, and until you have determined the status of the title and the existence of liens, judgments, bonds, taxes due, and so forth. Furthermore, if the seller doesn't clean the property or leave it in a good state of repair, such costs will all be borne by you, the buyer. So, pay as little as possible until the costs are all revealed.

Transferring the Property

The seller did not cancel the second Home Equity Purchase contract (the signed Notice of Cancellation is reproduced as Figure 1.5), so the property was transferred

NOV 24 1971

100867 BOOK **6527** PAGE **684**

RECORDED AT REQUEST OF
**TRANSAMERICA TITLE
INSURANCE COMPANY**
NOVEMBER 24, 1971
AT 03:00 O'CLOCK AM
OFFICIAL RECORDS OF
CONTRA COSTA COUNTY
W. T. PAASCH
COUNTY RECORDER
FEE $2.00 PD

AND WHEN RECORDED MAIL TO

⌐ Bert Biddles ¬
9829 Broadmoor Drive
San Ramon, CA
⌐ ¬

(stamp: NOV 24 1971 CONTRA COSTA CO. TRAN FER TAX PAID $ 34.10)

SPACE ABOVE THIS LINE FOR RECORDER'S USE

MAIL TAX STATEMENTS TO

⌐ The Colwell Company ¬
Post Office Box "N"
San Mateo, CA 94402
⌐ ¬

DOCUMENTARY TRANSFER TAX $ 34.10
  X COMPUTED ON FULL VALUE OF PROPERTY CONVEYED.
___ OR COMPUTED ON FULL VALUE LESS LIENS AND
ENCUMBRANCES REMAINING AT TIME OF SALE.

Johanna C. Harper
Signature of Declarant or Agent determining tax.   Firm Name

GRANT DEED
(CORPORATION)

(Escrow No. 212311)

By this instrument dated ....November 20, 1971........, for a valuable consideration,

TRANSAMERICA TITLE INSURANCE COMPANY, a California corporation

hereby GRANTS to Bert Biddles and Barbara Biddles

the following described Real Property of the State of California, County of..Contra Costa

City of ..unincorporated.........

Lot 11 of Tract 3478, filed September 19, 1970 in Book 132, page 32 of
Maps, in the Office of the County Recorder of said County

TRANSAMERICA TITLE INSURANCE CO.

BY: ......*D B Lantz*......
D. B. LANTZ ASSISTANT CORPORATE SECRETARY

STATE OF CALIFORNIA
COUNTY OF CONTRA COSTA

On this.....20..... day of .....November........ in the year ...1971...., before me,
...., a Notary Public, State of California duly commissioned and sworn,
personally appeared ....D. B. Lantz.................... personally known to be (or proved to me on the
basis of satisfactory evidence) to be the person whose name .... subscribed to this instrument,
and acknowledged that ....he... executed it.
   IN WITNESS WHEREOF I have hereunto set my hand and affixed my official seal in the State of
...California..........County of ..Contra Costa................ on the date set forth above this certificate.

Johanna C. Harper
Notary Public, State of California

Figure 1.3   Grant Deed

BIGLAND TITLE INSURANCE COMPANY
379 DIABLO ROAD, SUITE 102, DANVILLE, CA 94526
(415) 820-5700
PAGE 1
P R E L I M I N A R Y   R E P O R T

                    Order No.:   86884
            Escrow Officer: Wendy Watts
             Title Officer: Patricia Laird
          Property Address: 9829 BROADMOOR DRIVE
                              SAN RAMON, CALIFORNIA

In response to the above referenced application for a policy of
title insurance, Bigland Title Insurance Company hereby reports that
it is prepared to issue, or cause to be issued, as of the date
hereof, a policy or policies of title insurance describing the land
and the estate or interest therein hereinafter set forth, insuring
against loss which may be sustained by reason of any defect, lien or
encumbrance not shown or referred to as an exception below, or not
excluded from coverage pursuant to the printed schedules, conditions
and stipulations of said policy forms.

The printed exceptions and exclusions from the coverage of said
policy or policies are set forth in Exhibit A attached. Copies of
the policy forms should be read. They are available from the office
which issued this report.

This report (and any supplements or amendments thereto) is issued
solely for the purpose of facilitating the issuance of a policy of
title insurance and no liability is assumed hereby. If it is
desired that liability be assumed prior to the issuance of a policy
of title insurance, a binder or commitment should be requested.

Dated as of   OCTOBER 2, 1987   at 7:30 A.M.
           ────────────────────

The form of policy of title insurance contemplated by this report
is:

  CALIFORNIA LAND TITLE ASSOCIATION - 1973 OR AMERICAN LAND TITLE
     ASSOCIATION RESIDENTIAL TITLE INSURANCE POLICY - (6/1/87) OR
  AMERICAN LAND TITLE ASSOCIATION LEASEHOLD LOAN POLICY - (6/1/87) OR
     AMERICAN LAND TITLE ASSOCIATION OWNER'S POLICY - (6/1/87) OR
  AMERICAN LAND TITLE ASSOCIATION LEASEHOLD OWNER'S POLICY - (6/1/87)
  AND/OR AMERICAN LAND TITLE ASSOCIATION LENDERS POLICY - (6/1/87),
                 (STANDARD OR EXTENDED COVERAGE)

The estate or interest in the land hereinafter described or referred
to covered by this report is: A FEE

Title to said estate or interest at the date hereof is vested in:

Figure 1.4   Extracts from Preliminary Title Report

ORDER NO. 86884

PAGE 2

At the date hereof exceptions to coverage in addition to the printed exceptions and exclusions in said policy form would be as follows:

1. THE LIEN OF SUPPLEMENTAL TAXES, IF ANY, ASSESSED PURSUANT TO THE PROVISIONS OF CHAPTER 3.5, REVENUE AND TAXATION CODE, SECTIONS 75 ET SEQ.

2. COUNTY AND CITY TAXES FOR THE FISCAL YEAR 1987 - 1988
    1ST INSTALLMENT: $203.16 NOT DUE
    2ND INSTALLMENT: $203.16 NOT DUE
    LAND   : $8,630.00
    IMPROVEMENTS   : $33,422.00
    EXEMPTION   : $7,000.00
    A.P. NO.   : 212-161-003
    CODE AREA   : 17-005

3. SALE TO THE STATE OF CALIFORNIA OF DELINQUENT COUNTY AND CITY TAXES FOR THE FISCAL YEAR 1986 - 1987, AND SUBSEQUENT FISCAL YEARS, SALE NO. 86-05232. THE AMOUNT NECESSARY TO REDEEM THIS SALE IS $486.30 ON OR BEFORE OCTOBER 31, 1987 AND $492.26 ON OR BEFORE NOVEMBER 30, 1987.

4. COVENANTS, CONDITIONS AND RESTRICTIONS, BUT DELETING RESTRICTIONS, IF ANY, BASED ON RACE, COLOR, RELIGION OR NATIONAL ORIGIN, CONTAINED IN THE DECLARATION
    BY   : TRANSAMERICA TITLE INSURANCE COMPANY
    RECORDED   : SEPTEMBER 10, 1970, BOOK 6210, PAGE 471, OFFICIAL RECORDS

    CONTAINS NO REVERSIONARY CLAUSE.

    CONTAINS A MORTGAGEE PROTECTION CLAUSE.

5. DEED OF TRUST TO SECURE AN INDEBTEDNESS OF
    AMOUNT   : $56,000.00
    DATED   : JUNE 19, 1978
    TRUSTOR   : Bert Biddles and Barbara Biddles

    TRUSTEE   : ALPHA   SAVINGS AND LOAN ASSOCIATION OF SAN DIEGO, A CORPORATION
    BENEFICIARY   : ALPHA   SAVINGS AND LOAN ASSOCIATION OF SAN DIEGO, A CORPORATION
    ADDRESS   : P. O. BOX 2279, WALNUT CREEK, CA. 94595
    LOAN NO.   : 526990
    RECORDED   : JULY 14, 1978, BOOK 8923, PAGE 697, SERIES NO. 78-95519, OFFICIAL RECORDS

Figure 1.4 *(continued)*

ORDER NO. 86884

PAGE 3

NOTICE OF DEFAULT UNDER THE TERMS OF SAID DEED OF TRUST
RECORDED   : JULY 16, 1987, BOOK 13776, PAGE 145, SERIES
                    NO. 87-151825, OFFICIAL RECORDS

6. ANY POSSIBLE INVALIDITY OF TITLE OR EFFECT THEREON, BY REASON OF
    EXERCISE OF ANY RIGHTS OF RESCISSION OR CANCELLATION, OR
    OTHERWISE, OR ASSERTION OF ANY RIGHTS PURSUANT TO CHAPTERS 655,
    819, 1015 AND 1029, STATUTES OF 1979, CALIFORNIA STATUTES,
    ENACTED FOR THE PROTECTION OF RESIDENTIAL PROPERTY OWNERS IN
    FORECLOSURE AS SET FORTH IN SAID STATUTES.

7. DEED OF TRUST TO SECURE AN INDEBTEDNESS OF
    AMOUNT   : $53,800.00
    DATED   : SEPTEMBER 12, 1986
    TRUSTOR   : Bert Biddles and Barbara Biddles

    TRUSTEE   : PIONEER TITLE COMPANY OF CALIFORNIA, INC.
    BENEFICIARY   : I.L.S. MORTGAGE CORPORATION, A CORPORATION
    ADDRESS   : 1875 SOUTH GRANT, SUITE 700
                      SAN MATEO, CA 94402
    LOAN NO.   : PB02-32030
    RECORDED   : SEPTEMBER 26, 1986, BOOK 13156, PAGE 488,
                      SERIES NO. 86-169111, OFFICIAL RECORDS

    THE BENEFICIAL INTEREST THEREUNDER HAS BEEN ASSIGNED, BY MESNE
    TO   : HALE & RANDALL MORTGAGE CO., INC. A DELAWARE
                      CORPORATION
    RECORDED   : AUGUST 26, 1987, BOOK 13860, PAGE 977, SERIES
                      NO. 87-182068, OFFICIAL RECORDS
    ADDRESS   : 4695 CHABOT DRIVE #102, PLEASANTON, CA 94566
    LOAN NO.   : 79556462

    NOTICE OF DEFAULT UNDER THE TERMS OF SAID DEED OF TRUST
    RECORDED   : AUGUST 26, 1987, BOOK 13860, PAGE 979, SERIES
                      NO. 87-182070, OFFICIAL RECORDS

8. ANY POSSIBLE INVALIDITY OF TITLE OR EFFECT THEREON, BY REASON OF
    EXERCISE OF ANY RIGHTS OF RESCISSION OR CANCELLATION, OR
    OTHERWISE, OR ASSERTION OF ANY RIGHTS PURSUANT TO CHAPTERS 655,
    819, 1015 AND 1029, STATUTES OF 1979, CALIFORNIA STATUTES,
    ENACTED FOR THE PROTECTION OF RESIDENTIAL PROPERTY OWNERS IN
    FORECLOSURE AS SET FORTH IN SAID STATUTES.

9. THE EFFECT OF INSTRUMENTS, PROCEEDINGS, LIENS, DECREES OR OTHER
    MATTERS WHICH DO NOT SPECIFICALLY DESCRIBE SAID LAND BUT WHICH,
    IF ANY EXIST, MAY AFFECT THE TITLE OR IMPOSE LIENS OR
    ENCUMBRANCES THEREON. THE NAME SEARCH NECESSARY TO ASCERTAIN
    THE EXISTENCE OF SUCH MATTERS HAS NOT BEEN COMPLETED AND IN
    ORDER TO DO SO WE REQUIRE A STATEMENT OF IDENTITY FROM
    BERT BIDDLES AND BARBARA BIDDLES.

Figure 1.4   *(continued)*

ORDER NO. 86884

The land referred to in this report is situated in the State of
California, County of CONTRA COSTA, and is described as follows:

CITY OF SAN RAMON

LOT 11 OF TRACT 3478, FILED SEPTEMBER 19, 1970 IN BOOK 132, PAGE 32
OF MAPS, IN THE OFFICE OF THE COUNTY RECORDER OF SAID COUNTY.

EXCEPTING THEREFROM:

ALL OIL, GAS, MINERALS AND OTHER HYDROCARBON SUBSTANCES IN AND UNDER
OR THAT MAY BE PRODUCED FROM A DEPTH BELOW 500 FEET FROM THE SURFACE
OF SAID LAND, WITHOUT RIGHT OF ENTRY UPON THE SURFACE OF SAID LAND,
AS RESERVED IN DEED FROM VOLK-MC LAIN COMMUNITIES, INC., A
CALIFORNIA CORPORATION, RECORDED JUNE 27, 1967, AS SERIES NO. 38550
OF OFFICIAL RECORDS.

ASSESSOR'S PARCEL NO. 212-161-003

Figure 1.4   *(continued)*

NOTICE OF CANCELLATION

DATE _10-5-87_

YOU MAY CANCEL THIS CONTRACT FOR THE SALE OF YOUR HOUSE WITHOUT PENALTY OR OBLIGATION AT ANY TIME BEFORE _10-12-87_ TIME _MIDNIGHT_

Seller has the right to cancel until midnight of the 5th business day following the day on which Seller signs contract. ("Business day" means any day except Sunday/holidays) or until 8:00 A.M. on day of foreclosure sale, whichever occurs first.

NOTICE OF CANCELLATION (Separate document, but attached to contract.)

TO CANCEL THIS TRANSACTION, PERSONALLY DELIVER A SIGNED AND DATED COPY OF THIS CANCELLATION NOTICE OR SEND A TELEGRAM TO:

BUYER _New Growth Financial_   ADDRESS _185 FRONT ST. #207_
DANVILLE, CA 94526

NOT LATER THAN DATE _10-12-87_ TIME _MIDNIGHT_

I HEREBY CANCEL THIS TRANSACTION

Seller_____ Date_____

Seller_____ Date_____

I have received this notice to cancel.

Seller _(signature)_ Date _10-5-87_

Seller _Barbara Biddles_ Date _10-5-87_

Figure 1.5   Notice of Cancellation

from him to the corporation of which the author is an employee by the Grant Deed that is reproduced as Figure 1.6.

Now You Own the Property, Let's Inspect It

You own the property so now you better inspect it and see what you own. Roof reports, along with structural and termite damage reports, are essential. Use professionals. In order to treat the seller fairly and not expose yourself to question, you should employ the best professionals available.

The reports, contracts, and estimates become a permanent record that may be reviewed and referred to later. Keep in mind that the seller is generally extremely skeptical. Your intentions and your performance will be evaluated on the way in which you and the professionals you hire treat the homeowner.

Upon receipt of the inspection reports, *read* them. The two reports made on the San Ramon property are reproduced in Figure 1.7. Many foreclosure buyers neglect to read the reports. This oversight could be costly. Some buyers prefer to be at the property when the inspectors perform the work. However, I believe that it is better to hire a professional to do the inspection and stay at home to await his or her report. You are thus less likely to be considered to be in a position to influence the report. After the professional completes the inspection, telephone and have the inspector review the report with you. There will be a lot of items in these reports that you won't understand on the first two or three homes. It won't take long until you'll be an old hand. Stay with the professionals and they will get to know what you are doing and become part of your team.

There is neither space nor time enough at this writing to caution you adequately about the disclaimers written into termite and roof inspection contracts. Read them again and again. Then remember the magic, three-letter work: *ASK.* Keep asking! Ask about the warranties, guarantees, notices, limitations; ask about the findings on each report. It will be an education. If you neglect it, you will pay dearly. Remember, it is the seller who is responsible for making good any damage done to the roof and other parts of the structure and any damage done by termites. If you don't pay attention at this point in the transaction, while you are still a buyer, you will foot the bill later, when you become the seller. The seller understands that the contract he or she signed requires him to be responsible for the termite and roof repairs. As you receive these reports, make a photocopy and then make an excuse to drop by to visit. At that time, you can advise the seller of your progress. This will give you an additional chance to re-inspect the property and let the sellers know, if necessary, that the check they are expecting is getting just a little smaller.

Know What You're Really Buying—Sorting Out the Liens and Encumbrances

While the inspections are in progress, take the time to review the Preliminary Title Report. Loan data and tax information are shown on the last two pages of the report.

Taxes are always listed first. By taxes we are referring to property taxes, not to income or personal property taxes. In reviewing the Title Report, we find that Items 1 and 2 are normal. Item 1 is a standard clause that refers to the fact that the

RECORDING REQUESTED BY **87 | 222135**   RECORDED AT REQUEST OF
                                             CHICAGO TITLE CO.

And When Recorded Mail This Deed
and, Unless Otherwise Shown Below,
Mail Tax Statements To: OCTOBER 15, 1987

NEW GROWTH ENTERPRISES   AT 08:00 O'CLOCK AM
601 Hartz Ave., #220   CONTRA COSTA COUNTY RECORDS
Danville, CA 94526   J. R. OLSSON
                                             COUNTY RECORDER
                                             FEE $5.00

Title Order No. _____ Escrow No. 86884   **SPACE ABOVE THIS LINE FOR RECORDER'S USE**

DOCUMENTARY TRANSFER TAX $ 23.10
_____ COMPUTED ON FULL VALUE OF PROPERTY CONVEYED.
_____ OR COMPUTED ON FULL VALUE LESS LIENS AND
ENCUMBRANCES REMAINING AT TIME OF SALE.

Judi Johnson   Chicago Title Co.
Signature of Declarant or Agent determining tax.   Firm Name

GRANT DEED

FOR A VALUABLE CONSIDERATION, receipt of which is hereby
acknowledged.

ASSESSOR'S PARCEL NO. 212-161-003

Bert Biddles and Barbara Biddles
hereby GRANT(S) to
NEW GROWTH ENTERPRISES, a California corporation

the following described real property in the City of San Ramon county
of Contra Costa , state of California:

Lot 11 of Tract 3478, filed September 19, 1970 in Book 132,
Page 32 of Maps, in the Office of the County Recorder of
said County.

EXCEPTING THEREFROM:
All oil, gas, minerals

Figure 1.6   Grant Deed

Mailing Address: P.O. Box 396
Walnut Creek, CA 94596
Phone: 934-4842

License No. 360240

DATE ___10-14-87___
CUST. PHONE ___820-2511___
I 385

ROOFING--GUTTERS--DOWNSPOUTS

REQUESTING AGENT Nancy Patterson _____ SELLER _____

AGENT'S ADDRESS "New Growth Enterprises"
P.O. Box 5000 Suite 412   PURCHASER _____
Danville

TITLE COMPANY _____N/A_____ ESCROW NO._____

ADDRESS OF INSPECTION ____9829 Broadmore, San Ramon_____

REMARKS ___SEE ATTACHED REPORT_____

ATTACHED REPORT:

Patterson
Page 2
October 13, 1987

Re: 9829 Broadmore, San Ramon

This home has a medium shake roof on it. The roof is approximately twelve to fourteen years old. Following are the results of my inspection:

3) There are some felt exposures on the roof. The felt is the waterproofing agent of a shake roof and must be protected from the sun. We recommend this be done by tin shingling, which is the insertion of a tin shingle under the shake and over the felt to close off the exposure. A wood shingle could be used instead, but we feel there is greater potential for damaging the felt.

5) There are trees overhanging and dragging on the roof. They should be trimmed off of the roof to prevent damage to the roof.

6) The hip and ridge shingles on the rear gable are missing or loose. They need to be replaced or renailed.

11) There are some missing shingles. This causes the same problem as in item 3 and is corrected in a similar manner.

14) The bottom course of felt is missing around the eave edge of the home. This is typical of homes in this area. This is a code violation, as felt is required on all courses. What this actually does is make the eave edge more susceptible to leaks and can cause dryrot at this point. As the damage that can occur is minimal, we suggest this condition be left alone until the roof is replaced. However, this area should be checked periodically and any leaks occurring be tin shingled off.

We do not inspect any projections above or below the roof line, such as gutters, windows, chimneys, walls, skylights, heating or air conditioning and take no liability for their condition. Nor do we inspect solar panels or the roof underneath unless easily accessible.

Estimated costs to repair - $400.00.

Figure 1.7   Walnut Creek Roofing Report

STANDARD STRUCTURE PEST CONTROL INSPECTION REPORT
(WOOD DESTROYING PESTS OR ORGANISMS)
This is an inspection report only — not a Notice of Completion

ADDRESS OF PROPERTY INSPECTED	BLDG. NO. 9829	STREET BROADMOOR DR.	CITY SAN RAMON CO. CODE 07	DATE OF INSPECTION 10-7-87

DOLLAR $AVER$
TERMITE &PEST CONTROL
21018 CORSAIR BLVD. • HAYWARD, CA 94545
(415) 887-4080

Affix stamp here on Board copy only
A LICENSED PEST CONTROL OPERATOR IS AN EXPERT IN HIS FIELD. ANY QUESTIONS RELATIVE TO THIS REPORT SHOULD BE REFERRED TO HIM.

FIRM LICENSE NUMBER OC 6389	CO. REPORT NO. (If any) T-1997	STAMP NO. 349720P

Inspection Ordered by (Name and Address)   NEW GROWTH (NANCY PATTERSON) 9829 BROADMOOR DR., SAN RAMON, CA
Report Sent to (Name and Address)   NANCY PATTERSON P. O. BOX 5000 SUITE 412 DANVILLE, CA 94526
Owner's Name and Address   SAME AS ABOVE
Name and Address of a Party in Interest   SAME AS ABOVE

Limited Inspection   Reinspection   Original Report [X]   Supplemental Report   Number of Pages 4

PRICE BREAKDOWN

ITEMS	PRICE	ITEMS	PRICE
1	85.00		
2	550.00		
3	650.00		
4	REFER		
5	85.00		
6	425.00		
7	525.00		
8	1175.00		
9	125.00		
10	OWNER		
11	REFER		

TOTAL COST **$3,620.00**

PROPERTY ADDRESS: 9829 BROADMOOR DRIVE
SAN RAMON, CA 94583
REPORT NUMBER: T-1997

TITLE COMPANY _____

ESCROW NUMBER _____

Please list item numbers to be completed

ITEMS _____

COST _____

IF A CHEMICAL TREATMENT IS REQUIRED
Persons with respiratory or allergic conditions or others who may be concered about their health, relative to any chemical treatment should contact their physicians concerning occpancy during and after chemnical treatment prior to signing this authorization.

ACCEPTANCE CUSTOMER_____Date_____

ACCEPTANCE AGENT_____Date_____
AUTHORIZATION MUST BE SIGNED PRIOR TO COMMENCING WORK

Please sign and return one copy

Figure 1.7 *(continued)*

terms of the title insurance are subject to change if any tax liens are recorded against the property. Item 2 is merely a summary of the tax assessed on the property. Item 3 is not normal. Item 3 shows that the State of California has filed a lien against the property for back taxes. If these taxes remain unpaid, the state will ultimately sell the property at a tax sale. In California, the state will allow the taxes to become delinquent for five years before announcing the tax sale. The tax rules in your particular state may differ. Taxes on real property and personal property should be reviewed with your attorney, title company, and accountant.

Taxes and tax liens require special knowledge. Your CPA and your attorney will be helpful in guiding you through the maze of regulations, and the title officer at your local title company can also be extremely helpful. You should check the rules applicable to your state. To review even briefly the California law in layman's terms would take many pages, too many for this text. Item 3 is a report that the seller has not paid his taxes for the past year. California accepts two payments, one in December and one in April, and sends a notification as a regular reminder. The lien against the property is recorded at the local County Recorder's Office, which is how the title company found out about it. The owner failed to mention the matter to us. That lien, called an *Abstract of Delinquent Property Taxes and Certificate of Redemption,* is reproduced as Figure 1.8. The cashier's check that paid off the lien (removed the encumbrance), and so cleared the title report of a future encumbrance is shown as Figure 1.9.

Foreclosure is usually not an isolated action and is likely to be only the latest in a succession of financial misfortunes for the seller. Therefore, you should expect to find liens, abstracts, judgments, and encumbrances varying from mechanic's liens to alimony and child support payments.

Items 5 and 7 give the details of the two Deeds of Trust that are securing the loan against this property. The report indicates that both Deeds of Trust are in default. It is important to you if you are the new purchaser to note the date of default and to determine which loan has first right.

For example, if the lender of the first loan has filed a notice of default and the lender of the second loan takes no action to cure (bring current) the first note, the second note will be in jeopardy at the Trustee's Sale. The Trustee's Sale process will eliminate all junior Deeds of Trust. It is important to understand that the first note is the note that was filed at the County Recorder's Office first, regardless of the amount.

It is not unusual for the lender of the second note to cure the first note and then file a foreclosure action to redeem the property. If the second lender successfully purchases the property at the Trustee's Sale, the owner of the second Deed of Trust would own the property for the full amount of the first note plus the principal, back payments on the first, and the associated fees and costs on the second note.

It is crucial for a buyer at the Trustee's Sale to understand, before the sale, the liens and encumbrances against the property. The County Recorder's Office will have all the records regarding the purchase. Most title companies maintain title plants that also have accurate records showing the liens and encumbrances on real property.

Lien priority is determined by date and time and not the amount of the lien or who recorded it. If, for example, a builder/developer constructed a home on a

COUNTY OF CONTRA COSTA

ABSTRACT OF DELINQUENT PROPERTY TAXES AND CERTIFICATE OF REDEMPTION

STATE OF CALIFORNIA

YEAR	ASSESSEE	YEAR	PROPERTY DESCRIPTION	POWER OF SALE
86	BIDDLES, Bert and Barbara	86	103478 L0011 B EX MR	DATE VOLUME PAGE O.R. RECISSION OF POWER TO SELL TAX DEFAULTED PROPERTY DATE VOLUME PAGE O.R.

SCHOOL DISTRICT	TAX - DEFAULT AMOUNT	TAX - DEFAULT DATE	DEFAULT YEAR & NUMBER
	$447.44	JUNE 30, 1987	86-05232

TAX YEAR	PARCEL NUMBER / TAX RATE AREA/LEVY CODE	TAXED VALUATIONS: LAND	TAXED VALUATIONS: IMPROVEMENTS	TAXED VALUATIONS: PERSONAL PROPERTY	EXEMPTIONS: CODE	EXEMPTIONS: VALUE	TAXES AND ASSESSMENTS	DELINQUENT PENALTIES	DELINQUENT COSTS	TOTAL BEFORE REDEMPTIONS PENALTIES
86	212-161-003-0 17005 JT	8461 ST LIGHT/LNUSCP	32767		HO	7000	365.68 32.00	39.76	10.00	447.44

PAID

Current Taxes Not Included

TOTAL ALL YEARS BEFORE REDEMPTION PENALTIES	447.44
ADD: REDEMPTION PENALTIES	23.86
TOTAL ALL YEARS WITH REDEMPTION PENALTIES	471.30
ADD: INTEREST ON INSTALLMENT CONTRACTS	.00
STATE REDEMPTION FEE	15.00
LESS: CREDIT FOR AMOUNTS PREVIOUSLY PAID	.00
TOTAL COST TO REDEEM	486.30
ADD: FEE FOR RECISSION OF POWER TO SELL.	.00
R & T SEC. 4112 FEES	.00
TOTAL AMOUNT PAYABLE	486.30

I hereby certify the above to be a full and correct estimate of the total amount necessary, on the date shown, to redeem the above-described property in accordance with the provisions of law.
Receipt is Hereby Acknowledged of the Sum Shown as Total Cost to Redeem from:

NEW GROWTH ENTERPRISES
P O BOX 5030 SUITE 412
DANVILLE CA 94526

M. P. Lujinez
Deputy Tax Collector

CERTIFICATE OF REDEMPTION

DATE 10/15/1987 NUMBER 152169

(Y 18 Rev. 11/85)

Figure 1.8 Property Tax Lien

CASHIER'S CHECK CUSTOMER RECEIPT

142-3431542

DANVILLE 142
(OFFICE OF ISSUE)

90-49
1222

REMITTER   TED THOMAS   DATE   OCTOBER 14, 1987

PAY TO THE
ORDER OF   ALFRED P. LOMELI, TAX COLLECTOR $892.62

892 62

**CALIFORNIA
FIRST BANK**   1ST   HEAD OFFICE
350 CALIFORNIA STREET
SAN FRANCISCO, CALIFORNIA 94104

NON-NEGOTIABLE

AUTHORIZED SIGNATURE

FORM 247 (REV 8/80)

① 72288	10-15-87	86-5232		✓	486	30
TEMPORARY RECEIPT NO	DATE	BILL NUMBER	CASH	CHECK	AMOUNT RECEIVED	

CONTRA COSTA COUNTY   **TEMPORARY RECEIPT**   OFFICE OF TAX COLLECTOR

THIS IS A TEMPORARY RECEIPT, RECORDING YOUR PAYMENT WITH THE CASHIER. IT IS NECESSARY FOR THE
CASHIER TO RETAIN YOUR INSTALLMENT CARD (S) UNTIL IT IS PROCESSED. IF THERE ARE ANY INQUIRIES,
PLEASE REFER TO THE DATE AND NUMBER SHOWN ABOVE. IF A PERMANENT RECEIPT IS DESIRED, SEND A
SELF ADDRESSED STAMPED ENVELOPE TO:

CONTRA COSTA COUNTY TAX COLLECTOR
P.O. BOX 631
MARTINEZ, CA 94553

② 72289	10-15-87	212-161-003		✓	406	32
TEMPORARY RECEIPT NO	DATE	BILL NUMBER	CASH	CHECK	AMOUNT RECEIVED	

CONTRA COSTA COUNTY   **TEMPORARY RECEIPT**   OFFICE OF TAX COLLECTOR

THIS IS A TEMPORARY RECEIPT, RECORDING YOUR PAYMENT WITH THE CASHIER. IT IS NECESSARY FOR THE
CASHIER TO RETAIN YOUR INSTALLMENT CARD (S) UNTIL IT IS PROCESSED. IF THERE ARE ANY INQUIRIES,
PLEASE REFER TO THE DATE AND NUMBER SHOWN ABOVE. IF A PERMANENT RECEIPT IS DESIRED, SEND A
SELF ADDRESSED STAMPED ENVELOPE TO:

CONTRA COSTA COUNTY TAX COLLECTOR
P.O. BOX 631
MARTINEZ, CA 94553

Figure 1.9   Cashier's Check

parcel of land that was free of encumbrances or liens and sold it to a buyer who was depending on a loan from a bank or lending institution to finance the transaction, the following would take place. The purchaser would apply for a loan, the lender would approve it, and the purchaser/borrower would sign a Deed of Trust or Mortgage and be granted the necessary funds.

The act of executing (signing) the Deed of Trust has the effect of the borrower's pledging the property to the lender as security for the loan (collateral). In other words, the property, house and land in the above case, is now hypothecated (pledged) to the lender and, in the event of a default in payment, the lender is authorized to claim the property as his payment. As security instruments, mortgages are common in some states and Deeds of Trust in others; some states use both.

Properties with no liens or encumbrances are said to have *clear title*, meaning that they are clear of liens. However, immediately after the purchaser signs the Deed of Trust or Mortgage instrument and usually before taking possession of the new property, the lender records the Deed of Trust at the County Recorder's Office in the county in which the property is located. This recording, or filing, thus becomes part of the public records.

Additional or subsequent borrowing, judgments, or encumbrances will also be recorded in the public records. It is important to understand that subsequent loans or encumbrances will be junior in right of collection. The rule is: first to record at the Recorder's Office is first in right or seniority.

Let us return to the example of our newly constructed home that has been built on land that is free and clear—according to the County Recorder's Office. The property would be considered to have a clear title. When the lending institution files its lien, the property would then be encumbered with a First Deed of Trust. Let's set a value of $20,000 for our example and date that loan 1 January 1989. The owner later decides to borrow additional funds on 10 February 1990 in the amount of $50,000. This loan would be considered to be a junior Mortgage or Deed of Trust not because of the dollar amount but because it was filed (recorded) at a later date. First to record is first in right.

If, on June 16, 1990, the State of California records a tax lien for nonpayment of taxes, this lien will not take priority over the two previous liens. It will take its place in priority by date. It could be considered a third lien.

To review: The first party to reach the County Recorder's Office and officially file (record) a Deed of Trust will be first in right or priority. Deeds of Trust filed thereafter will assume position of second, third, or fourth, depending upon the date they were recorded.

In terms of Default Notices, the first default filed will be first in priority. However, if the owner of a Deed of Trust filing a Notice of Default is in a junior—second, third, or fourth—position, the foreclosure will be for the total dollar amount plus payments in arrears and fees and penalties and will include the obligation of any liens—first Deed of Trust, taxes that have been recorded earlier, and so on.

Remember: First to file is first in priority. Second, third, and fourth lenders charge higher interest rates and points on their loans because they have considerably more risk. They also must be prepared to obligate themselves for the payments on the first note in the event of a default. The risk requires a higher return on investment for most speculators.

The first loan in our case study was dated 19 June 1978. A second loan, noted in Item 7, is dated 12 September 1986. Just as taxes have priority over everything, one of these loans has priority over the other. The rule is: First to record is first in priority. So the loan dated and recorded on 16 July 1978 is the priority or senior loan. One does not determine position or seniority by dollar amount.

The lender of the first loan is Prosperity Savings and Loan Association, and that company is also referred to as the beneficiary. The second loan, as shown in Item 7, was made by D.D.G. Mortgage Corporation who then assigned the beneficial interest in it to the Hale and Randall Mortgage Corporation. So it was Hale and Randall Mortgage that issued the Notice of Default, dated 26 August 1987, for the second loan. The fact that ownership of the loan has changed *does not* stop the foreclosure clock.

BRINGING THE LOANS CURRENT

It is important to bring the loans current, that is, to pay the unpaid installments (and any penalties) to cure the default as soon as possible. How you do it is a matter of tactics. To ensure that the default be cured as quickly as possible, we made our payments by cashier's checks (see Figures 1.10 and 1.11).

By bringing the loans current immediately, the foreclosure clock is stopped. However, if you plan to hold the property to rehabilitate or sell, the payment books will be important. In the frenzy of completing the purchase and satisfying the sellers' needs, the payment books may be overlooked, or as happened in this case, the seller had given up on the future and just threw them away. Shortly after curing the loan, we requested that the seller sign a letter asking for new payment books (see Figures 1.12 and 1.13). You may need to do some research to find the specific lenders because many savings and loan offices have numerous branches. If your lender happens to be a private party, you may have to find the address from the seller.

Most loans written today include a clause that enables the lender to accelerate the loan if the property is "alienated" (title is transferred). In effect, such a clause could require the immediate payment of the balance of the loan if the property is transferred to a new owner or leased for any extended period of time. It is desirable, as a general rule, not to alert the lender of the property transfer, lest the loan be accelerated. The few thousands of dollars needed to make the delinquent loan payments are reasonable costs of doing business; repayment of the entire loan is not.

The question arises, can or will the lender accelerate the loan? Federal law gives the lender the right to accelerate or make the entire loan balance due and payable upon the alienation or conveyance of title. In the practical world, this rarely if ever occurs. Lenders are generally happy just to be receiving the payments on time. Loans that have fallen into default usually end up in special departments of the institutions, such as the Foreclosure Department, Foreclosure Section, Trustee Productions, and so forth. These departments all have their own

October 15, 1987

Prosperity Savings and Loan
Trustee Section
590 Morehouse Drive
San Diego, CA 92121

Attn: Denise Parks

Dear Denise:

Enclosed is our cashier's check to reinstate loan number
4-526990 in the name of Bert and Barbara Biddles.

Also, we've enclosed the receipt showing all property
taxes are current.

CASHIER'S CHECK

DANVILLE 142
(OFFICE OF ISSUE)   142- 3431544
                                                              80-49
REMITTER TED THOMAS   DATE OCTOBER 14, 1987   1222

PAY TO THE
ORDER OF PROSPERITY SAVINGS AND LOAN * * * * * * * * * * * * * * * * $**3,655.72*****

CALIFORNIA
FIRST BANK 3655 DOLS 72 CTS

CALIFORNIA FIRST BANK ST   HEAD OFFICE
                            350 CALIFORNIA STREET
                            SAN FRANCISCO, CALIFORNIA 94104   AUTHORIZED SIGNATURE

FORM 247 (REV. 8-80)

⑅3431544⑅ ⑈122200490⑉053 5000004⑅

Figure 1.10   Loan Payment for the First Deed of Trust

October 15, 1987

Hale & Randall Mortgage Company
4695 Chabot Drive, Suite 102
Pleasanton, CA 94566-9044

Attn: Stewart Kramer

Dear Stewart:

Enclosed is our cashier's check for $4,855.60 to reinstate
loan number 79556462 in the name of Bert Biddles.

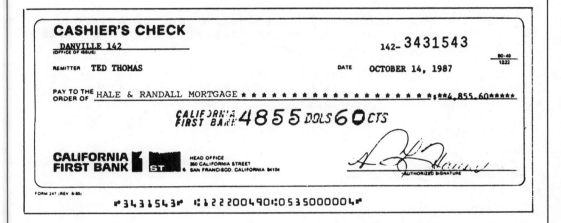

Figure 1.11   Loan Payment for the Second Deed of Trust

October 22, 1987

PROSPERITY SAVINGS AND LOAN
590 Morehouse Drive
San Diego, CA   92121

Attn: Loan Department

Gentlemen:

Please re-issue a coupon payment book for loan #4-526990
in the name of   Bert and Barbara Biddles   as we have
misplaced ours.

Also, please forward the invoice amount which is due
for insurance coverage on the property located at 9829
Broadmore Drive in San Ramon, California.

Mailing Address: Bert Biddles
                  c/o P. O. Box 5000, Suite 412
                  Danville, CA 94526

Sincerely,

Bert Biddles

Bert Biddles

Figure 1.12   Request for Coupon Payment Book (Letter)

October 22, 1987

HALE AND RANDALL MORTGAGE COMPANY
4695 Chabot Drive, Suite 102
Pleasanton, CA 94566-9044

Gentlemen:

Please re-issue a coupon payment book for loan #79556462
in the name of Bert and Barbara Biddles   as we have
misplaced ours.

Thank you.

Bert Biddles

Figure 1.13   Request for Coupon Payment Book on Second Loan (Letter)

priorities. Their primary function is to get the loan payments and they rarely worry about accelerating the loans and requesting the full balance.

What are your alternatives? You could approach the lender prior to the purchase and request an assumption agreement. Or you could inform the lender that you will bring the loan current if you are given a written notice that the loan will not be accelerated.

In this case, we brought the loans current and proceeded with our rehabilitation. It was not our intention to alert the lender of our purchase. Readers will need to decide if they want to assume loans, just make payments, or bargain with the lenders. The simple procedure used in the example was to make payments, fix up the property, and sell it to a new purchaser, who then paid off both loans.

Expect the lenders to know what is going on and recognize the rights they have under the law. However, as mentioned earlier, the defaulting loan will often get transferred to a different department and it could be months before you get any correspondence from the lender. This is exactly what happened with Prosperity Savings and Loan.

The second loan was treated differently. Hale and Randall operates local offices and bad loans are not sent off to a special department. They sit right on the local manager's desk and are his responsibility. We were not surprised when Hale and Randall responded to our cashier's check with a package of loan request documents.

Keep in mind we did not request these documents. The astute manager at Hale and Randall figured out exactly what was taking place and viewed the situation as a profit opportunity. He now had a loan out of default and, second, he had the opportunity to charge us a rather large assumption fee. The loan package included data about the present condition of the loan and then two pages of all the documentation that they require on loan assumptions. Figure 1.14 is a good example of what you'll need to prepare when you do request a loan from almost any institutional lender.

Note item 6 of Figure 1.14: The assumption fee for this loan is $25.00 plus 2 percent. This is a huge profit for Hale and Randall, considering that the loan was in default. Prosperity Savings did not correspond with us other than to send the required payment books.

A Place to Live

Your curing the loan default and paying the back taxes have ensured that the property you have just bought is saved from foreclosure and is free of liens and encumbrances. You have also solved the seller's long-term problems. But, until the seller is out of the house, both seller and buyer have a short-term problem. You need possession and the seller needs money. Many sellers in foreclosure have little or no money. They don't have enough to pay the first and last months' rent on a new dwelling. If you don't get them out, you'll never get possession. If, after you have deducted the costs of the termite and roof repairs and other liens, you see that you still have money due to the seller, you should consider assisting the seller in finding a new home. However, be cautious about how you spend these funds. Your only guarantee that the seller will indeed leave is to refrain

HALE and RANDALL MORTGAGE COMPANY

Dear

Thank you for your recent inquiry regarding an advance or refinance of your account.

Enclosed are some forms which we need for you to complete and return to us in order to process your loan application.

Upon forwarding these forms back to us, please include <u>photocopies</u> of the following items checked below:

X Most recent first mortgage statement showing the balance on all properties owned

X <u>Complete</u> Income Tax Returns for the years   and (Federal returns only)

X Homeowner's Insurance policy face sheet (in force)

X Most recent payroll stub or verification of income for both or all parties on loan

X <u>Complete</u> Statement of Identity (attached)

X Other: *If self-employed, send 12 months worth of checking account statements*

We have enclosed a large, self-addressed envelope for your convenience in mailing these items to us.

Your quick response will speed up the processing of your request. If you have any questions, please feel free to call me.

Very truly yours,

Figure 1.14   Loan Assumption Documents (Hale and Randall)

HALE and RANDALL
MORTGAGE COMPANY

RE: Assumption
    Escrow #   Account #

The following information must be furnished prior to close of escrow:

1. The enclosed loan information packet completed on the new owner and returned to Hale & Randall Mortgage Company so we may qualify the customer.

2. Copy of signed purchase agreement.

3. Copy of most recent preliminary Title Report.

The following information must be furnished upon close of escrow before we can consider this transaction complete:

1. Loss Payable on dwelling sufficient to insure our balance plus senior liens 100%. Please request we be sent an endorsement and a copy of the policy.

2. Statement of Condition on First Deed of Trust (showing First Deed of Trust Current).

3. Certified copy of recorded Assumption Agreement. Properly signed and acknowledged.

4. Certified copy of recorded Grant Deed.

5. Certified copy of final Closing Statement.

6. Assumption fee of $_25 + 2 %_ payable to Hale and Randall Mortgage Company.

Our Assumption Agreement will be forwarded upon completion of our qualifying the buyer. Normal processing time is 5-7 working days.

If there are any questions, please contact us.

Sincerely,

Nigel Hale

Nigel Hale

Figure 1.14   *(continued)*

HALE and RANDALL MORTGAGE COMPANY

RE:

Escrow # Loan # *79556462*

The following is a Statement of Condition requested by your company: *New Growth Financial*

Date of Loan:	*10/1/86*
Original Amount:	*53,800.00*
Terms:	*180 mos.*
Balance:	*53,731.43*
Interest Paid to:	*10/3/87*
Date Last Paid:	*10/20/87*
Date Next Due:	*11/1/87*
Interest:	*14.25%*
Late Charges After 10 Days:	*6*
Foreclosure/Attorney Fees:	*0*
Other Fees:	
Final Due Date:	*May apply*
Prepayment Penalty:	*10/1/01*
Rate Increase if Assumed:	*May apply*

If you have requested the above information because of an assumption you have in process, you should be aware that this loan is not assumable on a "Subject To" basis. We will consider a formal assumption of this loan based on our current lending guidelines.

Before approving this transaction, it is necessary that we have a completed assumption package on the new borrower.

Thank you.

Sincerely,

Figure 1.14 *(continued)*

November 13, 1987

New Growth Enterprises
601 Hartz Avenue, Suite 235
Danville, CA 94526

Gentlemen:

I, Amy Lee, am the legal owner of the property located at 101 Valdivia Circle in San Ramon, California.

I hereby accept cashier's check in the amount of $3,000 which represents first and last month's rent for a total of $2,200 and a $800 security deposit per rental agreement dated November 13, 1987 between Bert Biddles, lessee, and Amy Lee, lessor.

Amy Lee
Amy Lee Owner

                                        STATE OF CALIFORNIA
                                        COUNTY OF CONTRA COSTA

On this .....13..... day of ...*November*......... in the year ...*1987*....., before me, ...*Nancy M. Patterson*....., a Notary Public, State of California duly commissioned and sworn, personally appeared ...*Amy Lee*......................... personally known to be (or proved to me on the basis of satisfactory evidence) to be the person whose name ......*is*.......... subscribed to this instrument, and acknowledged that ..*She*... executed it.

   IN WITNESS WHEREOF I have hereunto set my hand and affixed my official seal in the State of ..*California*.............. County of .*Contra Costa*.... on the date set forth above this certificate.

                              Nancy M. Patterson
                              Notary Public, State of California

OFFICIAL SEAL
NANCY M. PATTERSON
NOTARY PUBLIC · CALIFORNIA
CONTRA COSTA COUNTY
My Comm Expires March 27 1990

Figure 1.15   Letter of Ownership of Property in San Ramon

from making the final payment until after the property has been vacated. *Don't violate this rule.*

Once again, it's a matter of solving problems. For both parties, the solution in this case was to have the seller find a new home. For the seller, this is difficult as prospective landlords will request a complete credit application and expect the prospective tenant to pay for the credit report. When you are in default, your credit report is likely to be a mess of everything from late payments to liens on the house, to abstracts of judgments from department stores. This is an extremely embarrassing and humiliating experience for the seller and may cause him to reconsider the transaction with you and attempt to cancel your contract.

Help the seller out of trouble. Instruct the seller to find a place to live and tell him that you will guarantee the rent. Have the landlord call you to confirm the arrangement.

Landlords want the rent and you want the property. So pay the rent in advance for the defaulting seller. This, too, becomes an expense and is deducted from the price paid for the equity. Figure 1.15 shows the notarized receipt signed by the landlord. Using a cashier's check assures the new landlord that the funds are available at the bank.

Unquestionably, the final settlement with the seller could be a time of disillusion for the seller. In keeping with our approach that we use only professionals for our series of reports—termite inspections, roof inspections, and so forth—notarize your payment of the seller's rent. That document will then become part of your settlement documents and not be subject to further inquiry.

Settle with the Owner

The final procedure in the purchase of distressed property is to settle with the owner. The contract stated that you would deduct the costs of repairs, taxes, and other expenses. Draw up a detailed billing of the expenses, making sure that your statement of account is as simple as possible. When you have completed your final walk-through, have determined that no additional damage has been incurred, and that the owners have removed all of their personal belongings, present the seller with the final statement and a cashier's check for the balance due, if any. Figure 1.16 shows the final statement for the property in San Ramon. Structural repairs required $4,000; payment of taxes due, $892.62; and the $3,025 described as Equity Paid to Date consists of the $25 paid as consideration for the Home Equity Contract and the $3,000 paid to the seller's new landlord.

We agreed to buy the equity for $12,000 more than those loans or a minimum of $7,000. When you buy from the owner, you buy what the owner has. The tax lien is a good example. If the owner did not have enough money coming to him as the equity payment to clear the tax lien, then you as the new owner will be responsible for the tax lien.

RESELLING DISTRESSED PROPERTY

If you decide to use a broker to sell the property, try to help the broker as much as possible. Do not wait for a buyer. If you can't advertise your property, you will

New Growth Enterprises

(415) 837-2106

November 17, 1987

Mr. & Mrs. Bert Biddles
101 Valdivia Circle
San Ramon, CA 94583

Dear Bert & Barbara:

Per the Home Equity Purchase Agreement dated October 3, 1987
between New Growth Enterprises and Bert and Barbara Biddles
the amount due seller is $12,000 less the following expenses:

Gross to Seller	$12,000.00
Less:	
Termite Repairs	3,620.00
Roof Repairs	400.00
Taxes	892.62
Equity paid to date	3,025.00
Equity Balance Due	$ 4,062.38

Sincerely,

NEW GROWTH ENTERPRISES

Ted Thomas

Ted Thomas
Vice President

Figure 1.16   Final Statement of Account (Letter to the Biddles)

hold it for a long time and use up all your profits in taxes and house payments. Selling real estate is easy if you price the property correctly and let the world know that it is available. The broker needs your help and support. If the broker won't advertise the property regularly, then you must either change the broker's contract to require it or you must advertise it yourself.

Let the neighbors know about your sale. Hold an Open House. Make up fliers with the broker's name on them and pay a high-school student to put one on each door for at least one mile around the house you want to sell. Do not put the fliers in mail boxes. Mail boxes are for mail and the post office will be annoyed with you. Figure 1.17 shows the memo we received from the broker who was handling this house; Figure 1.18 shows the flier we used to advertise the house in the immediate (one-mile) vicinity.

The brokerage community will be helpful. It is recommended that you work closely with all real estate brokers. The brokers and agents are your friends and they can show you many short cuts to the final sale. Don't wait for the brokers; your responsibility is to make money for yourself and investors. If you advertise aggressively, distribute fliers, and conduct Open Houses and parties for the neighborhood, you will be successful. Exclusive listings by the brokerage community may require that they do all the promotion and advertising. If that is the case, don't sign the contract. Sales, promotion, and advertising will find you your clients. I'm not suggesting that you alienate the brokerage community, but I am suggesting that you conduct the sale and that includes the advertisement, promotion, Open Houses, and the contacting of local charities and fraternal organizations.

Pricing is the key to selling. Don't get too greedy. Know your competition. Don't try for top dollar. You may get it—eventually, but you will spend a lot in carrying costs to get it.

PAYDAY

This transaction took a long time (the seller's contract was signed at the beginning of October, 1987, and escrow didn't close until the end of February, 1988) and a considerable amount in actual selling costs. But the property was very profitable as you can see by reviewing the final escrow papers (Figure 1.19). Even so, notice the high selling costs, especially the brokerage fees. Those fees could have purchased an enormous amount of advertising and promotion. You as the owner must control your costs; to do so, you must control what happens on the property. The purchasing, repairing, and selling are all your responsibilities.

Learn from your mistakes. It is not necessary to pay a full brokerage commission. Brokers and agents will be happy to bargain for a more equitable arrangement. It is cheaper to buy your own advertisements and fliers than it is to pay brokers. When you advertise, record the names of people who reply to your classified advertising. These are your future purchasers. Their names will be important when you have foreclosure property to sell in the future.

We thought you'd like
to see the ad we're running
on your home.
Our experience tells us that an ad
like this will attract qualified buyers.

OPEN SUNDAY 1–4:30
BE FIRST
to see this before it hits the open
market. Open rooms, open yard,
open feeling, open for an offer!
Like new at $169,500. Take
Montevideo to:
9829 BROADMORE DRIVE
Your host, Glenn Rose

Better Homes Realty   1838
Tice Valley Blvd.
**WALNUT
CREEK**
939-1131

Of course, advertising isn't the only way
we market your home.
Our relationships with other Better Homes Realty offices
and our nationwide referral and relocation services are
just two of the other methods we use to
give your property full exposure.

We want to give you a Better way.

Better Homes Realty

Each office is independently owned
& operated

Figure 1.17   Broker's Memo (Ad in *Contra Costa Times*)

FOR SALE

LARGE FAMILY HOME

OPEN HOUSE SUNDAY 1 p.m. - 5 p.m.

- NEW PAINT
- NEW CARPET
- 1450 SQUARE FEET
- 4 BEDROOMS
- 2 BATHS

- FIREPLACE
- DISHWASHER
- 2 CAR GARAGE
- FAMILY ROOM
- AIR CONDITIONING

LOCATED IN QUIET, RESIDENTIAL NEIGHBORHOOD
EASY ACCESS TO FREEWAY
LOOKS LIKE NEW

PRICE: $169,500

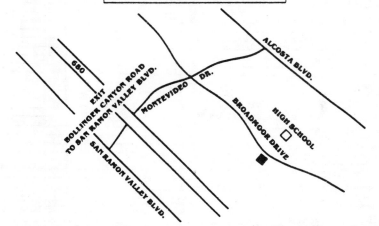

9829 BROADMOOR DRIVE, SAN RAMON
CONTACT GLEN ROSE 939-1131

Figure 1.18   "For Sale" Flier for San Ramon Property

SELLER'S INSTRUCTIONS

BIGLAND TITLE   DATE February 29, 1988
590 Ygnacio Valley Rd. Walnut Creek, Calif.   ESCROW NUMBER 36381 CH
ESCROW OFFICER CATHY HAMPTON   PROPERTY ADDRESS 9829 Broadmoor Driv
ENCLOSED ARE THE FOLLOWING: Corp Grant Deed, Instructions, & San Ramon, California
Corporation resolution.
Which you may deliver and / or record when you have collected for me the sum of $ 170,000.00   as follows:
LESS A _____ DEED OF TRUST FOR $ _____ IN FAVOR OF _____

SELLER'S COPY

ABOVE DEED OF TRUST TO BE RECORDED SUBJECT TO: _____

PRO RATE AS OF: CLOSE OF ESCROW - TAXES

ESTIMATED STATEMENT	DEBITS	CREDITS
PURCHASE PRICE		170,000.00
RECEIVED FROM BUYER OUTSIDE OF ESCROW		
DEPOSITS TO ESCROW $ BROKER $		
DEED OF TRUST ☐ FIRST ☐ SECOND		
Federal Express Payoff	15.00	
DEMAND OF: HOME FEDERAL NO. 0526990 TOTAL - EST	52,317.94	
PRINCIPAL $50,670.86		
INT. @ $14.08 FR 1-1-88 TO receipt,est 1,013.76		
INT. @ FR TO		
PREPAYMENT CHARGE		
RECONVEYANCE / FORWARDING FEE /Fax Fee	115.00	
XXXXXXXXXXXXXXXXX unpaid Late Charges due 98.32		
Impound Deficit 420.00		
DEMAND OF: BENEFICIAL MORTGAGE CO. - TOTAL - EST	54,821.75	
PRINCIPAL $53,634.01		
INTEREST @ FR 2-4 TO 3-25 1,082.74		
Trustee Fee $65.00 Forwarding Fee $40.00		
EXISTING LOAN BALANCE		
PRO RATA INT. ON $ @ % FR TO		
LOAN TRUST FUND BALANCE		
PRO RATA FIRE INS. PREM. $ FOR YR. PD TO		
PRO RATA RENT @ PER FR TO		
PRO RATA COUNTY TAXES FOR ½YR $ 203.16 PD TO 7-1-88 est		67.00
TAXES PAID to 7-1-88 (Both Installment, 1987-88 Paid)		
COMMISSION BETTER HOMES/$4,930.00	8,250.00	
Wallace & Anderson $3,320.00		
COUNTY TRANSFER TAX	187.00	
3 R REPORT - REFUND TO:		
NOTARY FEE est	10.00	
RECONVEYANCE FEE	85.00	
RECORDING FEE est	20.00	
Home Warranty - Western	295.00	
Credit to Buyer for Landscape Allowance	1,000.00	
Credit to Buyer for non-recurring closing costs	4,000.00	
	$	
ESTIMATED BALANCE TO: ☒ SELLER ( ) BIGLAND TITLE INS. CO.	49,065.31	
TOTALS	$ 170,067.00	$ 170,067.00

These instructions are effective until revoked by written demand on you by the undersigned or any one of them. I hereby agree to pay all my proper costs and
fees, including any adjustments, and authorize you to deduct same from funds due me and remit balance to NEW GROWTH ENTERPRISES, INC.,
A CALIFORNIA CORPORATION

c/o _____   NEW GROWTH ENTERPRISES, INC.
Received _____ , 19 ____ . Time _____

       BY: TED THOMAS

By _____
F. 2962 - (SF)   BY: NANCY PATTERSON

Figure 1.19   Final Escrow Papers

The property sold for $170,000 less the following expenses:

Demand to pay off Prosperity Savings	$52,317.94
Federal Express (see document)	15.00
Transfers	
Pay off demand from Hale and Randall	54,821.75
Real Estate Commission to Better Homes and Wallace Anderson Realtors	8,250.00
County transfer tax	187.00
Notary fee	10.00
Recording fee	20.00
Reconveyance fee	85.00
Home warranty	295.00
Credit to buyer for landscape allowance	1,000.00
Credit to buyer for nonrecurring closing costs	4,000.00
Net payment to seller	$49,065.30

TESTIMONIALS

The final illustration for this chapter is a testimonial from the seller (Figure 1.20). Testimonials and guarantees are probably the most important attributes of a good sales presentation. Customers who sell their property need reassurance that they will be treated fairly and equitably. The skepticism that your clients have will be reduced considerably by your effective use of testimonials. Carefully read any testimonials you might get in the mail. Note that if they are convincing, you will consider the product. If the person writing has the same problem you have and the testimonial claiming that the problem could be solved using this particular company's service, your interest will be sparked. Ask your sellers if they are happy with your service. If they are, get them to write a convincing testimonial. Be sure you obtain a release to use the testimonial in your promotional or direct mail. If your seller is prepared to tell you on a piece of paper what problem it was that you solved and how efficiently you solved it, new prospective clients will find the testimonial believable. If you take care of your clients and treat them as you would like to be treated, you will succeed.

October 28, 1987

To Whom It May Concern:

Selling ones home under duress of foreclosure can never be a pleasant experience. It touches ones sense of dignity and is terribly destabilizing to ones family.

Having endured such an experience, I would like to recommend that anyone else finding himself in similar circumstances contact Ted Thomas of New Growth Enterprises.

Mr. Thomas not only correctly advised me of my options, but outlined a plan that helped me in resettling my family and regaining a measure of stability in our lives.

Mr. Thomas and his staff performed efficiently and with sensitivity to our problems at a time which that kind of professionalism and attitude was essential to me and my family.

Bert Biddles
Bert Biddles

Figure 1.20   Biddles' Testimonial Letter

2

Real Estate at 20 to 30 Percent Discount

How to Find the Bargains

Where are those foreclosures that will make you rich? This chapter is loaded with money-making ideas:

- Sources of information
- Tips on finding properties
- The benefits of direct mail
- Letters that bring results
- Planning presentations
- List of dos and don'ts.

It is no secret. It is all in the public record, but you need to know how to use it. You also need a systematic approach to finding motivated sellers. However, don't let this take all of your time. If you do, you won't have time for appraisal, negotiation, and purchasing. To be successful, you must expect a continuous, unending search for the winners. You must do thorough, diligent homework to be ready when that right property comes along.

The distressed sellers will take your time in negotiations. This is valuable time spent as you will be solving a problem. Remember, if you can't solve the seller's problem, you probably can't do any business. The sellers are motivated but they will rarely just hand you the keys. The normal purchase will require time to locate, appraise, and negotiate.

SOURCES OF INFORMATION

When a borrower does not live up to the terms of his or her loan agreement, the lender requests that the trustee file a Notice of Default with the County Recorder's Office. These public records are available to anyone who has the desire to seek the information. In most populated areas, a few enterprising businesspeople provide the service of researching and compiling lists of defaulting homeowners and foreclosure auctions and sales. These lists are usually mailed regularly to subscribers. The lists include information on defaults, trustee's sales, and properties owned by the banks, known as REO (real estate owned). These compiling services range from a simple copy of the legal notice to sophisticated computer-generated reports that show everything from the Assessor's Parcel Number to the Trust Deed that is foreclosing.

In the state of California at the time the trustee files a Notice of Default at the County Recorder's Office, the foreclosure time clock starts running. The homeowner/trustor is granted by law three months to reinstate the defaulting loan. The reinstatement process simply requires the full payment of past due payments and penalties such as late charges.

If the defaulting loan has not been cured in the three months, the homeowner is issued a Notice of Trustee's Sale. The announcement of Trustee's Sale is the notification to the public that the property will be sold at public auction, often on the courthouse steps. The Notice of Trustee's Sale is issued to the homeowner/trustor at least 21 days before the actual auction/sale. This notice will be published three times in a newspaper of general circulation and posted on public bulletin boards. The 21-day period is referred to as the publication or advertising period. Sheriff's Sales and Trustee's Sales are open to the public and anyone qualified (with the cash or equivalent) may purchase property at the sale.

Detailed reports are helpful for property analysis and appraisal. The default reporting services list hundreds of properties being foreclosed upon weekly. You could easily spend all day, every day, driving from property to property trying to find that gem that will turn into a gold mine. You don't have that time. One such service, provided by the Daily Default Infoservice of Antioch, California, is shown in Figure 2.1.

In addition to reporting services such as the Daily Default Infoservice, most areas have a legal newspaper in which is published virtually everything that is recorded: sales tax permits, bankruptcies, divorces, probates, liquor licenses, and so on. Figure 2.2 shows a page of the *News Register*, published in Walnut Creek, California, in which legal notices of default are printed. Figure 2.3 shows a summary of similar information. *The Inter-City Express*, the legal newspaper of Alameda County, California (see Figure 2.4), displays the notices according to the stage of foreclosure. Legal newspapers are very inexpensive. The volume of defaults, Trustee's Sales, and REO in most counties will overwhelm you unless you eliminate the properties that do not have a high income potential. The more data you have, the easier the elimination becomes. It is instructive to compare legal newspaper listings with the Daily Default listings. The reader can easily see how the extra data provided by the Daily Default Infoservice will save hundreds of hours of wasted time. A comparison of the Daily Default Infoservice and the competitor, *L & A Publications* (see Figure 2.5), shows again that the more information you get the better your chances of eliminating the time wasters before you leave your home or office.

If you can't find a reporting service for default and foreclosure information, go to the County Recorder's Office and get it and, while you're there, ask the clerks if there is a reporting service for your county. Some buyers of distressed

DAILY DEFAULT INFOSERVICE BOX 456 ANTIOCH CA 94509 * 415/754-7039 W1

INSTRUMENT NO.: DFLT-83481 RECORD DATE: 05/08/89 AP# 400-651-1 TAX ASSESSED VALUE: $139,000.00: 1985

LOAN DATE: 08/02/84 | TRUSTOR: DAVID S. CANLAS, ET AL SINCE SOLD TO:
BOOK-PAGE: 11907 -92 | TRUSTOR ADD: 301 BRIGHTON, HERCULES, 94547
ORIG. LN. AMT.: $117,300.00 | TRUSTEE: CAL RECON PHONE: 818/701-2575 TS#:116433
DELINQ. DATE: 02/01/89 | ADDRESS: PO BOX 6200, NORTHRIDGE, CA 91328
DELINQUENT AMT.: $8,352.00 | LENDER: GREAT WESTERN BANK PHONE: 818/701-2013 LN#:353525-1
AS OF: 05/08/89 | ADDRESS: PO BOX 1900, NORTHRIDGE, CA 91328
ADD'L INFO: SFR: 1475 SQFT; 3/2.5; ATTACHED 2-CAR GARAGE; POOL; LOT 65 X 120; 1984 SUBDIVIDED
INSTRUMENT NO.: DFLT-83482 RECORD DATE: 05/08/89 AP#: 95-91-10 TAX ASSESSED VALUE: $58,000.00: 1987

LOAN DATE: 01/09/89 | TRUSTOR: HANS-JUERGEN JOHNSON, ET AL SINCE SOLD TO:
BOOK-PAGE: 14820-711 | TRUSTOR ADD: 127 MT. TRINITY CT., CLAYTON, 94517
ORIG. LN. AMT.: $16,000.00 | TRUSTEE: GOLDEN PACIFIC TD SERVICE PHONE: 415/935-1421 TS#:60321-DK-03
DELINQ. DATE: 04/09/89 | ADDRESS: 800 S. BROADWAY #410, WALNUT CREEK, CA 94596
DELINQUENT AMT.: $665.00 | LENDER: REDWOOD EMPIRE MTG. PHONE:707/546-5511 LN#:8863
AS OF: 05/08/89 | ADDRESS: 513 'E' ST., SANTA ROSA, CA 95404
ADD'L INFO: SFR: TRUSTOR PHONE 672-4070;2261 SQFT; ATTACHED 3-CAR GARAGE; 4/2; 1979 SUBDIVIDED
INSTRUMENT NO.: TS-81768 RECORD DATE: 05/08/89 AP#: 413-213-2 TAX ASSESSED VALUE: $63,500.00 : 1986

LOAN DATE: 10/27/82 | TRUSTOR: DANNY L. DUGAN, ET AL SINCE SOLD TO:
BOOK-PAGE: 10984-295 | TRUSTOR ADD: 3375 WALNUT AVE, CONCORD, 94519
APROX MINM BID.: $93,345.99 | TRUSTEE: ROBERT WEISS INC. PHONE: 818/967-4302 TS#:A-2122
DATE OF SALE: 05/31/89 | ADDRESS: PO BOX 3269 COVINA, CA 91722
TIME OF SALE: 3 PM | LENDER: MISSION BAY MTG. PHONE: 415/828-3730 LN#:8019331
PLACE OF SALE: ENTRANCE TO COUNTY COURTHOUSE, 27TH & BARRETT ST., RICH
ADD'L INFO: SFR: ; 912 SQFT; 3/1; TRUSTOR PHONE 827-1170; .2 ACRES
INSTRUMENT NO.: REO-80493 RECORD DATE: 05/03/89 AP#:400-681-17 TAX ASSESSED VALUE: $91,000.00 : 1988

Figure 2.1 Daily Default Notice from Infoservice

Figure 2.2   News Ad from News Register for Legal Notices

JULY 19, 1988

TS   2470 20th St San Pablo sale to be 8/11/88 at 9:30 at the
      Broadway side entrance to the City Hall 1666 N Main St
      Walnut Creek Trustor Sarah J Chilton rec 11/20/87 14030OR707
      TS#W84122 $21,074.79 Trustee TD
      Service (415)944-9015 opening bid (415)946-4357

TS   1009 Santa Monica Ct Pleasant Hill sale to be 8/16/88 at 10:00 at
      the main entrance to the City Hall 1666 N Main St Walnut Creek
      Trustor Roland Mallory rec 7/23/79 9451OR681 TS# 88 2057
      $60,678.60 Trustee First Interstate Mtg Co (818)356-7638

TS   878 Redwood Ct Crockett sale to be 8/11/88 at 11:30 at the Court St
      entrance to the CCC Courthouse corner of Main & Court St Mtz
      Trustor Bryan & Diane Schwab rec 9/25/81 10511OR475 TS#3673
      02 $102,971.13 Trustee Westwood Assoc (714)996-6815

TS   45 El Gavilan Orinda sale to be 8/24/88 at 3:00 at the Main entrance
      to the City Hall 27th St & Barrett Ave Richmond Trustor Ted Carroll
      & Gwendolyn Belle rec 12/6/85 12649OR195 TS#213941
      $360,692.41 Trustee Calif Recon Co (818)701-2575

TS   1438 Ventura Blvd Pitts sale to be 8/11/88 at 11:30 at the Court St
      entrance to the CCC Courthouse Main & Court St Mtz
      Trustor Warren Jr & Ruth Alexander rec 8/13/86 13057OR868
      TS#88024 $47,142.74 Trustee Red Shield Servicing Inc
      (916)485-5753

$388.50   Davidson Homes to Carlo & Paula Petricola
          Lot 68 subdiv 6685 1005 Jennifers Ct Danville
          Weyerhaeuser Mtg Co $165,000

$120.45   Kevin & Melanie Gambetti to Ulpinao Jr & Anita Tongol
          Lot 88 Park View Terrace Unit #3 2677 Gill Dr Concord
          Far West S&L $105,097

DT   Ray & Brigitta Turnipseed
          7301 Gladys Ave El Cerrito lot 1 Holly Tract
          Wells Fargo $30,000

DT   ERol & Vicki Akin
          440 Moraga Way Orinda lot 9 Moraga Woodlands
          Lakeshore Properties Retirement Trust $75,000

Figure 2.3   News Ad from News Register with Listings

The Inter-City Express

Established in 1909

Contra Costa County

DEFAULT NOTICES

Filed: Oct 21

Legal: Lt 20, Pleasantimes sub,
  Bethel Island
Owner of Record: Rich & Gayla Loza
Owner's Address: PO Box 1134,
  Bethel Island
PI: $4,012.54 as of 10-18-88
Beneficiary: Eileen L. Simpson &
  James P. Sharp
TS #: 183406JE
TD $: $100,000
TD Date: 7-17-87 as #13779/525
Default Recorded: 10-21-88 as #194296
Trustee: Fidelity Nat'l Title Ins. Co.
  707-443-8013

Legal: Ut 179, 1/209 Int. lt 1, sub 5195
Owner of Record: Linda M. Rupprecht
Owner's Address: 2742 Oak Rd
  #179, Walnut Creek
PI: $4,066.76
Beneficiary: Investor's Mtg Svc Co
TS #: 5368869
TD $: $64,500
TD Date: 8-13-82 as #10891/243
Default Recorded: 10-21-88 as #194166
Trustee: IMCO Realty Svcs Inc.
  707-546-3310 X 5251

TRUSTEE'S SALES

Filed: Oct 21

Legal: Lt 55 Manor Crest Village#2.
Street Address: 2859 La Salle Ave,
  Concord
Doc #: #194292 as filed 10-21-88
Owner of Record: Danielle Meginness
TD Date: 9-2-87 as #13876/38
Beneficiary: Weyerhauser Mfg Co
Unpaid: $101,666.63
TS #: 4349-02
Trustee: Advanced Trust Deed
Svc for Westwood Assocs,
  714-996-6815
Sale Date: 11-16-88, 10am, Court
  & Main Streets Martinez

Legal: Pcl A,, 4/18/79 bk 75, pg 37
Street Address: 24 Amber Pl, Alamo
Doc#: #194201 as filed 10-21-88
Owner of Record: Frank & Nancy
  Guarascio
TD Date: 7-30-87 as #13806/125
Beneficiary: Argent Mtg & Investment Co
Unpaid: $98,982.76
TS #: 88-07-13
Trustee: A/C Trust Deed Svcs Inc,
  415-284-4644
Sale Date: 11-22-88, 10am, 1666 N. Main
  St, Walnut Creek

Figure 2.4 Ad from Inter-City Express (Contra Costa County)—Default Notices

```
                L & A  Real Estate Publications,  Inc.
                      NOTICES OF  DEFAULT
                      Santa  Clara  County


DEFAULT(Rec'd Date/Instr.No.): 02/03/89        DEFAULT  AMT.: $730.41
TRUST DEED: 11/07/85  J513/1655                ORIGINAL AMT.: $None given
PROPERTY ADDRESS: 3145 Ludlow Court, San Jose  95148
LEGAL: Lot 92, Tract 4983  APN: 673-17-056
TRUSTOR: Canales, Raul & Mary S.
OWNER: Same
MAILING ADDRESS: Same
BENEFICIARY: Jacobs, Frank K. & Judith
BENE'S ADDRESS: c/o World Equities


DEFAULT(Rec'd Date/Instr.No.): 02/03/89        DEFAULT  AMT.: $1,901.70
TRUST DEED: 07/24/87  K236/2179                ORIGINAL AMT.: $2,867.95
PROPERTY ADDRESS: 2828 Broken Oak Court, San Jose  95148
LEGAL: Lot 67, Tract 6067  APN: 652-28-062
TRUSTOR: Pena, Rosie E.
OWNER: Same
MAILING ADDRESS: Same
BENEFICIARY: Century Loan Corp.
BENE'S ADDRESS: c/o Bay Counties Foreclosure Services Inc.


DEFAULT(Rec'd Date/Instr.No.): 02/03/89        DEFAULT  AMT.: $None given
TRUST DEED: 07/06/78  D792/398                 ORIGINAL AMT.: $73,200.00
PROPERTY ADDRESS: 109 Cadwell Court, San Jose  95138
LEGAL: Lot 22, Tract 5842  APN: 678-33-038
TRUSTOR: Lindsey, Albert M. & Patricia Y.
OWNER: Same
MAILING ADDRESS: Same
BENEFICIARY: Home Savings of America
BENE'S ADDRESS: PO Box 7075, Pasadena


DEFAULT(Rec'd Date/Instr.No.): 02/03/89        DEFAULT  AMT.: $1,771.68
TRUST DEED: 08/12/87  K256/1559                ORIGINAL AMT.: $48,000.00
PROPERTY ADDRESS: 3250 East Hills Drive, San Jose  95127
LEGAL: None given          APN: 601-24-057
TRUSTOR: Lewis, Raul A. & Alice C.
OWNER: Same
MAILING ADDRESS: Same
BENEFICIARY: Frain, Mary J. etal
BENE'S ADDRESS: c/o Global Equities
```

Figure 2.5   Default Report (L and A Real Estate Publication, Santa Clara)

property spend one day a week researching the records and the remaining time contacting the property owners or following the Trustee's Sales.

FINDING PROPERTIES

Your system for finding properties may include reviewing and tracking notices of default, notices of impending Trustee's Sales, and notices of real estate owned by the banks (REO). Many buyers of distressed property also follow the county tax sale auctions and the Small Business Administration foreclosure sales and auctions. Foreclosure on Housing & Urban Development (HUD) and Veterans Administration (VA) properties is a business in itself. Ask a broker to take you to one of the HUD auctions or a VA property sales seminar. You'll find hundreds of brokers at those meetings.

Segmenting your market is probably the best way to start. After you review the defaults and Trustee's Sale listings thoroughly, you may decide to start with the defaults. Before doing anything else, review the foreclosure consultants law in your state. The specific statute in the State of California is in Sections 1695.1 to 1695.14 of the Civil Code. (See the Appendix to Chapter 6.)

The appropriate foreclosure laws may have a different name or reference in your state. A visit to the local library should answer your questions. If the public library does not have the codes or statutes, check with a business school, university, or law school library, or as a last resort, contact a real estate attorney.

SEEING THE CLIENTS

Armed with your knowledge of which properties are in default and of the legal requirements, you then contact the homeowner or person in default either by letter, post card, telephone, or a personal visit. Remember, you are in the problem-solving business. You are there to solve, not sell. Try to discover the owner's reason for needing to sell. Why is he or she in this situation? You're in the business of meeting needs, so it helps if you discover the seller's needs and wants.

KNOW YOUR LOCAL MARKET

The more you know about your local market, the easier it is to control it. Study your territory as precisely as possible. This work should be done methodically on a regular basis. You should be able to determine how many prospects you have, where they are, and how much of your type of service they probably will buy each year. When you have this information, you can decide how much of the potential sales volume you want. Then you must plan to be in the right place at the right time.

The big chain and discount stores study and research every market to find the most profitable locations. They look for high concentrations of potential customers. You must do the same.

FINDING FORECLOSED PROPERTIES BY DIRECT MAIL MARKETING

The information services described thus far will identify local foreclosed properties for you to pursue. But to make the system really work for you, you need to put yourself in the broader marketplace. That is where direct mail advertising of your services comes in.

Most businesses prospect in their own community. For example, if you have a retail dress shop, you'll probably get most of your business from the local area. No matter how much advertising you do, women from the other side of town will usually shop on the other side of town.

Direct mail is different. The whole city, the whole state, and perhaps the whole country, is your marketplace. And you get all those free employees (the mail carriers) helping you deliver your message to hundreds of people every day.

Direct marketing, whether it is of coupons, solicitations, sales announcements, catalogs, or sales memos can effectively expand your business by taking you out of the local community. Who are the potential buyers of your products or services? It is easier to find out than you think: the hundreds of defaults every week; the owners of thousands of properties throughout the United States that are auctioned at Trustee's Sales each week.

Size, weight, and price are not factors to be considered in the marketing of your services by mail. The only consideration is whether or not there are potential customers beyond your local community who could be invited and enticed to buy your service. Think about it. There are far more potential customers outside your local community (marketplace) than in it. In other words, you judge your results by how much profit you make on each purchase and subsequent sale, not on how many telephone responses you receive.

What does mail order really mean? Mail order is direct marketing. You are writing directly to one segment of a market, not to the market as a whole. You are segmenting the market down to a narrow slice (or segment) which you will call *distressed properties*. You could narrow down that segment into just Trustee's Sales or just REO or possibly just properties seized by the IRS. Direct mail goes from you straight to the customer.

HOW DO PEOPLE BUY?

People buy for convenience and availability. You'll probably not buy too many houses through the mail, but you can easily let all the homeowners who are in default know about your service with this direct response method.

One of the keys to success in direct marketing is the return on investment. You must reach enough people by whatever method you use, make your presentation, and get a response from them. If you send out a hundred letters offering to purchase houses in default and you get only one response, that is a 1 percent return. If you purchase that house, fix it up, and sell it at a profit of, say $5,000, that is a great response. So whether you get a 1 percent or 10 percent response is less important than the amount you make in net profit from each sale. The critical question is not rate of response but return on investment. In other words, you judge your results by how much profit you make on each purchase and subsequent sale and not on how many telephone responses you receive.

Keep in mind your customers need information. First they want to know that your services are available. Then they will want to know what your services consist of. Then they'll have a host of other questions.

Personal visits can be productive, but they are also time consuming, especially if you travel any distance. And you may not get in the door. Women are sometimes more able than men to convince homeowners to let them in. It seems that defaulted homeowners have been called on by process servers, bill collectors and disgruntled people in general. Their answer to the door is usually hostile and aggressive. In most cases the door will not be answered even though you can hear the television playing and people talking. Direct mail will allow you to tell your customers, inexpensively, about what you can do to help them.

Telephone calls are effective, but homeowners are usually available only before and after normal business hours. Bill collectors and other creditors attempt to contact homeowners by telephone. If you are planning to use the telephone to contact the defaulting homeowners, expect them to hang up frequently and offer considerable resistance. The defaulting homeowners are street-wise. Plan your telephone presentation and try to establish a rapport that will convince the homeowner you are trying to solve the foreclosure problem.

WHAT DOES THE CUSTOMER WANT?

What does the customer (in this case the homeowner whose loan is in default) want to know? The same things you want to know each time you buy something: What's in it for me? That's a realistic question to ask yourself, because the customer will. The customer will want to know what you can do for him. So tell him—more than once. Give him a good answer or your letter will be in the trash. What do you want him or her to do? Telephone? Write? Wait? Do nothing? You must tell him what you want him to do, exactly, specifically, and repeatedly. Will you pay cash? Or will the customer expect deferred payments? What about a guarantee? Do you offer a free consultation? Should you? You must make an offer your customer *can't* refuse.

APPEAL TO THE RIGHT PERSON

Once you have targeted your prospects, people who appear likely to be interested in your product and capable of using the services you offer, you know to whom you will be addressing your appeals and your qualifications. Having researched the county records or the default listing services, you'll not waste your time with people who are not motivated to use your service.

LETTERS THAT BRING RESULTS

Use a series of letters, coupons, fliers, and seminars to inform prospects of your services and clarify for them the procedures of a foreclosure action. But mere information is not enough; repetition is important. Recognize that buying and selling decisions are emotional decisions, not necessarily logical decisions. This means that you'll need to be in the prospect's mind when he or she makes the decision to sell the defaulted property. People usually buy benefits or whatever it is that a product will do for them. Remember, the customer is saying over and over again in his or her mind: What's in it for me? The benefits of doing business with you must be stated clearly and expressed repeatedly. Your customer will buy results and benefits from you; not things or services. Don't offer things; offer proven or guaranteed results. Tell the customers about the wonderful things that will happen as a result of doing business with you: have them envisage no more bill collectors, no more tax payments, no more judgments on the public record. Sell them on fast relief, just as the cold remedies or aspirins do on television: fast, easy relief.

What Makes Customer Respond?

You must appeal to your customers' fundamental human needs. You experience these needs every day of your life, but it is sometimes difficult to reduce them to written form. The fear of loss is a tremendous motivator and, when the defaulted homeowner finally realizes that his house will be sold at auction and all of the funds will go to others, he will become motivated. That is the time when your letter should arrive.

Profitable sales letters will bring prospects to you. Write your letter to capture attention with the first paragraph. Get right to the point. (See Figure 2.6 for an example of the sort of information-packed letter that is an effective introduction for your services.) Don't take a long time to promise an important benefit of your service. If you don't get attention and promise benefits in the first paragraph, you'll lose the prospect and your letter will be thrown into the waste basket.

The question the recipient of your letter is asking is: What is in it for me? Your letter must answer this question and solve the homeowner's problem.

Continue to describe all of your other benefits within the body of the letter. If possible, make your prospect visualize himself enjoying the benefits. Show him how easily he can get the benefits.

Once the prospect knows what he gains by doing what you suggest, then tell him what he will lose by not taking action. Tell him what to do and how to do it. Then repeat the information. Tell him again what he stands to lose by not acting immediately.

Why, you ask, will the customer respond to my letter? He will not, unless you have credibility. If you send post cards and letters that are poorly drafted, misspelled, and not professionally reproduced, you will lose them to the trash can. On receiving the letter, the customer will require proof: Show me. He will want proof, or at least some evidence, that you can perform as your letter says you will. It is not enough to make a promise; you must back it up with proof, such as a copy of a testimonial from a satisfied customer or an unconditional, written guarantee. In short, the promises and claims must be made creditable.

FOLLOW UP—FOLLOW UP—FOLLOW UP

You will need to repeat your prospecting letters again and again. (See Figure 2.7 for an example of a follow-up letter and Figure 2.8 for an example of a coupon

New Growth Enterprises

(415) 837-2106

April 15, 1988

&fname& &lname&
&address1&
&city&, &state& &zip&

Dear &fname&:

Isn't it about time you did something about the <u>FORECLOSURE</u> that
is hanging over your head???

If you do nothing, hoping for a miracle, the law will take its
course and you will lose your house at PUBLIC AUCTION. Not only
will you lose your house but also your equity, because houses sold
at PUBLIC AUCTION usually go for twenty five (25%) to fifty
(50%) percent less than houses sold on the open market. This
isn't surprising when you think of it.

You need help today. <u>We</u> <u>will</u> <u>provide</u> <u>you</u> <u>with</u> <u>cash</u> <u>for</u> <u>your</u>
<u>equity</u> <u>within</u> <u>10</u> <u>days.</u>

<u>You</u> <u>need</u> <u>cash</u> <u>right</u> <u>now</u> <u>and</u> <u>we</u> <u>provide</u> <u>you</u> <u>with</u> <u>the</u> <u>cash</u> <u>you</u>
<u>need.</u>

What is the "unpardonable sin" in life? What one thing brings
its own punishment? What surely spells extinction?
PROCRASTINATION!! That is the "unpardonable sin".
What are you waiting for? In just days you
will lose your home to foreclosure sale. Don't
stick your head in the sand!

Lord knows what it is like to be broke!
The company I worked for went out of
business. The local economy was in
bad shape and it was hard to find
a job. If you have ever looked for
employment in a depressed economy
you know how frustrating and
humiliating that can be.

Soon things got worse. My car was repossessed
because I missed a couple of payments. One day,
I reached for the telephone to continue my
job search only to find it disconnected. A
few days later my eviction notice arrived in
the mail.

(please turn to page 2)

© 1988 New Growth Financial.

Figure 2.6   Introductory Letter from New Growth

My situation became so desperate that I had to borrow money from friends just to feed my family. I felt awful doing this because I didn't know when I could pay them back. I thought that things couldn't get any worse, but they did. My youngest child became seriously ill and needed surgery I couldn't afford.

I couldn't believe this was really happening to me. What made it even more difficult to bear was watching my wife and children suffer. I dreaded waking up in the morning and facing my hurt and disappointed family.

Does this sound familiar?

The foreclosure clock is running. In just a short time your home will be sold at PUBLIC AUCTION (trustee sale).

Don't turn your back on a sure thing.

WE CARE. We have taken the time to write you a letter which could save you a dreadful experience. This isn't another one of those xerox copies of some bland letter. Of course, you are skeptical. That just proves you are a responsible person.

Let's fact it. Your life would be better if you had some cash to deal with the present difficult circumstances.

We will provide you with cash for the equity in your home and then you will have the comfort of knowing and planning your future.

Think about it. Cash will bring freedom to make choices that will make you a happier person. The certainty of knowing that you can control the next steps in your life.

Freedom from loan companies.

What have you got to lose?? The equity in your home is what you will lose if you don't take action immediately.

Of course, you can throw this letter in the trash and maybe miss your best chance to recover; that is up to you. But what about your family; don't they deserve a chance to start again?

Don't turn your back on a sure thing. Take action right away. Make this the turning point in your life.

(please turn to page 3)

Figure 2.6   *(continued)*

****

OUR GUARANTEE TO YOU: Let's be perfectly frank. You are afraid someone will take advantage of you. Let's relieve you of that anxiety. If you get a better written offer (and we know you won't) that is more beneficial than our proposal, we will cancel our contract. Yes! That is correct! We will release you from the contract if you get a better deal. You are the judge. Is that fair treatment? How can you lose? Stop procrastinating; indecision could cost you thousands of dollars if your property is sold at public auction (trustee sale).

****

P.S. You need cash to solve your problem!!

We have the cash you need!!! Just pick up the telephone and dial 837-2106. Ask for Ted or Nancy.

The cash you need will be in your hands in TEN (10) DAYS.

Remember: If you take no action, your home will be sold at public auction and you will be evicted. That is the law. Make sure this doesn't happen to you.

Figure 2.6   *(continued)*

?\WS4\DEFAULTS .op

New Growth Enterprises
(415) 837-2106

April 17, 1988

&fname& &lname&
&addesss1&
&city&, &state&   &zip&

Dear &fname&:

Be honest with yourself for a minute. Do you really think the lender cares what happens to you? Aren't they really only interested in getting their money back?

Many people panic when they receive a Notice of Default. This is a moment of careful planning, not procrastination, not self-defeating panic.

If you do nothing - hoping for a miracle - the law will take its course and you will lose your house at Public Auction. Not only will you lose your equity in your home, because houses sold at Public Auction usually sell for for twenty five percent (25%) to fifty percent (50%) less than houses sold on the open market. This isn't very surprising when you think about it.

We will buy your house and pay you cash.

By the time the lender forces the public auction, he is really only interested in getting his money back. The fact that you want to get your money out of the house isn't of much interest to me.

You can save the equity in your house and stop the legal hassle.

If you sit back and do nothing you will lose not only your house, but you will lose the equity you have earned.

Many people in your situation fall victim to their fears and anxieties and simply decide to do nothing. They can't believe that their home will be taken away from them by a bank or lending institution. They can't believe the law allows this and they hope that some legal angle will resuce them. They therefore HIDE inside their homes hoping the problem will simply go away, procrastinating about taking no action; meanwhile, they are running out of time and options.

(please turn to page 2)

© New Growth Financial.

Figure 2.7   Follow-Up Letter from New Growth

Let's review. The moment you were sent the NOTICE OF DEFAULT notifying you that you weren't making your mortgage payments, the law took over. If you take no action your home can and will be sold right out from under you. The company that loaned you the money to buy your home has the power to do this. And if you don't pay them what you owe them, they will.

We know you are in a difficult situation. We have helped many others through it. I'm including a <u>notarized</u> <u>testimonial</u> from one of our recent clients so you can see for yourself.

<u>We</u> <u>pay</u> <u>cash</u> <u>for</u> <u>houses</u> <u>in</u> <u>10</u> <u>days.</u> You owe it to your family to seek a money solution!! We do the work for you; we guide you every step of the way. You can turn to us with confidence. Make this the turning point in your life. Reach for the telephone and dial 837-2106. Ask for Ted or Nancy.

P. S.

You need cash to solve your problem!!

We have the cash you need!!!

Just pick up the telephone and dial 837-2106.

The CASH you need will be in your hands in TEN (10) DAYS.

<u>Remember</u>: If you take no action, your home will be sold at public auction. And you will be evicted. That is the law.

<u>Make</u> <u>sure</u> <u>this</u> <u>doesn't</u> <u>happen</u> <u>to</u> <u>you.</u>

© New Growth Financial.

Figure 2.7 *(continued)*

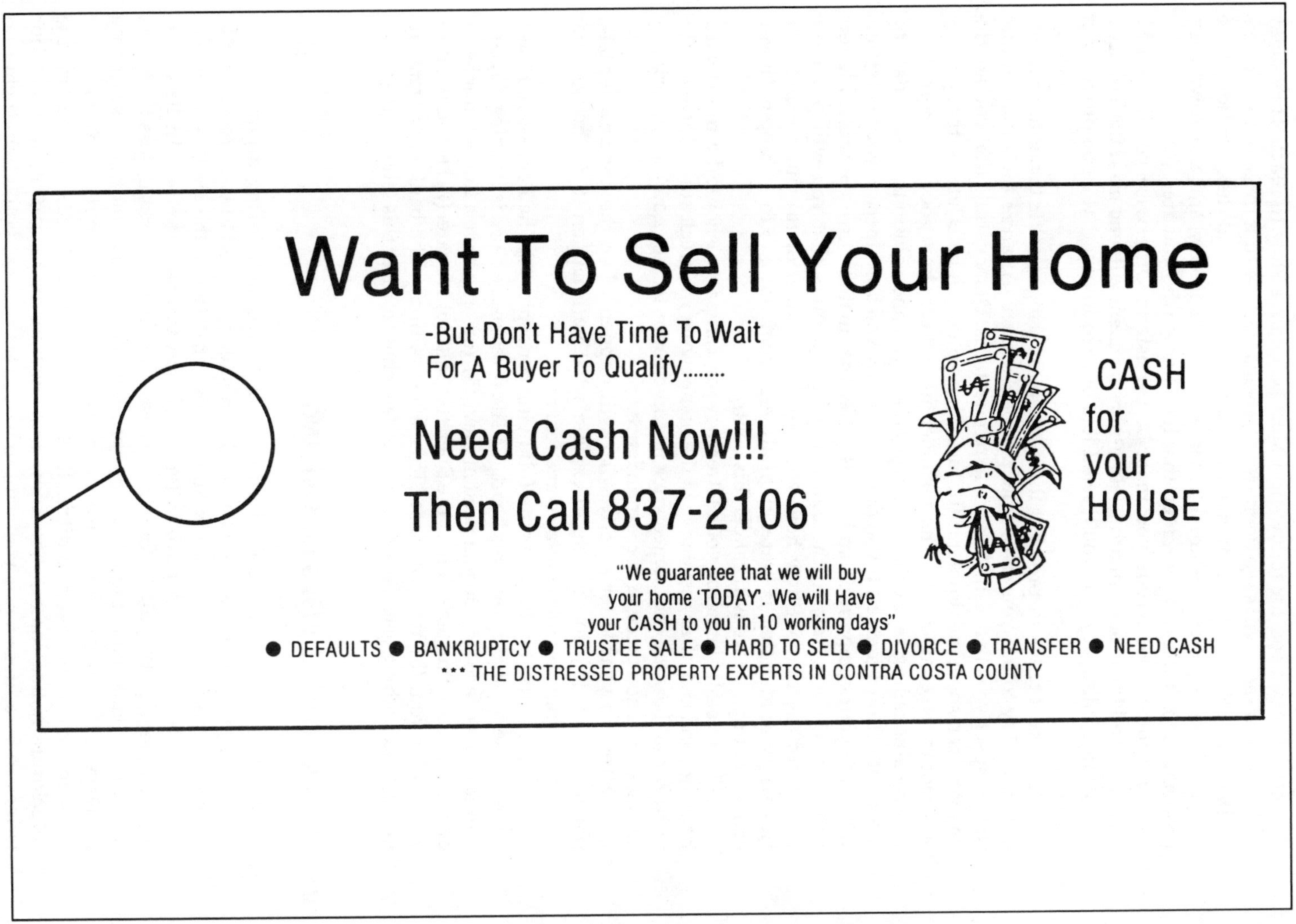

Figure 2.8 Sample of "Door Hanger" Flier to Sell Home

that can also be used for follow-up.) Most people are slow to react. They delay and hope a miracle will save them from foreclosure. The first three or four letters probably go into the waste basket. So you must try to build their confidence so that they believe that you are a reliable source of money and can solve their problems. Don't take it for granted that they know who you are.

In repeat sales letters you must be persistent. Otherwise you'll soon be forgotten and the procrastinating, slow-moving client will end up at the Trustee's Sale or in bankruptcy and you'll need lots of cash to buy that same property at those sales.

You must tell your prospect that you are offering specific benefits he needs or wants. Try to put yourself in the prospect's place. Analyze the situation that the prospective seller is in. Ask the hard questions. Demonstrate that you are the one who can solve the problems for him. Show proof, in your letters, that you are superior to the competition. The customer doesn't care how good you might be at buying and selling real estate. He wants benefits and solutions: cash today; no more collection agencies. If you don't show why you are superior, your prospects will go to your competition and you'll suffer the financial costs of wasted letters and time. Demonstrate to the defaulting homeowners that you will pay more money for the home. Show how your service is superior to your competition. Have a guarantee that is better than all your competitors'; for example, "if you can beat our price we will cancel this contract."

The overall theme of your letter writing campaign should be to extend a helping hand and offer assistance to the homeowner in foreclosure. However, the need for action, for the homeowner in foreclosure to "act now" is the primary emphasis of each piece of correspondence.

Stress in your letter exactly what will happen when the homeowner telephones you. It is also sensible to explain what will happen if the homeowner takes no action; you might allay some fears.

Your letters should cover the following concepts: (1) The homeowner has a large problem hanging over his head. (2) The foreclosure clock is running. (3) Isn't it time to save face? (4) Do you need money? (5) You only have a limited number of days left till the Trustee's Sale or the Sheriff's Sale. (6) We care. (7) Here is what we will do for you. (8) You *can't* lose. This is a sure thing. The bank only wants its money and nothing else. (10) This is your last chance; after this letter I give up.

REMIND SELLERS OF THE RISKS OF WAITING

Your letters should be planned with an objective, convincing argument that moves the prospect to call you and makes him eager to sell to you. You've got to help your prospect make up his mind. Prove that this is the right time to sell. Point out that the prospective seller will begin to enjoy the benefit he or she wants as soon as the sale is completed. Also point out the risks of loss if he does not sell to you. Keep in mind that your prospective seller is continually searching for ways to find money. Foreclosure actions don't spring up out of nowhere. Your prospective clients have had difficulties with money for a while. By the time the foreclosure notice comes, they know that they are at the end of the line. Your letter can be a lifesaver. If you want to be a great success, you'll help them find ways to solve their problems. Study their needs for your service and you'll gain them as your clients. Show them how they will get more of what they need when they sell to you.

Analyze their needs. Ask questions, questions that push the customers to admit their problem and allow you to solve it for them. Be specific when you tell them you can save money for them or help them avoid losses. Then spell out the specific terms and make sure that they understand each benefit you offer. Learn enough about your potential clients so that you can anticipate and answer *their* questions. Determine exactly when and how you will ask them to sell to you. Ask for the order in the letter, otherwise you miss your objective.

MAP OUT YOUR TERRITORY

When you have responses to your letter writing campaign, don't run haphazardly from one place to another. Get a clear picture of the location of your prospects. Get a map of your territory or territories. Plot your calls and know exactly where you are going so that you don't crisscross the territory and waste time.

Become the best known buyer in your territory. We have all heard the old saying: Out of sight, out of mind. In the foreclosure business, this is especially true. After all, your prospect is living through a time of great stress and tension. More than likely he is not thinking as practically and rationally as he should. You need to keep your name in front of him as a problem solver. Follow up with additional letters (see Figures 2.9 to 2.11). Most people give up after the first refusal or even sign of resistance. Don't let this happen to you. Persistence will get you the great property purchases. Most of your competitors will only call upon the seller once. It is your job to prove you are superior and you'll do so by being persistent.

Your letters will get results because they are planned with a methodical follow-up. Owners of distressed property will sell to you when you prove by persistence that you are interested in solving their problems. Keep accurate records of your letters and your follow-up. Such records let you evaluate just how motivated the sellers are.

SUCCESS IS NOT AN ACCIDENT

Success is not accidental. Success is the result of using proven techniques and money-making formulas on a regular and systematic basis. Dominate your territory by being the best known buyer in it and send follow-up letters again and again to your prospective sellers.

TRIPLE YOUR DOLLARS WITH A PLANNED PRESENTATION

Once you meet your prospective seller, get him to focus his attention on you. To do this you need a planned presentation.

At times you will have the feeling that the people you are talking to aren't listening to you; their minds are on other things. Even as they are talking to you,

New Growth Enterprises
"The Distressed Property Experts"
(415) 837-2106

June 3, 1988

&fname& &lname&
&address1&
&city& &state&   &zip&

Dear &fname&:

In less than three months, your home will be sold at public auction if you don't correct the problem you've got with your home lender.

You are now in the midst of a legal process that, if not solved, will result in your home being sold at auction -- and you losing not only your home but also most of your equity money.

I wrote to you two weeks ago so that this won't happen to you.

You need money and you need it now. Why not schedule a no-fee, no-obligation consultation meeting with me so I can discuss your options and, if this seems to be the best thing to do, buy your home. <u>You</u> <u>can</u> <u>have</u> <u>a</u> <u>bank</u> <u>check</u> <u>within</u> <u>ten</u> <u>days</u>. A check that will enable you to pay off the lender, keep the maximum amount of equity in your home, and end the legal hassle you are now facing.

I can help. But I need to see you! Call me now at 837-2106 to start things going. You can have a bank check for your home within ten days and an end to the anxiety you are now going though.

Please call or fill out the enclosed coupon and return it to me.

P.S.   If you've already solved your cash problems and squared things with your lender, we'd like to know so that we don't send you any more letters! But if you haven't, why don't you let us help??

© 1988 New Growth Financial.

Figure 2.9   Follow-Up Letter from New Growth

New Growth Enterprises

"The Distressed Property Experts"
(415) 837-2106

June 3, 1988

&fname& &lname&
&address1&
&city&, &state& &zip&

Dear &fname&:

You have about ten weeks -- just 10 weeks!!! -- remaining before your home is sold at public auction by the lender.

You can save the equity in your home, pay off the lender and stop the legal hassle -- BUT YOU'VE GOT TO STOP PROCRASTINATING.

Call us today for a no fee, no obligation consultation on what you should do now. Your time is running out. But <u>we</u> <u>can</u> <u>give</u> <u>you</u> <u>a</u> <u>bank</u> <u>check</u> <u>for</u> <u>your</u> <u>home</u> <u>within</u> <u>ten</u> <u>days</u>. TO GET THIS CHECK AND SOLVE YOUR PROBLEMS YOU MUST TAKE ACTION.

Call us at (415) 837-2106. We'll get your lender off your back, stop the embarrassment and distress of your home being sold at public auction and you being evicted, and help you -- without cost -- to find a new place to move. <u>And</u> <u>we'll</u> <u>give</u> <u>you</u> <u>a</u> <u>bank</u> <u>check</u> <u>for</u> <u>your</u> <u>home</u> <u>within</u> <u>ten</u> <u>days</u>.

If you sit back and do nothing, you will not only lose your home but you'll lose the equity you've built up in it.

Act now while there's still time.

P.S. If you've already solved your cash problems and squared things with your lender, we'd like to know so that we don't send you any more letters! But if you haven't why don't you let us help??

Figure 2.10   Second Follow-Up Letter from New Growth

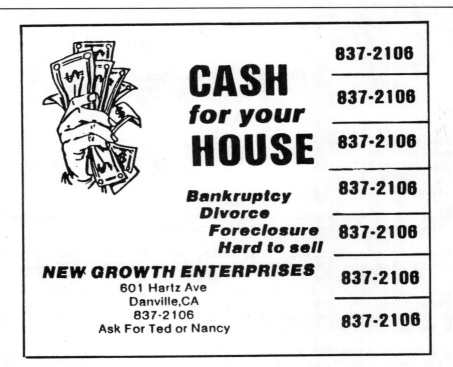

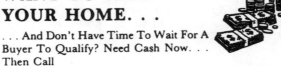

Figure 2.11   Examples of Notices and Cards to Sell Home from New Growth

they are searching for the miracle that will rescue them. And they are *still* asking themselves: What is in it for me? You must focus the prospective seller's attention on what you have to say.

Demonstrate your interest in the seller's predicament. Give him a booklet or information about seminars on the ways in which your business can help. (See Figures 2.12 and 2.13.) Give him something that will help solve his problems. If you are solving the seller's problems and talking about benefits he will attain, you will have his attention.

Remember, too, that you must demonstrate the benefits you can offer are superior or you will just be an also-ran. Why are your services more valuable than those of your competition? Think this over and be prepared to demonstrate your superiority. When your prospect is convinced by your benefits and demonstrated superiority, he will sell his distressed property to you. If you want to succeed in this business, you must be solving problems. Think about what makes you different. If your services are different, you will be successful. The prospective seller will not be convinced until you demonstrate that you can solve his particular problem better than any other competitor can. In summary, analyze your prospect, try to visualize the individual and understand what motivates him, and then tailor yourpresentation to suit him.

The testimonials reproduced as Figure 2.14 are an example of the type of proof that helps convince sellers. Our presentation to Mr. Biddles was planned and structured to solve his problems. We demonstrated our superiority by writing a contract which allowed Mr. Biddles to stay in the home for an additional month at no cost and solved his problem of having no access to ready cash by guaranteeing him a cash payment of $7,000 even if the termite and roof inspection revealed severe problems. He was expecting to receive little or no money out of the deal. By stipulating a minimum payment of $7,000 to the seller, we demonstrated that we were superior to our competitor. We were able to buy the house, and even received a recommendation for our services.

CAUTION: SOME DOS AND DON'TS

To emphasize the necessity of doing your homework and to give you some pointers for the all-important planned, individually tailored presentation, we offer some dos and don'ts.

- Don't argue with the homeowner, even if he or she is wrong. Remember time is on your side.
- Do keep in contact. Sellers will rarely make up their minds the first time they receive your letter, or even the first time you meet them.
- Do ask questions. Estimate your repair cost before you make a money commitment.
- Don't get discouraged if the homeowner brings his payments current (cures the loan). Keep an eye on the default list. Many of these owners, a surprising number, will be back in default within the next six months. By then they will have more debts to pay.

GET THE
INSIDE STORY
ON
FORECLOSURE

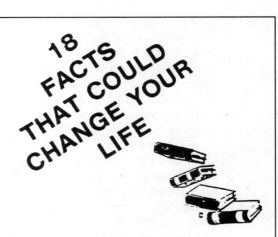

AMAZING BOOKLET!!!

18 FACTS THAT COULD CHANGE YOUR LIFE!

Exactly what you need to know and to make sure your house is **NOT** sold at PUBLIC AUCTION by the Lender.

Send only $2.00 in the enclosed self-addressed envelope with your address and we will immediately forward this information packed booklet to you.

Eye Opening Facts About Foreclosure: This booklet will give you 18 ways to avoid foreclosure.

Your problem can be solved and this booklet will give you the solution. Get facts that help! Gain knowledge and security. Send only two dollars. You have nothing to lose and everything to gain.

NEW GROWTH ENTERPRISES
P.O. Box 5000, Suite 412
Danville, CA 94526

Figure 2.12   Cover to Informational Book (Mailer Piece) about Foreclosure

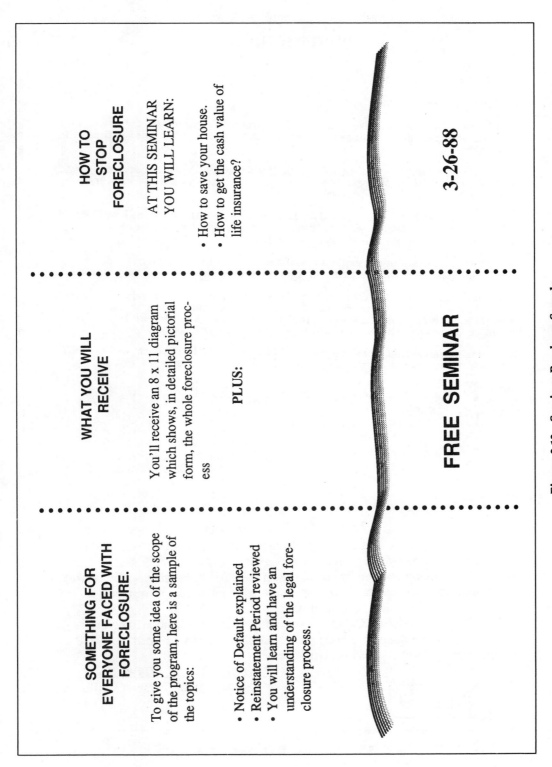

SOMETHING FOR EVERYONE FACED WITH FORECLOSURE.

To give you some idea of the scope of the program, here is a sample of the topics:

- Notice of Default explained
- Reinstatement Period reviewed
- You will learn and have an understanding of the legal foreclosure process.

WHAT YOU WILL RECEIVE

You'll receive an 8 x 11 diagram which shows, in detailed pictorial form, the whole foreclosure process

PLUS:

HOW TO STOP FORECLOSURE

AT THIS SEMINAR YOU WILL LEARN:

- How to save your house.
- How to get the cash value of life insurance?

FREE SEMINAR

3-26-88

Figure 2.13   Seminar Brochure Sample

TESTIMONIAL

March 22, 1988

To Whom It May Concern:

I had received a letter from New Growth Enterprises offering to help me. I was very skeptical after reading it because I'd never heard of a company like this so I threw the letter away.

A couple weeks went by, my time was running out, and another letter arrived. I read the letter and filled out the response coupon because I didn't want to lose everything when my house was sold at trustee sale.

Shortly after that Ted Thomas called me to discuss my situation and see how he could help. At first I didn't know what to think, but after reading other testimonials that they sent to me, I began to feel more comfortable.

Ted Thomas took the time to explain how his service worked. He did not pressure me but let me make my own decision. I felt he treated me honestly and very sincerely.

Without the help from New Growth Enterprises, it would have been very hard to find a new place to live. But, the money he gave me more than made up the deposit I needed to move into an apartment. Without that money, I don't know where I would have ended up. New Growth Enterprises helped me get started again.

If I come up against this problem again, Ted Thomas would be the first person I'd call. If I know of someone in a similar situation, I will highly recommend him.

Sincerely,

Clyde Cutter

Clyde Cutter

STATE OF CALIFORNIA
COUNTY OF CONTRA COSTA

On this....30.... day of .....*March*......... in the year ..*1988*.., before me, ...*Nancy M. Patterson*......., a Notary Public, State of California duly commissioned and sworn, personally appeared ..*Clyde Cutter*............... personally known to be (or proved to me on the basis of satisfactory evidence) to be the person whose name ......*is*......... subscribed to this instrument, and acknowledged that ....he... executed it.

IN WITNESS WHEREOF I have hereunto set my hand and affixed my official seal in the State of ..*California*............ County of *Contra Costa*... on the date set forth above this certificate.

Nancy M. Patterson

Notary Public, State of California

Figure 2.14   Testimonial from Clyde Cutter

- Do caution the homeowner that, if he or she signs an exclusive "Right to Sell" agreement with a real estate broker, a commission will be due and deducted from the proceeds of the sale.
- Do appraise the property. Does it need paint, carpet, wallpaper, linoleum, repairs? The seller, in most cases, knows whether the home has serious structural problems. If you are not careful, these sellers will take advantage of your ignorance. Keep in mind that the prospective seller is obligated to take care of himself and his family. He is not interested in making you wealthy. Your contract should include various cancellation or escape clauses to allow you to reject the purchase if you do discover serious structural problems.
- Do expect a no to your first offer.
- Do leave the door open for new talks with the owner if you get an initial rejection.
- Do tell the owners that time is of the essence and that you have limited capital that must be put to work.
- Do tell the homeowner that foreclosure causes other credit problems if the bank or savings and loan association reports the action to the credit bureaus.
- Do remind the homeowner that each day the situation gets worse: payments are further behind, late charges are accruing, and property taxes and penalties are adding up.
- Do get all the owners to sign the purchase contract. Review the Grant Deed to make sure you know who owns the property and what the legal description consists of.
- Do be Mr. Good Guy, the man in the white hat. Yes, you're saving them from foreclosure and embarrassment.
- Do think about the financing for the new buyer before you put the house up for sale. Financing is the most important part of the sale.
- Do review the default list daily.
- Do establish an attitude that tells the world: "I know it can be done."

Once again, remember the millionaire's secret of success: prepare—prepare—prepare; do your homework—do your homework—do your homework.

3

Contracts, Title, and Escrow

The Small Print Explained

Real estate has such great value and is so basic a form of wealth that many special laws have been enacted for its protection. As a result, the owner of land has well-established rights as do the family and heirs of the owner. In this chapter, you will learn:

- To write a contract with the owner of distressed property that will be fair to both parties.
- To understand title procedures and claims against the property.
- To understand escrow procedures, which are an essential part of real estate transactions.

HIGHLIGHTS OF THE EQUITY PURCHASE AGREEMENT

Experience in real estate can be a very costly commodity. Take advantage of the contract provisions shown in the *Equity Purchase Agreement* shown in Figure 3.1. This contract will help keep you out of trouble and save you thousands of dollars in repair costs. The provisions written into the contract on the subject of inspections are not there to give you legal advice. However, they will give you ideas and a chance to think about relevant considerations before you visit your attorney and draw up your own contract.

It is impossible to cover every aspect of this contract, so only the highlights of the money-saving points will be dealt with in the following paragraphs. California law may be different from the laws of your state; make note of the contract provisions but do not copy the exact terms. Modifications will be necessary for the state in which you live. Contact your legal counsel and certified public accountant.

EQUITY PURCHASE AGREEMENT
Page 1 of 3

THIS AGREEMENT, made this_____day of_____, 19_____
between New Growth Financial and/or assignees (hereinafter "Buyer"); in consideration of the
covenants and agreements hereinafter contained, Seller agrees to sell and convey to Buyer and
Buyer agrees to purchase from Seller, the following real property located in (city) _____
County_____,California (street address)_____
Assessor's parcel no.) _____Tract_____Lot_____Block _____
Page(s)_____(Attach legal description as Exhibit "A"). The following personal property is also
included in this purchase:_____

Said real and personal property is collectively known as the "Property".

1. In consideration for said property, Buyer agrees to pay to Seller, as Seller's equity in the
Property, the total sum ($), payable at the time Seller delivers to Buyer both (1) A
properly prepared, notarized and valid Grant Deed to the Property (and bill of sale for any
personal property included in the sale) and, (2) Subject to section 2 (f) hereof, the transfer of
possession of the Property to Buyer, including all improvements, vacant, clean, and in good repair.
IN NO EVENT SHALL ANY MONEY OR OTHER CONSIDERATION BE TRANSFERRED TO SELLER
BY BUYER AT ANY TIME PRIOR TO THE EXPIRATION OF SELLER'S RIGHT TO CANCEL THIS
CONTRACT, PROVIDED FOR HEREINBELOW, AS SUCH TRANSFER IS PROHIBITED BY
CALIFORNIA LAW.

2. (a) Seller represents that the following are the deeds of trusts, liens, encumbrances, judgments,
bonds assessments (hereinafter "Encumbrances")

1st TD $_____payable $_____per month_____% int. incl. T & I

2nd TD $_____payable $_____per month_____%_____due date

3rd TD $_____payable $_____per month_____%_____due date

   (b) Seller represents that said Encumbrances each have the following amounts which are now
due or past due: _____
From the NET amount due Seller may be deducted all payments on existing encumbrances
through the payments due_____, 19_____. Also, any taxes, judgments,
assessment bonds, prepayment penalties, and other liens if any. Impounds, if any, are to be
assigned without charge to the Buyer, in any amount satisfactory to the lending institution. Any
impound shortage will be deducted from the funds due Seller. Insurance Fire Casualty Policy will
be assigned to the Buyer without charge.

   (c) Buyer shall take title to the property subject to all of said Encumbrances and amounts due
or past due, except _____
Buyer shall further take title subject to all easements, zoning and land-use restrictions, and
covenants, conditions and restrictions of record, so long as the same do not adversely affect the
continued use of the Property for its present use.

   (d) Buyer shall have the right to rescind this agreement and to receive a refund of all
consideration paid to Seller if within (5) days after receiving a Grant Deed to the Property Buyer
notifies Seller in writing that the principal amounts of, and/or the amounts due or past due on,
one or more of the Encumbrances are greater than as represented hereinabove, or that there are
one or more easements, zoning or land use restrictions, or covenants, conditions and restrictions
concerning the Property which adversely affect the continued use of the Property for its present
use. Said notice shall demand rescission and shall specify the Encumbrance(s) which are not in
compliance with the representations made by Seller or the easements, etc. which interfere with
the continued use of the Property for its present use. Upon receipt of said notice Seller shall
immediately cooperate with Buyer to execute all documents and do all things necessary to fully
rescind the sale and return the full amount of money and/or other property transferred to Seller in
connection with this sale. If Seller shall fail or refuse to so cooperate, Seller shall be liable for all
loss or harm caused by said failure or refussi.

(Page 1 of 3)

Figure 3.1   Equity Purchase Agreement

NEW GROWTH FINANCIAL

EQUITY PURCHASE AGREEMENT
Page 2 of 3

(e) Buyer shall pay all the following, if any: escrow fees, title insurance fees, transfer taxes, recording fees, notary fees. Seller agrees to pay for any damages found by termite and roof inspections.

(f) Possession of the Property shall be transferred to Buyer on _____, 19_____. Any and all risk of loss of the Property or any part thereof shall be born by Seller until possession of the Property has passed to Buyer. Any possession, occupancy or tenancy by the Seller at any time after the Grant Deed has been delivered to Buyer shall be on the following terms: Rent to be paid by Seller to Buyer: ($_____) per day_____, month_____ year_____. Seller to vacate Property on or before:_____. Other terms of rental: Seller agrees to pay for any damage done to the Property that is caused by Seller or tenants after the date this contract is signed. Balance of funds due Seller are to be paid after the premises are vacated.

3. ATTORNEY'S FEES.

In the event that any legal or equitable action is brought to enforce the terms of this agreement, including but not limited to specific performance, or rescission of contract, the prevailing party in such action shall be entitled to collect reasonable attorney's fees, expert witness fees and cost of suit, as determined by the court.

4. EFFECT OF PARTIAL INVALIDITY.

The provisions of this Agreement are agreed to severally by the undersigned, and the invalidity or partial invalidity of one or more provisions of this Agreement shall not render the remaining provisions invalid or unenforceable.

5. AGREEMENT BINDING UPON HEIRS, ASSIGNS.

This Agreement, and all terms hereof, shall be binding on the heirs, devisees, executors, personal representative, conservators, successors, and assigns of the undersigned Buyer and Seller.

6. WARRANTY OF TITLE; WARRANTIES TO SURVIVE DELIVERY OF DEED.

Seller hereby warrants, jointly and severally, that each of the undersigned, as Seller, is the lawful owner of any ownership interest in the Property, and that collectively the Property and Seller has the right and authority to convey said ownership to Buyer. This warranty, and all warranties, terms and conditions hereof, shall survive the delivery and recordation of any deed to buyer, and the close of any escrow.

(a) Seller is not entitled to receive any other consideration or thing of value or services from Buyer, in connection with or incident to the sale of the Property to Buyer, except as stated hereinabove and except the following: _____

Ted Thomas is an employee of New Growth Financial and holds a valid Broker's License issued by the State of California.

7. PHYSICAL CONDITION OF PROPERTY

The Property is free of all defects in its structure and its operating systems such as plumbing, electrical, roof and metal work, gas and sewer, except for the following: _____ _____Seller agrees to pay for all damages and repairs found by termite and roof inspectors. Buyer takes the property subject to the above disclosed defects. Seller hereby warrants that the property is free of other defects, as of the date of delivery of a Grant Deed to the Property to Buyer.

8. COMMISSIONS

Seller hereby represents that there is no licensed real estate salesperson or broker representing Seller in any way in connection with this purchase and sale, and Seller agrees to hold Buyer harmless and defend Buyer from any claim to commission in connection with this purchase and sale.

9. UNCONSCIONABILITY

Seller hereby represents that all negotiations and dealings with Buyer have been and are at arm's length, and that no duress or undue influence has been exerted by Buyer over Seller or Seller's family in connection with this purchase and sale. Seller is aware that the Buyer may be purchasing property for immediate resale.

Figure 3.1 *(continued)*

NEW GROWTH FINANCIAL

EQUITY PURCHASE AGREEMENT
Page 3 of 3

10. Property MUST appraise at $_____. Less than that amount will be DEDUCTED from net to seller.

(c) Seller is aware and understands that the present fair market value of the Property probably is higher than the purchase price set forth herein. Seller hereby expressly waives any and all claim to any potential or actual income, profits or other sums in excess of the above mentioned purchase price, which may be realized by Buyer or others as a result of any transaction involving the Property. Seller acknowledges that the purchase price stated herein is fair and equitable and is in Seller's best interests, and that Seller's decision to sell was based on Seller, and that Seller has not relied on any representations of Buyer which are not contained expressly herein.

NOTICE REQUIRED BY CALIFORNIA LAW UNTIL YOUR RIGHT TO CANCEL THIS CONTRACT HAS ENDED NEW GROWTH FINANCIAL AND OR ASSIGNEES OR ANYONE WORKING FOR NEW GROWTH FINANCIAL CANNOT ASK YOU TO SIGN OR HAVE YOU SIGN ANY DEED OR ANY OTHER DOCUMENT.

YOU MAY CANCEL THIS CONTRACT FOR THE SALE OF YOUR HOUSE WITHOUT ANY PENALTY OR OBLIGATION AT ANY TIME BEFORE _____ (DATE AND TIME OF DAY). SEE THE ATTACHED NOTICE OF CANCELLATION FORM FOR AN EXPLANATION OF THIS RIGHT

Signed:

_____   _____
Seller   **Date**

Signed:

_____   _____
Seller   **Date**

BUYERS NAME, BUSINESS ADDRESS AND TELEPHONE NUMBER

New Growth Financial   Offices Located at:
P.O. Box 5000, Suite 412   177 Front Street, #207
Danville, CA 94526   Danville, CA 94526
(415) 837-2106

(Seller's time for cancellation ends at midnight on the fifth business day following the day the Seller signs this Agreement, or until 8:00 a.m. on the day scheduled for sale of the Property under power of sale conferred by deed of trust, whichever comes first.)

(Page 3 of 3)

Figure 3.1   *(continued)*

Section 1: Payment

Notice when the seller is to be paid and under what circumstances: when the Grant Deed has been signed, when the bill of sale for personal property is completed, and when possession of the property (vacant, clean, and in good repair) has been transferred. (A Grant Deed is shown in Figure 3.2 and a Bill of Sale is available at the stationery store.) Transfer of possession is important. "Vacant, clean, and in good repair" means exactly that. If you do not enforce this stipulation and the seller leaves mountains of trash in and around the house, the cost of removal will be borne by you. Unless you use diligence at this point, you might find that the property has been severely damaged in the interval between the date of the agreement and the day on which the seller finally moves out. Remember, too, to arrange for an inspection after the owner has departed—before you pay the seller the monies due. If you should unwisely pay out before the property is vacant, the seller may not move. Keep in the front of the seller's mind at all times the incentive to move as a prerequisite of receiving the cash payment. The motivation to search for a new dwelling and make that final departure must be continually reinforced.

The procedure of transferring the title from one party to another is as follows:

- The seller signs a Grant Deed and delivers the deed to you at the title or escrow company
- You in turn deliver funds to the seller
- Then you record the Grant Deed at the County Recorder's Office.

Possession is another matter. The seller will more than likely stay in possession after transferring the title to you. The seller will be awaiting your period of rescission or what I call the *due diligence period*. Immediately after the seller grant deeds the property to you, you will contract with professional inspectors to perform a termite report, roof report, home inspection, appraisal, and preliminary title report. If additional reports such as the water quality in a well or soils and slide conditions are needed, you will be checking these during your right of rescission period.

After you have received the professionals' reports, reviewed them and found no unsatisfactory or damaging facts, your next step will be to get possession from the seller. Payment to the seller of the agreed equity purchase price less the contracts for termite repairs, roof repairs, past-due taxes, and prepayment penalties is the *final* act of the transaction. It is extremely important that the payment or transfer of the remaining funds takes place only *after* the seller has removed his possessions from the home. If the seller or possessions remain in the property, do not make the final disbursement. The only incentive the seller has at this point is to get the final disbursement. If you pay while the seller is still in residence, the seller will have your money and the property and no incentive to depart short of a costly and aggravating legal eviction process. Needless to say, the payments, taxes, and other expenses will be your responsibility even if you don't have possession.

RECORDING REQUESTED BY

And When Recorded Mail This Deed
and, Unless Otherwise Shown Below,
Mail Tax Statements To:

NAME

STREET
ADDRESS

CITY,
STATE
ZIP

Title Order No. _____ Escrow No. _____

SPACE ABOVE THIS LINE FOR RECORDER'S USE

DOCUMENTARY TRANSFER TAX $_____
_____ COMPUTED ON FULL VALUE OF PROPERTY CONVEYED.
_____ OR COMPUTED ON FULL VALUE LESS LIENS AND
ENCUMBRANCES REMAINING AT TIME OF SALE.

_____
Signature of Declarant or Agent determining tax.   Firm Name

GRANT DEED

FOR A VALUABLE CONSIDERATION, receipt of which is hereby acknowledged,

hereby GRANT(S) to

the following described real property in the
county of _____, state of California:

Dated
STATE OF CALIFORNIA
COUNTY OF

On _____before me, the under-
signed, a Notary Puboic in and for said County and
State, personally appeared_____

_____

_____

_____, known to me
to be the person____whose name____subscribed to the
within instrument and acknowledged that _____
executed the same.

_____

Name (Typed or Printed)
Notary Public in and for Said County and State

(Space above for official notarial seal)

MAIL TAX STATEMENTS TO PARTY SHOWN ON FOLLOWING LINE; IF NO PARTY SO SHOWN, MAIL
AS DIRECTED ABOVE

| Name | Street Address | City & State |

Figure 3.2   Grant Deed

Section 2: Encumbrances

Encumbrances can create a real problem for the foreclosure buyer. Know what you are buying and be positive you understand all the loans, judgments, bonds, and assessments that are due on (encumbering) the real estate. If you don't know or understand what is owed on the property, do not buy it.

The County Records Office is open to the public daily. Take the time to research the title on the real estate you are attempting to purchase. If you buy from an owner, you buy exactly what the seller owns. There are professionals who will help you in this area. Telephone your local title company or request that your attorney research the chain of title and the amounts due on any encumbrances or liens.

By having an acknowledgment in the contract of all the liens due on the property, you will be alerting the seller to your intention of checking and confirming the status of all loans. It is impossible to make people honest, but it won't hurt your negotiations or purchase to state clearly your intentions to review the title records. If you should locate (and you will) undisclosed liens, most sellers will say, "Oh, I forgot about that tax payment." Property taxes in some states are allowed to accrue or stay delinquent for as long as five years. If you purchase property for which the taxes are not paid, it will be your responsibility to bring them current. This provision in the Equity Purchase Agreement allows you to deduct the money for back taxes or other payments owed from the net payment that will be due the seller.

Section 2b: Prepayment Penalties

Many sellers in default throw the loan papers away or simply misplace them. You need the loan documents if you intend to assume the loan or even if you just plan to bring the loan current and stop the foreclosure auction. If you are planning to repair the property and then resell, you may decide to assume the loan or to purchase the property subject to the existing loan. However, lenders frequently choose at the time of the sale to extract a prepayment penalty. It is not unusual for this penalty to take the form of the payment of six months' interest. Think about a $100,000 loan at an annual interest rate of 12 percent. This translates to $12,000 per year or a penalty of $6,000. If the loan has a prepayment penalty, you will want your contract to allow you to deduct that amount from the proceeds that the seller expects.

Section 2d: Buyer's Right to Cancel

If the property has more encumbrances than those described by the seller, you must make a choice. Do your homework and make sure you find out about the liens due and encumbrances on the property. Confirm your findings by requesting a Preliminary Title Report from your local title company or abstracting service. It is important to get written evidence of any lien. Then you will have to decide whether you take the property with its existing debt and encumbrances or not. In the contract, you will observe a provision (Section 2d) that allows you to deed the property back to the seller if the debt is more than the amount disclosed when the contract was signed.

Section 7: Physical Condition of Property

The physical and mechanical condition of property in foreclosure could easily be the subject of an entire book. The wise foreclosure buyer will include books, manuals, and a list of important volumes on the subject as part of his library.

Contractors will provide excellent information on what is needed to bring homes to standard. Professional inspectors ferret out the problems and make recommendations about repairs. If your contract allows for inspections (and it should), expect the seller to view the reports with skepticism and plan to negotiate at length about who pays for the termite and roof repairs. For this reason, be sure to employ well-known, well-respected inspectors, whose reputation will support their estimates of repair costs. If your state requires inspections other than those specified in the agreement we use, be sure to include these inspections in your contract.

Section 8: Commissions

Real estate brokers and agents have a difficult profession. They walk a tightrope most of the time, attempting to keep sellers and buyers together. Most sellers want about 110 percent of value for their home and most buyers are willing to pay about 90 percent of the value for a home. Conflicts, egos, pricing, and the economy all keep the real estate brokers in the middle of controversy. If the property you are purchasing is listed for sale with a real estate broker, contractually the seller owes a commission to the broker upon sale. Be sure that the seller understands this and is prepared to pay the broker or cancel the broker's right to sell. Keep in mind all the while that the seller might be leaving the community. You, however, are planning to be around for some time and business relationships are important to your future. If your contract has a provision that no broker is included in the transaction, be sure the seller places his initials near that section after he reads it. A broker who feels deprived of his commission will not suffer in silence. Your reputation will also suffer.

Section 9: Unconscionability

Are you treating the buyer fairly? The purchase of foreclosure and distressed property must be a win-win situation. If it is not, someone will get hurt and, in the long term, that will be your problem. Bargain for the best price but, if it's too good to be true, expect to hear from an attorney or the Bankruptcy Court after you have spent your money. Hundreds of properties are foreclosed on weekly throughout the United States. There is enough business for all the foreclosure buyers in the country well into the future. If you deal at arm's length and treat people fairly, you'll never have a problem. However, if your deal is really unbelievable and entirely in your favor, you'll have left yourself open to question . . . think about that.

Section 10: Appraisals

The decision to get a professional appraisal is always wise. The appraisal will prevent you from overspending when you buy the property and will give you information on the comparable properties in the neighborhood. You can then evaluate the property you are purchasing and compare it with others of similar value. A contract that includes an appraisal provision will allow you the additional benefit of reducing the purchase price if you have inadvertently overvalued the property.

THE CANCELLATION CLAUSE

California law requires that buyers who are dealing with foreclosure property before the Trustee's Sale must allow the seller five full days to rescind (cancel) the contract. This provision of the civil code is very specific. The number of days required for cancellation must be written into the contract and spelled out for the seller in large type. The statute is designed to protect the seller and prevents buyers from taking advantage of sellers who are in a difficult position. It relieves the sellers from making quick decisions and possibly big mistakes. The cancellation period gives the sellers, who have written contracts, time to study the contract or find someone who will give them a better deal.

Of the five-day grace period, the day the contract is signed is not counted, nor are Sunday and major holidays. In effect, this gives the seller seven days. Don't count the first day and don't count Sunday and it is easy to see it will take one week before the contract is effective. Note, however—and be sure to point this out to the seller—that, if the transaction is really a race against the clock and if the Trustee's Sale is scheduled within the next few days, the five-day period does not apply. The seller will have until 8 o'clock on the morning of the Trustee's Sale to cancel the Agreement. Figure 3.3 shows the form that the author uses. This *Notice of Cancellation* is left with the seller who is instructed to sign and return it by a specified date and time if he wishes to cancel the Equity Purchase Agreement. Your state may have a different requirement and it is up to you to know that. Check with your attorney and review the codes and laws at your local library.

SOLVING THE MYSTERY OF TITLE PROCEDURES

As a property buyer you need to be aware that others may have rights in the property. If the owner has contracted for debt and the property has been pledged (hypothecated) as collateral for the debt, the creditors are in effect part owners of the property until the debt has been paid. The lien rights would apply to the holders of the mortgage, holders of any leasehold rights, mining and air rights, unpaid taxes, lawsuits pending against the owner, bankruptcy proceedings, or other liens (claims) such as mechanic's liens. (As an example of the last item, you may find that the owner had a new roof installed, but failed to pay the contractor's bill. The roofer may file a mechanic's lien in the hope that, when the property is sold, he will get some of the proceeds.) All those who hold such claims are, in a limited way, part owners. They cannot ordinarily be deprived of their interest except by having the claim settled or extinguished (canceled). The property may be sold without their knowledge, but the claim is still good until

NEW GROWTH FINANCIAL

NOTICE OF CANCELLATION

_____
(Enter Date Contract Signed)

You May Cancel This Contract For The Sale Of Your House Without Penalty Or Obligation At Any Time Before _____
(Enter Date and Time Of Day)

To Cancel This Transaction, Personally Deliver A Signed and Dated Copy Of This Cancellation Notice or Send a Telegram To:

New Growth Financial   1.77 Front St. #207 Danville, Ca 94526
(Name of Purchaser)   Street Address of Purchaser

Not Later Than _____
(Enter Date and Time of Day)

I HEREBY CANCEL THIS TRANSACTION

_____
(DATE)

_____
SELLER SIGNATURE

_____
SELLER SIGNATURE

I have received notice to cancel.

Seller _____ **Date**_____

Seller _____ **Date**_____

© 1988 New Growth Financial.

Figure 3.3   Notice of Cancellation from New Growth

satisfied. As a new owner, you may know nothing about such part-owners, but you are still subject to the claims on your property.

GRANT DEED DOES NOT GIVE CLEAR TITLE

"Aha," you say, "but I have the Grant Deed. Doesn't that give me clear title?" Not at all! A *deed* is merely an instrument (in the form of a piece of paper) whereby a seller transfers his or her right of ownership, whatever it may be, to you. It is not proof that the person described as the seller is actually the owner. It does not do away with claims or rights others may have in the property. Nor from the deed, can you determine what rights, liens, or claims may be outstanding against your title. In order for you—the new owner—to determine the status of the title, you must research the county records and determine the status of the liens and encumbrances. The hidden risks that may be discovered in a title search include:

- The marital status of the owner
- The existence of undisclosed heirs
- The owner's mental incompetence or status as a minor
- Instances of fraud and forgery
- Defective deeds
- Confusions due to similar or identical names
- Errors in the records.

TITLE INSURANCE

It is also possible to purchase a Title Insurance Policy. The title company is insuring that the property you purchase is free of liens and encumbrances. The title company searches records so that when you request title insurance it will be able to insure that you are buying the property free and clear of all liens and encumbrances. It is to your benefit that the property you purchase is subject to only the liens and encumbrances you want and agree to purchase, assume, or "take subject to." Your title policy insures that you run no risk of someone's claiming a lien or encumbrance against your ownership. Title companies work under the theory that, by thoroughly researching the public records to identify risks, they will expose any claims and eliminate them before you purchase. So you are buying peace of mind. If the title were clouded in any way and the impediment could not be resolved, it would be difficult or maybe impossible to obtain title insurance. However, once the title company agrees to issue a title policy, it is in effect insuring that you are free of risk should a claim be filed at a later date against your property and its chain of title. In summary, the title company is insuring you against defects or what is commonly referred to as a "cloud of title."

What Do the Title Companies Do?

Title insurance companies spend much of their time collecting, storing, maintaining, and analyzing official records. The staff members are trained to identify the rights (interests) you may have in real property and so be able to inform you of matters such as recorded liens, legal actions, rights of way, easements, and encumbrances of any kind. The title company personnel are qualified to conduct a thorough search and evaluation of the public records to become knowledgeable about the state of the records pertaining to the particular property about which you request information.

How Often Do I Need Title Insurance?

Title insurance is paid for once. You buy it when you close escrow. Unlike medical or casualty insurance, which require regular renewal, a title insurance policy will remain in effect as long as you own the property.

What If There Is a Defect in the Title That Doesn't Show Up in the Records?

The hidden risk of forgery or an overlooked lien or encumbrance is possible. Your ability to buy title insurance does not mean that there are no defects in the title report or that no claims against the title will be filed at a later date. Title insurance simply assures you that, as far as the title insurance company is concerned, the title is clear enough for them to sell you insurance. The hazards of future disclosures are transferred from the home buyer to the title insurance company by the purchase of insurance and payment of the premium.

What Happens If Someone Files a Claim Against My Property?

If a claim or lawsuit happens to be filed against your title and ownership, the title company is responsible, once you have bought insurance, for defending your title and bearing the costs of the defense.

How Will a Lawsuit Against the Former Owner Affect Me as the New Owner?

If a person is sued and a judgment is rendered against that person, any real estate he or she owns may become security for the debt. This means the property cannot be sold to a new owner and clear title delivered until that judgment is paid or otherwise satisfactorily disposed of.

What About Taxes?

Unpaid federal taxes constitute a lien on real property. See below, under Tax Liens, for more details.

What If the Seller Is a Corporation?

Be sure that the corporation has a Board of Directors and that the Board has authorized the sale.

ABSTRACT OF TITLE

An *abstract*, a document used in some parts of the country, is a history of the title to property as revealed by the public records. Deeds, mortgages, and other instruments and legal proceedings that have affected the property through the years are all included in the abstract. Local customs and rules dictate who compiles the summary or digest of the conveyances and other facts that show evidence of title. This summary is referred to as an *abstract*. Depending on the state, this research could be accomplished by a local attorney or his staff or a company that is referred to as an abstract or title company.

To purchase a property without an abstract (summary) of title would be extremely risky. The abstract report or title search will reveal all recorded liens, judgments, taxes, and encumbrances that are burdens on the property. Remember if you purchase from an owner you purchase what the owner owns, good and bad.

PITFALLS—UNDISCLOSED LIENS AND ENCUMBRANCES

Wise buyers always research title or purchase a Preliminary Title Report. Property owners have a tendency to forget liens that might have been filed by creditors or even unpaid secured or third trust deeds. If you are buying a property at the Trustee's Sale, you must identify positively and establish the seniority of the Deed of Trust (see Figure 3.4) that is foreclosing. For example, if the Deed of Trust foreclosing is for $25,000 and the trustee sells the property to you for $25,500, you will own the property for $25,500 assuming that there was no Deed of Trust in a senior or prior position (with an earlier date of recording). If you purchased a property at Trustee's Sale and a loan (Deed of Trust) was recorded before the Deed of Trust that you purchased was recorded, that Deed of Trust will become your obligation. You will own the property. However, you will own it for the $25,500 you paid the trustee plus the amount of the senior obligation. In other words, if you purchase property at the Trustee's Sale for $25,500 cash and a subsequent title report or records search shows a senior lien in the amount of $50,000, you own the property for $50,000 plus $25,500, or $75,500, because, as the new owner, you are obliged to pay the senior lien.

HOW TO FIND THE LIENS AND ENCUMBRANCES

Many owners do not know (some merely refrain from telling you) what is owed against the property, so you must determine what is owed.

So how do you find out? Keep on asking and you'll discover more than you ever dreamed about the property you are purchasing. To determine what is owed against any property:

- First, *ASK* the homeowner.
- Second, *ASK* the lender, if you know who it is.
- Third, *ASK* the Trustee.
- Fourth, *ASK* the title company to provide a Preliminary Title Report. Assuming the title company will insure the property you are purchasing from an owner, your risk of undisclosed liens will be eliminated. However, the wise foreclosure buyer will spend time with the county records researching the liens and encumbrances, thereby assuring himself that he is buying exactly what he thinks he is buying.
- Fifth, *ASK* a broker to look in the MLS book.

Order No. _____

Escrow or Loan No._____

RECORDING REQUESTED BY

_____

When Recorded Mail To:

SPACE ABOVE THIS LINE FOR RECORDER'S USE

DEED OF TRUST WITH ASSIGNMENT OF RENTS

This DEED OF TRUST, made　　　　　　　　　　　　　　　　　, between

herein called TRUSTOR,

whose address is
　　　　　　　(Number and Street)　　　　　　(City)　　　　　　(State)

BIGLAND TITLE INSURANCE COMPANY,　　a Missouri Corporation, herein called
TRUSTEE, and

,herein called BENEFICIARY,

WITNESSETH: That Trustor grants to Trustee in Trust, with Power of Sale, that propoerty in the　　　　　　　　　County of　　　　　　　, State of California, described as:

Together with the rents, issues and profits thereof, subject, however, to the right, power and authority hereinafter given to and conferred upon Beneficiary to collect and apply such rents, issues and profits.

For the Purpose of Securing (1) payment of the sum of $　　　　　with interest thereon according to the terms of a promissory note or notes of even date herewith made by Trustor, payable to order of Beneficiary, and extensions or renewals thereof, and (2) the performance of each agreement of Trustor incorporated by reference or contained herein (3) Payment of additional sums and interest thereon which may hereafter be loaned to Trustor, or his successors or assigns, when evidenced by a promissory note or notes reciting that they are secured by this Deed of Trust.

To protect the security of this Deed of Trust, and with respect to the property above described, Trustor expressly makes each and all of the agreements, and adopts and agrees to perform and be bound by each and all of the terms and provisions set forth in subdivision A. In the book and at the page of Official records in the office of the county recorder of the county where said property is located, noted below opposite the name of such county, namely:

COUNTY	BOOK	PAGE	COUNTY	BOOK	PAGE
Alameda	1288	556	Placer	1028	379
Alpine	3	130-31	Plumas	166	1307

The undersigned Trustor, requests that a copy of any notice of default and any notice of sale hereunder be mailed to him at his address herein before set...

Dated_____

STATE OF CALIFORNIA
COUNTY OF_____
On_____before me, the
undersigned, a Notary Public in and for said State, personally appeared

proven to me to be the person(s) whose name(s) is (are) subscribed to the within instrument and acknowledged that executed the same. Witness my hand and official seal.

Signature _____
　　　　　　　Name (Typed or Printed)

Signature of Trustor

_____

Figure 3.4　Deed of Trust with Rental Assignments

- Sixth, *ASK* the staff in the County Recorder's Office to assist you in getting records and researching the title for yourself.

The county records are available to the public. This is a vast source of information and you can only benefit by the knowledge you'll gain by searching the records. I suggest that you search the county records to determine if the property you plan to purchase has any liens or encumbrances upon it, whether or not it is in foreclosure. This is especially important if you buy at the Trustee's Sale where all the property is sold "as is." You get whatever is owned. That means you get not only the house but also all of the liens and encumbrances that are on file against the property.

USING THE PUBLIC RECORDS TO RESEARCH A TITLE

At first the records may seem overwhelming but in a short time you will become proficient at finding the properties and reading and researching the documents. The following description of the system should be helpful. Keep in mind that your county office might use a slightly different system, but the following description will give you a general knowledge of the process and the records.

Start with what is called the *General Index.* The General Index could be on microfiche, microfilm cassettes, or on computerized printouts. Look in the General Index under the name of the trustor or owner of the property that is being foreclosed upon. All of the documents that relate to that *person* will be filed here. Expect the General Index to be divided into different time periods. If you have a question, simply ask one of the Recorder's staff. In Alameda County (Oakland, California), the recorder's staff includes two people whose job it is to help members of the public find the various records.

Claims are filed according to an overall system called a Book and Page System or a Reel and Image System. If you live in a populous county, you could expect the Reel and Image System to be in use. Less populous counties may still be using the Book and Page System. If you live in a section of the country that has many older properties, expect to become familiar with an even older system by which claims are filed in Grantee and Grantor books.

In the Book and Page System, you look for property information that is to be found in a particular book, on a particular page, the number of which you find in the General Index. Then you simply pull the book, go to the correct page, and there's the information you need.

The more progressive counties use a simpler, modern system called the Reel and Image System. These counties have taken the time to put the property information on microfilm on large cassettes (reels), the contents of which have been indexed. Viewers are provided for the public. This system is easy to learn and one can thoroughly research many properties in a short time.

In your records research, you soon learn that each document is given an identifying number that indicates the order in which it was received by the Recorder's Office. This is important, as are the dates. Remember, a first Trust Deed is only first because it was recorded first. Expect to find the document numbers and dates on both the microfilm (Reel and Image) and the Book and Page systems.

With this knowledge of the records and system, you are now prepared to look for documents that pertain to your proposed purchase. Remember, you will rarely see a Deed of Trust that says: "This is the First Deed of Trust." The second loan will rarely say: "This is the Second Deed of Trust." You will know whether a Deed of Trust is a first or second loan only by the date upon which it was filed and recorded. (First in date means first in priority.)

Once you have found the Trust Deed, read it. It will show the specific date on which it was filed and recorded, and it will probably have the name of the party who requested the recording. Make a note of these items because you may need them later. Thoroughly check until you've found all the Trust Deeds recorded against the property. Also, be sure to find documents showing any judgments and tax liens filed against the property.

If you are buying at the Trustee's Sale, you may be purchasing a second Deed of Trust or junior loan. This is fine if you are aware of what you are buying. Even then, you should obtain as much information about the first Trust Deed, or senior lien, as possible. If it has a high interest rate or an imminent maturity date, you may not want to bid at the sale. The opposite position could also apply. For example, the first lender may want to refinance at favorable rates after you purchase the property. The lesson is, you need to make yourself knowledgeable. Don't just buy and hope for the best.

KNOW WHAT YOU OWN AND KNOW WHAT YOU ARE BUYING—LIENS AND ENCUMBRANCES THAT WILL BE YOURS

What Happens to the Other Liens and Judgments if You Buy a First Trust Deed at the Trustee's Sale?

At many Trustee's Sales, the owners of the second Trust Deed and those who filed the liens will not show up. If that is the case and you purchase a first Trust Deed from the Trustee, you will own the house for what you pay the Trustee and the other lenders or judgment holders will have their liens or judgments extinguished by the sale. (The status of tax liens is different and is explained below.)

If this were always the situation, the Trustee's Sales would be mobbed with interested buyers. In the real world, the owner or holders of the second Trust Deed will show up at the sale to bid. Many holders of junior Trust Deeds understand the situation and will attempt to bid more than you bid in order to salvage the loan they have already made on the property. So keep in mind that because loans recorded later than the foreclosing loan are extinguished by the foreclosing loan at the Trustee's Sale, the holders of the junior loan could be your competition.

Some foreclosure buyers approach the second lien holder and buy his or her interest at a discount, or less than its face value. They then cure, or reinstate, the defaulting first Trust Deed by paying what is in arrears. This procedure will take the property out of the foreclosure process temporarily.

If you then foreclose under the second Trust Deed and no one shows up at the Trustee's Sale to outbid you, you will own the property for the price of the discounted second Trust Deed plus whatever it took to cure the default on the first Trust Deed. If someone outbids you and is prepared to pay more than your note value plus penalties, costs, and back payments, you'll still profit, because you purchased the note at a discounted value and will be receiving the face value of the note.

Whether you buy real estate at the Trustee's Sale or from the owner, you get exactly what is owned by the seller: You will own all liens and encumbrances that are senior or recorded prior to the date that the Trust Deed (mortgage) that you are purchasing was recorded. Keep in mind that any liens or abstracts of judgment recorded *before* the foreclosing loan will still apply to the property after the Trustee's Sale. Most liens and abstracts of judgments recorded *after* the foreclosing loan will be extinguished by the Trustee's Sale.

The worst mistake you can make will be made in ignorance. If you don't know what is owed against the property and cannot get that information from title company or your own records search, *don't bid*.

LIS PENDENS

From time to time, you find a property with a *lis pendens* filed against it. This is simply a notice that some form of legal action has been filed against the property. This could be a lawsuit filed to obtain money from the owner. If the *lis pendens* was filed after the foreclosing trust deed, it will be extinguished; if it was filed before, it will have seniority.

QUITCLAIM DEED

In researching the records you may come across a document called a *Quitclaim Deed* (see Figure 3.5). Like a Grant Deed, this document shows a transfer of ownership, but its use is limited. It is considered legally binding only when the property is being transferred between spouses. The following statement should be included on the Quitclaim Deed: "It is the intention of the Grantor herein to relinquish all of his/her rights, title and interest whether community property or otherwise in and to the herein above described property and to vest said property in the above Grantee as his/her sole and separate property." Because of the Deed's limitations, most title companies prefer to have Grant Deeds as evidence of the transfer of ownership.

TAX LIENS

Tax liens are more complicated. They may be filed by municipal, state, or federal authorities. Any tax lien filed before the foreclosing Trust Deed was recorded will be senior in priority and (you guessed it) you will be assuming those liens if you buy from the owner or at the Trustee's Sale. Keep in mind all liens junior to the foreclosing lien get eliminated at the Trustee's Sale.

Municipal and county liens will be extinguished by the foreclosure (Trustee's Sale). The liens are eliminated from the property but will remain in force against the individual.

RECORDING REQUESTED BY
AND WHEN RECORDED MAIL TO

NAME
STREET
ADDRESS

CITY,
STATE
ZIP

MAIL TAX STATEMENTS TO

NAME
STREET
ADDRESS

CITY,
STATE
ZIP

SPACE A___ THIS LINE FOR RECORDER'S USE

DOCUMENTARY ___ ISFER TAX $_____
_____ COMPUTI___ FULL VALUE OF PROPERTY CONVEYED.
_____ OR COMP___ ON FULL VALUE LESS LIENS AND
_____ ENCUME___ ES REMAINING AT TIME OF SALE.

Signature of Declaran___ determining tax.   Firm Name

QUITCLAIM D___)

By this instrument dated ...., for valuable consideration,

do ....hereby remise, release and foreve___ ..aim to

the following described Real Property in the$___ .f California, County of..................................City of ....

STATE OF CALIFORNIA   On........................,19.......,before me, the undersigned, a Notary Public
COUNTY OF   in and for said County and State, personally appeared.......................
...., known to me to be
the person..........whose name................ubscribed to the within instrument and acknowledged that ....he...........executed the same.

Notary's Signature...
Type or Print Notary's Name ....:...

MAIL TAX STATEMENTS AS DIRECTED ABOVE

Figure 3.5   Quitclaim Deed

Likewise, state tax liens filed (recorded) after the foreclosing lien (loan) will be extinguished by the foreclosure. Extinguished, that is, with regard to the property you have just bought but still payable by the previous owner.

Federal tax liens are different. The buyer at the Trustee's Sale is required to wait 120 days for the federal government to exercise its right of redemption. If the federal government does not exercise its rights within 120 days, the new owner will be cleared by the title insurance company to purchase title insurance, as all other liens including state tax liens, trust deeds, mortgages, mechanic's liens, abstracts of judgment, and everything else are extinguished by the Trustee's Sale.

By researching the recorder's files, the purchaser-investor who plans to buy at the foreclosure sale can determine if a federal tax lien (filed by the IRS) is still in effect. If a lien is found, contact the party handling the sale and ask if the federal government has been notified of the approaching sale. The law requires the government be given a 25-day notice of the sale. If the government is not notified, the lien will not be extinguished by the sale. If it is notified, the lien will be extinguished with the expiration of the 120-day right of redemption.

WHAT IS AN ESCROW?

Buying or selling a home usually involves the transfer of large sums of money. This money and the related documents are usually handled by an escrow agent who is an independent third party. Until the transaction is completed, this third party holds the money and the documents and upon specific instructions (usually written) he or she disburses the money and supervises the exchange of documents.

The escrow agent will have received funds and documents necessary to comply with the instructions, completed or obtained any special forms, such as Grant Deeds, Quitclaim Deeds, Promissory Notes, and so on, and in due course will deliver those documents to the appropriate parties. The escrow holder, or company, impartially carries out the written instructions given by the parties involved in transaction and must be provided with the necessary information to complete the transaction. An example of escrow instructions is given as the Appendix to this chapter.

What Documents Should I Expect the Escrow Holder to Require?

- Loan documents
- Tax statements
- Fire and hazard insurance policies
- Title insurance policy
- Any document pertaining to financing of the sale
- Requests from outsiders requiring payment.

Who Does the Escrow Holder Work For?

The escrow holder serves as a neutral stakeholder and the link between the principal parties, the seller and the buyer.

What Should I Expect the Escrow Holder to Do?

Ask to be sure, but you can usually expect the escrow holder to:

- Prepare the escrow instructions
- Request a preliminary title search to determine the condition of the present title: outstanding loans, tax liens, judgments
- Request a beneficiary's statement if the debt is to be taken over by the new buyer
- Comply with the lenders' requests in the matters of, for instance, late fees, and prepayment penalties
- Prepare the Deed and other documents
- Pro-rate taxes, interest, insurance, and rents
- Secure releases on other encumbrances
- Record the Deed and any other documents as requested in the written escrow instructions
- Request title insurance
- Close the escrow when all the documents of the buyer and the seller have been completed
- Distribute the funds as authorized by the written escrow instructions.

WHAT ARE CLOSING COSTS?

A rule of thumb is that closing costs will be approximately 10 percent. This figure usually consists of:

- Real estate commissions
- Loan fees
- Escrow charge
- Title insurance premium
- Termite inspection payments
- Roof inspection payments.

Understanding these costs is important so that you are prepared and not surprised on the settlement day.

NEW GROWTH FINANCIAL

AGREEMENT FOR SALE OF REAL PROPERTY AND ESCROW INSTRUCTIONS

THIS AGREEMENT is made this _____ day of _____, 19_____, for purposes of reference, by and between _____, who together with his heirs, legal representatives, nominees and assigns is hereinafter referred to as "buyer," hereby agrees to purchase the real estate described in paragraph 1. hereinbelow, from _____, who together with successors and assigns is hereinafter referred to as "Seller," upon the following terms and conditions.

1. TRANSACTION

Seller agrees to sell and convey, and Buyer agrees to purchase for the price and upon the terms hereinafter set forth, the real property described in Exhibit "A" attached hereto and for address purposes known as the building and lot located at _____, together with all appurtenances, and heritaments belonging thereto, improvements situated thereon, the personal property located therein, if any, and all electrical, heating, plumbing and bathroom fixtures, attached wall-to-wall carpeting, other attached floor coverings, draperies including hardware, shades, blinds, window and door screens, trees and items permanently attached to the real property, all of which are hereinafter referred to collectively as the "Premises."

The Seller of this home has not resided in the home and therefore has no knowledge of defects, if any. Seller therefore requires the buyer satisfy to his/her own knowledge that the home meets the standards he/she expects.

2. PURCHASE PRICE AND METHOD OF PAYMENT

The purchase price shall be the sum of _____ ($_____)

for the following:

a. Land	$	_____
b. Building	$	_____
c. Personal Property	$	_____
TOTAL	$	_____

Said purchase shall be paid in the following manner:

d. Cash upon acceptance of offer: $ _____
(to be placed into escrow)

e. Increase of deposit upon removal $ _____
of contingencies (if any):
to be deposited on: _____
_____

f. Cash upon closing of transaction: $ _____

g. Financing – First Loan: _____

h. Financing – Other (if any) _____
_____

3. Buyer's success in obtaining financing, on the terms set forth above, is a condition precedent to Buyer's obligation to complete the purchase of the Premises. Buyer hereby agrees to use due diligence and good faith to apply for and obtain all financing set forth hereinabove. If, after _____ ( ) days after acceptance, Buyer has been unable to obtain all financing as stated hereinabove, Buyer may cancel this agreement and receive a full refund of all sums deposited toward the purchase price. This condition is for the benefit of Buyer and may be waived by Buyer.

4. CONTINGENCY – INSPECTION OF PREMISES

Regardless of any warranties made by Seller herein, if any, regarding the condition of the premises, and in addition to disclosures made by Seller to Buyer pursuant to Civil Code Sections 1102 et seq., or otherwise, Buyer shall obtain, at Buyer's expense, an inspection of the Premises performed by a qualified professional, part of whose regular business is the inspection of property similar to the Premises. Buyer shall obtain a written report from said professional, which report shall provide the results, in reasonable detail, of said professional's inspection of the various components of the premises, including but not limited to, as applicable, structural, plumbing, heating, electrical, built-in appliances, roof, soils, foundation, mechanical systems, pool and heater and filter, air conditioner, any environmental hazards such as asbestos, formaldehyde, radon gas, water impurities, etc. Buyer shall keep the Premises free of all liens and indemnify and hold Seller harmless from all claims, liability, costs, and damages, and shall repair all damage to the premises arising from inspections. All such reports concerning the Premises shall be in writing, delivered to Seller, at his cost to Seller, within _____ days after Seller's acceptance. When such reports disclose conditions or information unsatisfactory to Buyer, Buyer may cancel this agreement and receive back all of Buyer's deposit. Seller shall make the Premises available for all inspections. The completion of such inspections, to the reasonable satisfaction of Buyer and Seller, is a condition precedent to the obligations of Buyer and Seller, respectively, to complete this purchase. This provision is for the benefit of both Buyer and Seller, and may not be waived by either Buyer or Seller alone, but only by written waiver signed by both Buyer and Seller. If Buyer does approve of the Premises after these inspections, or otherwise waives this contingency, Buyer understands that Buyer takes the Premises in its present condition, subject only to such warranties and representations of Seller as may be contained in this agreement, and such disclosures as are contained in the Civic Code section 1102 disclosures received, or to be received by Buyer. Seller does not hereby covenant to repair any defect discovered by said inspection, unless it is also included as an item which Seller is required to repair pursuant to the structural pest control report provided for in paragraph 5 hereof, or unless it is required to be repaired under some other warranty given by Seller to Buyer hereunder, if any.

The Seller is in the business of selling and buying real estate wholesale and has not resided in this house and/or building.

5. STRUCTURAL PEST CONTROL INSPECTION

Within _____ days from the date of acceptance of this agreement, Buyer shall have the right to obtain, at Buyer's expense, a current written report of an inspection by a licensed pest control operator of Buyer's choice, of the main building and all structures on the property, except _____.

If no infestation by wood-destroying pests or organisms is found, the report shall include a written certification as provided in Business and Professions code section 8519(a) that on the date of the inspection "no evidence of active infestation or infection was found."

Any and all work recommended in said report to repair damage caused by infestation or infection by wood-destroying pests or organism found, including leaking shower stalls and replacement of tiles removed for repair, and all work to correct conditions that cause such infestation or infection shall be done at the expense of Buyer.

Buyer agrees that any work to correct conditions will be repaired at the expense of the Buyer. If there is evidence of existing infestation or infection, such conditions are not the responsibility of the Seller and that such work will be done only at the request of Buyer at the Buyer's expense.

If inspection of inaccessible areas is recommended by the report, Buyer has the option of accepting and approving the report or requesting further inspection be made at Buyer's expense. If further inspection is made and infestation, infection or damage is found, repair of such damage and all work to correct conditions that caused such infestation or infection and the cost of entry and closing inaccessible areas shall be at the expense of Buyer. If no infestation, infection or damage is found, the expense of opening and closing inaccessible areas shall be Buyer's.

6. ASSIGNMENT

None of the Buyer's rights or obligations under this agreement shall be assigned without the prior written consent of Seller, and any attempted assignment purported to be made without the prior consent of Seller shall be null and void and of no effect whatever.

7. DEFAULT

DEFAULT BY BUYER: IF BUYER FAILS TO COMPLETE SAID PURCHASE AS HEREIN PROVIDED BY REASON OF ANY DEFAULT OF BUYER, SELLER SHALL BE RELEASED FROM OBLIGATION TO SELL THE PREMISES TO BUYER AND MAY PROCEED AGAINST BUYER ON ANY CLAIM OR REMEDY WHICH SELLER MAY HAVE IN LAW OR EQUITY: PROVIDED, HOWEVER, THAT BY PLACING THEIR INITIALS HERE BUYER: ( ) SELLER: ( ) AGREE THAT SELLER SHALL RETAIN THE BUYER'S DEPOSIT, IN THE AMOUNT OF $ _____ OR 4% OF THE PURCHASE PRICE AS LIQUIDATED DAMAGES.

DEFAULT BY SELLER: If Seller fails to perform any of Seller's obligations under this contract, all money deposited by Buyer shall, at the option of Buyer, be immediately returned to Buyer, and Buyer may proceed against Seller on any claim or remedy which Buyer may have in law or equity, including but not limited to the right of specific performance.

8. DEED — TITLE

Seller agrees to convey marketable title to the Premises to Buyer by good and sufficient Grant Deed. Seller shall deposit said Grant Deed with Escrow Holder no later than seven (7) days prior to the date scheduled for close of escrow of this purchase. Seller shall grant title to the premises free from all liens and encumbrances whatsoever except covenants, conditions and restrictions of record, easements which do not substantially affect the continuing use of the Premises in its present manner, real estate taxes and assessments both general and special which are not yet due and payable, unless any of the foregoing are reasonably disapproved by Buyer within five (5) days after Buyer's receipt of a preliminary title report furnished at Buyer's expense, and any liens or encumbrances for new financing to finance this purchase, as stated in this agreement, or encumbrances which Buyer has agreed to take title subject to, or assume, elsewhere in this agreement. If Buyer does object to any title matter, Buyer shall so notify Seller in writing and Seller shall use due diligence to cure said title defect. Seller shall have sixty (60) days to remove or alter said title matter to Buyer's reasonable satisfaction, and if Seller is unable to do so, Buyer may cancel this contract and have return of all sums deposited, or Buyer may proceed with the purchase, at Buyer's option. A standard California Land Title Association policy of title insurance shall be furnished in the amount of the purchase price at Buyer's expense, showing title vested in Buyer subject only to the above.

9. REPRESENTATIONS AND WARRANTIES OF SELLER

Seller hereby makes the following representations and warranties which shall survive the closing of this transaction and delivery of Grant Deed to the premises:

a. Seller is the owner of the premises and has the right to sell and convey the Premises, and Seller has not previously conveyed the ownership of the Premises to any other person or entity;

b. No order of any municipal, county or state agency has been served upon Seller requiring work to be done or improvements to be made to the premises which have not already been performed and approved by such agency.

10. ESCROW, ESCROW AGENT

The last day for close of escrow under this agreement is agreed by Buyer and Seller to be _____, 19_____. _____ at _____ _____, or any other escrow agent acceptable to Buyer and Seller is hereby designated as Escrow Holder hereunder. Buyer and Seller appoint said Escrow Holder to perform all the usual duties of escrow agents in purchases and sales of real property in Northern California, including but not limited to the issuance of title insurance, and preparation and recordation of documents.

11. POSSESSION

Seller agrees to deliver possession of the Premises to Buyer on the date the Escrow Holder obtains recordation of the Grant Deed to Buyer hereunder.

12. TRANSFER OF PERSONAL PROPERTY

Seller agrees to execute a Bill of Sale containing the usual covenants to transfer ownership to Buyer of the personal property located on the Premises. The following personal property, located on the premises when inspected by Buyer, is included in the purchase price and shall be transferred in its present condition at the time of acceptance of this agreement, unless otherwise stated herein:

_____
_____

13. NO MERGER

Covenants, warranties, representations, and terms of this agreement shall in no way be merged or defeated by reason of delivery of deed to the Premises to Buyer or close of escrow of this purchase.

14. REAL ESTATE TAXES AND ASSESSMENT — PRORATIONS

All real estate taxes and assessments shall be prorated by the Escrow Holder on the basis of the last available tax duplicate as of the date of the recordation of the Grant Deed.

15. SECURITY DEPOSIT – LEASES – CONTINGENCY – ESTOPPEL STATEMENTS

Seller shall assign tenants' security deposits in Seller's possession or control as of the date of closing, to Buyer. Within _____ days after acceptance hereof by Buyer and Seller, Seller shall provide Buyer with copies of all written leases affecting the Premises, if any. Buyer shall have fifteen (15) days to review said leases and approve or disapprove of same. Said approval is a condition of Buyer's obligations under this agreement, and shall not be unreasonably withheld. This contingency is for the benefit of Buyer and shall be waivable by Buyer in writing. Seller shall provide estoppel statements from all tenants and subtenants on the Premises, prior to close of escrow, stating that there has been no prepayment of rents, credit given in lieu of rent, or promises of work to be done on the Premises which have not been fully performed.

16. PRORATION – TENANTS' RENTS

All rents shall be prorated by Escrow Holder as of the date of recordation of deed. Rents remaining unpaid during the escrow period shall be prorated as well as rents already paid for the month in which escrow closes.

17. INSURANCE PREMIUM

Premiums on insurance, if policy is acceptable to Buyer such that Buyer desires that existing policies be transferred to Buyer, shall be prorated as of the date of recordation of the deed hereunder. Seller will provide Buyer with the name of Seller's insurance agent so that Buyer may arrange to examine these policies should Buyer so desire.

18. RISK OF LOSS

Until such time as the Grant Deed provided for hereunder is recorded, or until Buyer takes possession of the Premises, whichever occurs first, Seller shall bear all risk of loss to the premises and shall insure the same, as the Premises are currently insured.

If after acceptance of this agreement, but prior to close of escrow, any part of the Premises is destroyed or damaged by fire or any other casualty, then if the aggregate amount of such losses is less than _____ ($_____) this transaction shall be completed and Seller shall pay to Buyer the proceeds of any insurance payable to Seller, if any, by reason of such losses.

If the aggregate of such losses exceeds the above-specified amount, then, at Buyer's option, either:

a. This agreement shall be terminated and Buyer may recover any funds theretofore deposited by Buyer hereunder; or

b. This transaction shall be completed and Buyer shall accept the Premises in their damaged condition, and recover from Seller the insurance proceeds payable to Seller in connection herewith, if any. Buyer shall notify Seller in writing within twenty (20) days after Buyer has received written or actual notice of such damage or destruction, as to which of the above options Buyer has chosen.

19. MAINTENANCE

Until possesion is delivered, Seller agrees to maintain heating, sewer, plumbing and electrical systems and any built-in appliances in the same condition as when this agreement was accepted.

20. KEYS

Prior to or upon close of escrow, Seller shall deposit all copies of all keys in Seller's possession or control to locks on the Premises with the Escrow Holder, for transmission to buyer.

21. BROKER

The Seller's business is purchase and sale of real estate. Seller has not resided within this building or house. Seller is acting as a principal not as a broker.

22. NOTICE

Any notices required or allowed hereunder shall be deemed properly served if mailed to the party entitled to such notice, by certified mail return receipt requested, at the following addresses:

Seller: _____
_____

Buyer: _____
_____

23. CLOSING

At such time that all funds and documents required for closing hereunder have been deposited with Escrow Holder, and when Escrow Holder is prepared to issue thereupon its C.L.T.A. policy in the amount of the purchase price as stated herein, Escrow Holder shall file the Grant Deed for record. At such time Escrow Holder shall disburse funds, after charging Seller with the following:

a. One-half of any documentary transfer tax imposed by the state, any county or any municipal authority;

b. The amount of any tenants' security deposits being held by Seller:

c. Any amounts due Buyer by reason of proration of tenants' rents as stated herein;

d. The amount of prorated real estate taxes or assessments payable by Seller;

e. Any brokerage commission due;

f. Any amounts due Buyer by reason of any other prorations hereunder;
Escrow Holder shall charge Buyer with the following:

a. The escrow fee;

b. Costs of recordation of documents required to complete this transaction, including deeds and deeds of trust, and any notary fees for notarization of Buyer's signature;

c. Any amount due Seller by reason of prorations of unpaid rent or other prorations stated herein;

d. The cost of the Title Insurance and of the preliminary title report required hereunder;

e. One-half of any documentary transfer tax imposed by the state, any county or any municipal authority;

Escrow Holder shall thereupon deliver to Seller its escrow statement, together with its check for the proceeds of sale, after the appropriate deductions; and shall deliver to Buyer the recorded deed or evidence thereof, the policy of title insurance, the bill of sale, its escrow statement, and any proceeds due to Buyer hereunder.

24. TIME
Time is of the essence of this agreement.

25. EXCHANGE COOPERATION
Buyer and Seller each reserve the right to transfer as part of an I.R.S. Section 1031 exchange or similar tax-related arrangement, and each party agrees to cooperate with the other in effecting such an exchange. Any party desiring to complete this transaction as part of such an exchange shall notify the other party and the Escrow Holder within 20 days after acceptance of such party's intention to exchange. Failure to so notify shall be deemed a waiver of the right to the other party's cooperation in an exchange.

26. ENTIRE CONTRACT - ADDENDUM
Except for additional terms and conditions of this purchase which are included on the attached ADDENDUM consisting of _____ (_____) pages, which are made a part of this agreement and incorporated herein by reference, this agreement contains the entire agreement between Buyer and Seller, and all prior negotiations promises, representations, warranties and statements relating to this transaction are of no force and effect, except insofar as they are included in this agreement. This agreement may not be modified, amended, or changed in any way except by a further agreement in writing signed by Buyer and Seller.

27. BENEFITS AND BURDENS
This agreement shall be binding upon and inure to the benefit of Buyer and Seller, and each of their heirs, legal representatives, nominees, successors and assigns.

28. VESTING
The name or names in which title to the premises shall vest in Buyer shall be provided by Buyer to Escrow Holder no later than ten (10) days prior to the date scheduled for close of escrow hereof.

29. ATTORNEY'S FEES
In the event of any action or proceeding arising out of this agreement the prevailing party shall be entitled to recover its reasonable costs and attorney's fees, as fixed by the court.

30. OCCUPANCY
Buyer (check one only) does _____ does not _____ intend to occupy the Premises as Buyer's primary residence.

31. TRANSFER DISCLOSURE
Unless exempt, Seller shall comply with Civic Code section 1102 et seq. by providing buyer with a Real Estate Transfer Disclosure statement. Unless said statement has already been provided, Seller shall provide said statement to Buyer within _____ days after acceptance hereof, after which Buyer shall have three days after delivery to Buyer in person, or five days after delivery by mail, to terminate this agreement by written notice of termination to Seller or Seller's agent.

The Seller has not resided in the house/building and therefore has no knowledge of defects if any. Seller therefore requires buyer to satisfy his/her knowledge that the home meets his/her purchase requirements.

32. TAX WITHHOLDING

Under Internal Revenue Code section 1445, every Buyer of U.S. real property must, unless an exemption applies, deduct and withhold from Seller's proceeds ten percent (10%) of the gross sales price. No withholding is required if: (a) Seller provides Buyer with an affidavit under penalty of perjury that Seller is not a "foreign person", or (b) Seller provides Buyer with a "qualifying statement" issued by the I.R.S.; or (c) if Buyer purchases the real property for use as his primary residence and the purchase price is $300,000.00 or less. Seller is not a "foreign person" and Seller will provide the necessary affidavit in escrow, so that no withholding of Seller's proceeds will be necessary.

33. CALIFORNIA LAW

Insofar as possible, this agreement shall be interpreted according to the laws of the State of California.

Buyer and Seller, by their respective signatures hereon, intend to form a binding agreement for the purchase and sale of the Premises, and Buyer and Seller hereby acknowledge that each of them has read, understands and accepts the terms of this agreement.

_____   _____

BUYER   **DATE**

_____

SELLER: NEW GROWTH FINANCIAL
By: Ted Thomas, Vice President

Amazing Profits in Fixer-Uppers

How to Buy and How to Sell Them

Everyone loves a fixer-upper—everyone, that is, who can recognize a bargain and appreciate the rewards that come to those who are prepared to work. Almost every neighborhood has at least one house that falls into disrepair for one reason or another: divorce, bankruptcy, the death of the breadwinner, economic changes that have closed industries. Such changes are all opportunities for the buyer of distressed property.

This case study describes the purchase of a run-down property that, with a few improvements, could become a highly desirable property that virtually sells itself—at a handsome profit.

In the course of reading the case study you will learn:

- How to make a 100 percent return with very little cash investment
- What action the County Assessor takes if you neglect to pay your personal property taxes (Certificate of Delinquency)
- What action the state can take for nonpayment of state income taxes
- About personal property tax and how you find out about it
- To turn those negative termite and roof inspection reports to advantage
- Who will buy your fixer-upper before you lift a hammer or a paint brush
- The benefit of using a conservative appraiser
- To price the property to sell
- To be a marketing genius.

Locating defaults and Trustee's Sales is the major investment in time that the foreclosure buyer must make. Legal newspapers, county records, bulletin boards in public buildings, professional service companies that specialize in researching records all will help you find these unusual properties.

Sales of distressed property are not part of the normal real estate market. Most agents don't want to handle distressed property. They consider this business, which is essentially one of solving the distressed owner's problems, beneath them. Take advantage of this market. Only a few hard workers will spend the time to seek out the bargains. It does take time because in most circumstances, you will find properties in which there is no equity or that require extensive repairs, modifications, or financing. These you will reject. But if you do have the patience to follow the market, send letters, make telephone calls, knock on doors, hang door hangers, and generally pursue the foreclosures, your persistence will pay off.

A CASE STUDY

$10,000 Profit in Six Weeks

The following case study describes the purchase of a foreclosure property in California that, with very little money, yielded a profit of more than 100 percent in less than six weeks.

The customer responded to a direct-mail letter and what we found was a real fixer-upper. In spite of looking bad, this property had the potential to produce significant profits for the investor who was willing to work, investigate local values, and research the buyers' needs.

The owner responded to one of the many direct mail pieces that we sent over the period of 12 weeks that is the reinstatement period affecting foreclosures and the sale of real estate under California laws.

You recall that the foreclosure period in California is rather lengthy, 111 days. The first step is the filing at the County Recorder's Office of a Notice of Default (NOD) by the Trustee. This recording of the notice begins a three-month reinstatement period. Upon the expiration of the reinstatement period, the Trustee will file a Notice of Trustee's Sale. The Trustee will also post this notice on the property and will publish it in a newspaper of general circulation at least three times in the next 21 days. According to California law, on the 22nd day, the property will be auctioned or sold at the Trustee's Sale. In your state it may be called a Sheriff's Sale and the process may be called a Judicial Foreclosure.

When sellers, the defaulting homeowners, respond to direct mail, we always complete a Property Evaluation Questionnaire and attempt to make an appointment to visit the property. Such visits will allow you to assess the neighborhood and the actual structure. If the neighborhood is deteriorating and the home is beyond repair, you will just cancel the appointment and not attempt to write an Equity Purchase Agreement. However if, after talking with brokers, checking the MLS for comparable sales and talking with homeowners in the vicinity, you find that the neighborhood is improving and property values are likely to rise (upward appreciation), you'll want to pursue the purchase further.

Sellers will always try to get as much as possible when selling their home. Many will have realistic expectations; others will have visions of prices that are far higher than you could pay and still make money. The easiest method of arriving at a price fair for both parties is to ask what the seller wants. Many times the response will be: "Oh, just give me a couple thousand dollars to move." The Equity Purchase Agreement has rights of rescission clauses protecting both the buyer and the seller. These are useful, especially when the seller asks too high a price and you, the buyer, find you cannot pay the seller, complete the repairs, and come out with a profit.

The seller in our case knew exactly what he wanted for his equity and we agreed to pay the amount he requested. The Equity Purchase Agreement (Figure 4.1) required a payment to the sellers of $14,550, less deductions for termite damage, roof repairs, and any liens that might have been filed against the property.

Figure 4.2 shows the Grant Deed by which William Wiggs granted the property to Alice Abels and her brother, Albert Abels. Notice that the Grant Deed shows the Assessor's Parcel Number for the property as 380-120-014; the number is also noted on the Equity Purchase Agreement. This detail is especially important: you need to confirm that you are buying the property that is owned by the seller.

We knew that the mortgage payments on the property had been in default for a number of months. After the owners had signed the Equity Purchase Agreement, we asked them to obtain from the mortgage holder a breakdown of the outstanding amount. According to the reply from Prosperity Savings of America (Figure 4.3), the owners had not paid the mortgage since September of the previous year, a total of eight months. This letter confirmed one of the major costs of our proposed purchase: more than $7,000 would be needed to cure the default.

Bigland Title Company provided additional information in the form of a *Property Profile*. The Property Profile includes, among other items, an assessor's map, a copy of the Grant Deed, and usually a copy of at least one Trust Deed or mortgage. The Property Profile is not a Preliminary Title Report; it is just an overview of the property at a certain date. From the Preliminary Title Report we learned the tax status of the property and the original loan amounts (Items 4 and 5 of the report). We also ascertained that the loan that was in default had originally been taken out by William Wiggs and Alice Abels. It appears from the Grant Deed (Figure 4.2) that Mr. Wiggs had subsequently deeded his interest in the property to Alice Abels and Albert Abels. We noted that his Deed was recorded on September 10, 1987 and that the first delinquent loan payment had fallen due on September 9, 1987.

Expect to find, as part of the Property Profile, information about comparable properties and their selling prices. It is possible to use the assessor's map (Figure 4.4) to confirm which parcel you are purchasing and its location and size compared to others on the same street.

After the five-day right of rescission, which is required by the California Civil Code, had expired and the sellers had chosen not to cancel the Home Equity Purchase Agreement (Figure 4.5), a more detailed Preliminary Title Report was requested. The report confirmed the loan from Prosperity Savings was in default and had been so since January 26, 1988 or some four months.

The Preliminary Title Report shows immediately after the Item 5 Deed of Trust information, that a Notice of Default was recorded on January 26, 1988, approximately four months before the Equity Purchase Agreement was signed. However, the sellers had been delinquent on the payment of the loan, according to the letter dated May 5, 1988, from Prosperity Savings of America, since

NEW GROWTH FINANCIAL

EQUITY PURCHASE AGREEMENT
Page 1 of 3

THIS AGREEMENT, made this ___14___ day of ___APRIL___, 19 _88_
between New Growth Financial and/or assignees (hereinafter "Buyer"); in consideration of the
covenants and agreements hereinafter contained, Seller agrees to sell and convey to Buyer and
Buyer agrees to purchase from Seller, the following real property located in (city) _MARTINEZ_
County _CONTRA COSTA_ California (street address) _4206 VALLEY AVE._
Assessor's parcel no.) _980-130-014_ Tract_____ Lot _6_ Block _MAP BOOK 25_
Page(s) _230_ (Attach legal description as Exhibit "A"). The following personal property is also
included in this purchase:_____

Said real and personal property is collectively known as the "Property".

1. In consideration for said property, Buyer agrees to pay to Seller, as Seller's equity in the
Property, the total sum ($ _14,550_), payable at the time Seller delivers to Buyer both (1) A
properly prepared, notarized and valid Grant Deed to the Property (and bill of sale for any
personal property included in the sale) and, (2) Subject to section 2 (f) hereof, the transfer of
possession of the Property to Buyer, including all improvements, vacant, clean, and in good repair.
IN NO EVENT SHALL ANY MONEY OR OTHER CONSIDERATION BE TRANSFERRED TO SELLER
BY BUYER AT ANY TIME PRIOR TO THE EXPIRATION OF SELLER'S RIGHT TO CANCEL THIS
CONTRACT, PROVIDED FOR HEREINBELOW, AS SUCH TRANSFER IS PROHIBITED BY
CALIFORNIA LAW.

2. (a) Seller represents that the following are the deeds of trusts, liens, encumbrances, judgments,
bonds assessments (hereinafter "Encumbrances")

1st TD $ _55,200 00_ payable $_____ per month_____% Int. incl. T & I

2nd TD $ _5,000 00_ payable $_____ per month_____% _____due date

3rd TD $_____ payable $_____ per month_____% _____due date

(b) Seller represents that said Encumbrances each have the following amounts which are now
due or past due: _55,200 PLUS 5,000 BACK PAYMENTS_
From the NET amount due Seller may be deducted all payments on existing encumbrances
through the payments due_____ _4-1_ , 19 _88_ . Also, any taxes, judgments,
assessment bonds, prepayment penalties, and other liens if any. Impounds, if any, are to be
assigned without charge to the Buyer, in any amount satisfactory to the lending institution. Any
impound shortage will be deducted from the funds due Seller. Insurance Fire Casualty Policy will
be assigned to the Buyer without charge.

(c) Buyer shall take title to the property subject to all of said Encumbrances and amounts due
or past due, except _NONE_
Buyer shall further take title subject to all easements, zoning and land-use restrictions, and
covenants, conditions and restrictions of record, so long as the same do not adversely affect the
continued use of the Property for its present use.

(d) Buyer shall have the right to rescind this agreement and to receive a refund of all
consideration paid to Seller if within (5) days after receiving a Grant Deed to the Property Buyer
notifies Seller in writing that the principal amounts of, and/or the amounts due or past due on,
one or more of the Encumbrances are greater than as represented hereinabove, or that there are
one or more easements, zoning or land use restrictions, or covenants, conditions and restrictions
concerning the Property which adversely affect the continued use of the Property for its present
use. Said notice shall demand rescission and shall specify the Encumbrance(s) which are not in
compliance with the representations made by Seller or the easements, etc. which interfere with
the continued use of the Property for its present use. Upon receipt of said notice Seller shall
immediately cooperate with Buyer to execute all documents and do all things necessary to fully
rescind the sale and return the full amount of money and/or other property transferred to Seller in
connection with this sale. If Seller shall fail or refuse to so cooperate, Seller shall be liable for all
loss or harm caused by said failure or refusal.

Copyright 1988 New Growth Financial

(Page 1 of 3)

Figure 4.1 Equity Purchase Agreement

NEW GROWTH FINANCIAL

EQUITY PURCHASE AGREEMENT

Page 2 of 3

(e) Buyer shall pay all the following, if any: escrow fees, title insurance fees, transfer taxes, recording fees, notary fees. Seller agrees to pay for any damages found by termite and roof inspections.

(f) Possession of the Property shall be transferred to Buyer on _____ 4-30 , 19 88 . Any and all risk of loss of the Property or any part thereof shall be born by Seller until possession of the Property has passed to Buyer. Any possession, occupancy or tenancy by the Seller at any time after the Grant Deed has been delivered to Buyer shall be on the following terms: Rent to be paid by Seller to Buyer: ($_____) per day 30.00 , month 900 00 year 10,800 00 . Seller to vacate Property on or before: 4-30-88 . Other terms of rental: Seller agrees to pay for any damage done to the Property that is caused by Seller or tenants after the date this contract is signed. Balance of funds due Seller are to be paid after the premises are vacated.

3. ATTORNEY'S FEES.

In the event that any legal or equitable action is brought to enforce the terms of this agreement, including but not limited to specific performance, or rescission of contract, the prevailing party in such action shall be entitled to collect reasonable attorney's fees, expert witness fees and cost of suit, as determined by the court.

4. EFFECT OF PARTIAL INVALIDITY.

The provisions of this Agreement are agreed to severally by the undersigned, and the invalidity or partial invalidity of one or more provisions of this Agreement shall not render the remaining provisions invalid or unenforceable.

5. AGREEMENT BINDING UPON HEIRS, ASSIGNS.

This Agreement, and all terms hereof, shall be binding on the heirs, devisees, executors, personal representative, conservators, successors, and assigns of the undersigned Buyer and Seller.

6. WARRANTY OF TITLE; WARRANTIES TO SURVIVE DELIVERY OF DEED.

Seller hereby warrants, jointly and severally, that each of the undersigned, as Seller, is the lawful owner of any ownership interest in the Property, and that collectively the Property and Seller has the right and authority to convey said ownership to Buyer. This warranty, and all warranties, terms and conditions hereof, shall survive the delivery and recordation of any deed to buyer, and the close of any escrow.

(a) Seller is not entitled to receive any other consideration or thing of value or services from Buyer, in connection with or incident to the sale of the Property to Buyer, except as stated hereinabove and except the following: _____ NONE _____

Ted Thomas is an employee of New Growth Financial and holds a valid Broker's License issued by the State of California.

7. PHYSICAL CONDITION OF PROPERTY

The Property is free of all defects in its structure and its operating systems such as plumbing, electrical, roof and metal work, gas and sewer, except for the following: EVERYTHING O.K. _____ Seller agrees to pay for all damages and repairs found by termite and roof inspectors. Buyer takes the property subject to the above disclosed defects. Seller hereby warrants that the property is free of other defects, as of the date of delivery of a Grant Deed to the Property to Buyer.

8. COMMISSIONS

Seller hereby represents that there is no licensed real estate salesperson or broker representing Seller in any way in connection with this purchase and sale, and Seller agrees to hold Buyer harmless and defend Buyer from any claim to commission in connection with this purchase and sale.

9. UNCONSCIONABILITY

Seller hereby represents that all negotiations and dealings with Buyer have been and are at arm's length, and that no duress or undue influence has been exerted by Buyer over Seller or Seller's family in connection with this purchase and sale. Seller is aware that the Buyer may be purchasing property for immediate resale.

(Page 2 of 3)

Figure 4.1 *(continued)*

NEW GROWTH FINANCIAL

EQUITY PURCHASE AGREEMENT
Page 3 of 3

10. Property MUST appraise at $ *80,000 00* . Less than that amount will be DEDUCTED from net to seller.

(c) Seller is aware and understands that the present fair market value of the Property probably is higher than the purchase price set forth herein. Seller hereby expressly waives any and all claim to any potential or actual income, profits or other sums in excess of the above mentioned purchase price, which may be realized by Buyer or others as a result of any transaction involving the Property. Seller acknowledges that the purchase price stated herein is fair and equitable and is in Seller's best interests, and that Seller's decision to sell was based on Seller, and that Seller has not relied on any representations of Buyer which are not contained expressly herein.

NOTICE REQUIRED BY CALIFORNIA LAW UNTIL YOUR RIGHT TO CANCEL THIS CONTRACT HAS ENDED NEW GROWTH FINANCIAL AND OR ASSIGNEES OR ANYONE WORKING FOR NEW GROWTH FINANCIAL CANNOT ASK YOU TO SIGN OR HAVE YOU SIGN ANY DEED OR ANY OTHER DOCUMENT.

YOU MAY CANCEL THIS CONTRACT FOR THE SALE OF YOUR HOUSE WITHOUT ANY PENALTY OR OBLIGATION AT ANY TIME BEFORE *4-20-88* **(DATE AND TIME OF DAY). SEE THE ATTACHED NOTICE OF CANCELLATION FORM FOR AN EXPLANATION OF THIS RIGHT**

Signed: *Alice Abels*   *4-14-88*
Seller   Date

Signed: *Albert Abels*   *4-14-88*
Seller   Date

BUYERS NAME, BUSINESS ADDRESS AND TELEPHONE NUMBER

New Growth Financial   Offices Located at:
P.O. Box 5000, Suite 412   177 Front Street, #207
Danville, CA 94526   Danville, CA 94526
(415) 837-2106

(Seller's time for cancellation ends at midnight on the fifth business day following the day the Seller signs this Agreement, or until 8:00 a.m. on the day scheduled for sale of the Property under power of sale conferred by deed of trust, whichever comes first.)

Copyright 1988 New Growth Financial

(Page 3 of 3)

Figure 4.1 *(continued)*

Order No.
Escrow No.
Loan No.

WHEN RECORDED MAIL TO
William Wiggs
4206 Valley Avenue
Martinez, California

RECORDED AT REQUEST OF

Grantor

87-191984

SEP 10 1987
OFFICIAL RECORDS
J. R. OLSSON
COUNTY RECORDER
FEE $7.00 PD

MAIL TAX STATEMENTS TO

——— SPACE ABOVE THIS LINE FOR RECORDER'S USE—
CITY TRANSFER TAX $ _8.25_
DOCUMENTARY TRANSFER TAX $ _____
SURVEY MONUMENT PRESERVATION FUND $ _____

AP # __380-120-014__

GRANT DEED

FOR A VALUABLE CONSIDERATION, receipt of which is hereby acknowledged,
 William Wiggs

hereby GRANT(S) to   **Alice Abels and Albert Abels**

the real property in the City of **Martinez** , County of **Contra Costa** , State of California,
described as

 More commonly known as 4206 Valley Avenue, Martinez, California.
 Description: **Attached**

Order No: 203862
Page: 3

LEGAL DESCRIPTION

Real property in the State of California, County of Contra Costa, unincorporated, described as
follows:

Portion of Lot 6, Map of Vine Hill Homesites, Unit No. 1, filed June 20, 1941, Map
Book 25, Page 838, Contra Costa County Records, described as follows:

Beginning on the west line of Valley Avenue, at the south line of the parcel of land
described in the deed to Egbert Allen Beverly, et al, recorded July 19, 1944, Book
696, Official Records, at Page 475, thence from said point of beginning, south 55
degrees 15' west, along the south line of said Beverly parcel, to the most southerly
corner thereof; thence south 34 degrees 38' east, 56 feet; thence north 55 degrees
15' east, to the west line of Valley Avenue; thence north 15 degrees west, along
said west line to the point of beginning.
A.P. No: 388-120-014

Figure 4.2 Wiggs Grant Deed for Transfer of Ownership

PROSPERITY SAVINGS
OF AMERICA

May 5, 1988

Mr. Albert Abels
Ms. Alice Abels
4206 Valley Avenue
Martinez, California 94553

Loan Number 00611552

Dear Mr. Abels and Ms. Abels:

Pursuant to your request, the following is a breakdown of the amount necessary to cure the default on the above-referenced loan:

5 payments @ $526.74 (09/10/87 to 01/10/88)	$2,633.70
1 payment @ $490.04 (02/10/88)	490.04
1 payment @ $2,517.95 (03/10/88)	2,517.95
1 payment @ $452.60 (04/10/88)	452.60
Late charges	487.31
Trustee fees	606.27
Insurance advance	18.06
TOTAL AMOUNT DUE	$7,225.93

The total amount due must be paid in certified funds (cash, cashier's check, or money order) and delivered to one of our branch offices on, or before, May 6, 1988. Please instruct the branch personnel to contact our office in order to effect an immediate rescission of the advertising.

If you have any further questions regarding this matter, please contact Leonard R. Perez of our Foreclosure/Bankruptcy Department at (818) 791-6187.

Sincerely,

Karen Cooper

Karen Cooper
Foreclosure/Bankruptcy Department

LP/pm/hk

cc: Mr. Ted Thomas
    Newgrowth Financial
    177 Front Street
    Danville, California 94526

Member Federal Savings and Loan Insurance Corporation • Federal Home Loan Bank

Figure 4.3   Statement of Loan from Prosperity Savings of America

Site Location

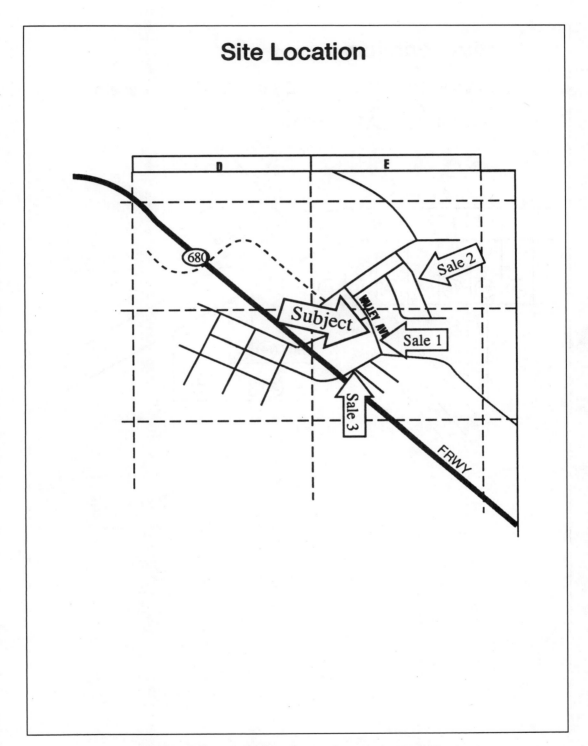

Figure 4.4   Site Location Maps (2) and Abels Grant Deed

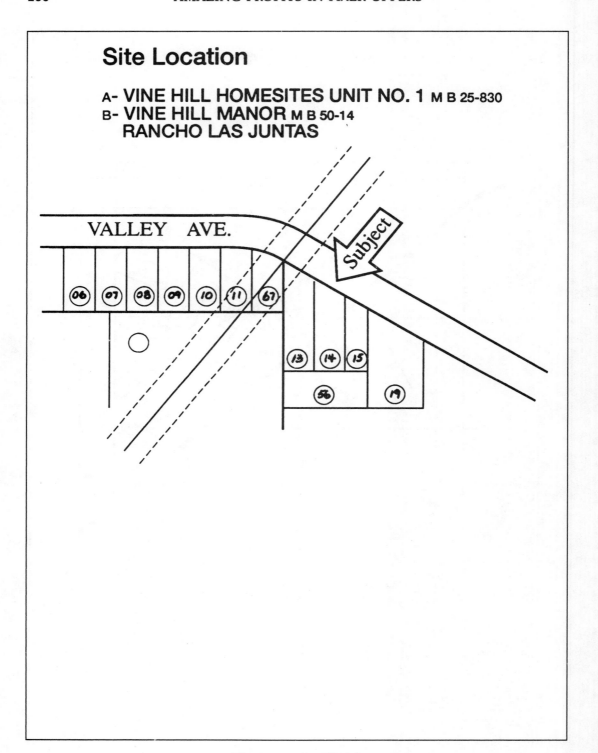

Figure 4.4 *(continued)*

Order No.
Escrow No.
Loan No.

WHEN RECORDED MAIL TO
William Wiggs
4206 Valley Avenue
Martinez, California

87-191984

RECORDED AT REQUEST OF

Grantor

SEP 10 1987
OFFICIAL RECORDS
J. R. OLSSON
COUNTY RECORDER
FEE $7.00 PD

MAIL TAX STATEMENTS TO

SPACE ABOVE THIS LINE FOR RECORDER'S USE—
CITY TRANSFER TAX $ 8.25
DOCUMENTARY TRANSFER TAX $
SURVEY MONUMENT PRESERVATION FUND $

AP # 380-120-014

GRANT DEED

FOR A VALUABLE CONSIDERATION, receipt of which is hereby acknowledged,
   William Wiggs

hereby GRANT(S) to   Alice Abels and Albert Abels

the real property in the City of Martinez , County of Contra Costa , State of California,
described as

   More commonly known as 4206 Valley Avenue, Martinez, California.
   Description: Attached

Order No: 203862
Page: 3

LEGAL DESCRIPTION

Real property in the State of California, County of Contra Costa, unincorporated, described as
follows:

Portion of Lot 6, Map of Vine Hill Homesites, Unit No. 1, filed June 20, 1941, Map
Book 25, Page 838, Contra Costa County Records, described as follows:

Beginning on the west line of Valley Avenue, at the south line of the parcel of land
described in the deed to Egbert Allen Beverly, et al, recorded July 19, 1944, Book
696, Official Records, at Page 475, thence from said point of beginning, south 55
degrees 15' west, along the south line of said Beverly parcel, to the most southerly
corner thereof; thence south 34 degrees 38' east, 56 feet; thence north 55 degrees
15' east, to the west line of Valley Avenue; thence north 15 degrees west, along
said west line to the point of beginning.
A.P. No: 388-120-014

Figure 4.4   *(continued)*

NEW GROWTH FINANCIAL

NOTICE OF CANCELLATION

4-14-88

(Enter Date Contract Signed)

You May Cancel This Contract For The Sale Of Your House Without Penalty Or Obligation At Any Time Before *4-20-88 MIDNIGHT*

(Enter Date and Time Of Day)

To Cancel This Transaction, Personally Deliver A Signed and Dated Copy Of This Cancellation Notice or Send a Telegram To:

New Growth Financial   177 Front St. #207 Danville, Ca 94526

(Name of Purchaser)   Street Address of Purchaser

Not Later Than *4-20-88*

(Enter Date and Time of Day)

I HEREBY CANCEL THIS TRANSACTION

(DATE)

SELLER SIGNATURE

SELLER SIGNATURE

I have received notice to cancel.

Seller *Alice Abels*   **Date** *4-14-88*

Seller *Albert Abels*   **Date** *4-14-88*

© 1988 New Growth Financial.

Figure 4.5   Notice of Cancellation for Abels

September 10, 1987. From a review of the delinquent dates and the actual recording of the NOD (Notice of Default) it appears that Prosperity Savings of America allows a Trustor (homeowner) to neglect the loan payment for some three months before recording a Notice of Default. Lenders differ in their policy toward delinquency; some allow only thirty days, although it is not unusual to see loans guaranteed by the Veterans Administration (the VA) unpaid for a year or more.

Tax Liens

The Preliminary Title Report also included other documents pertaining to the ownership of the property. We were particularly interested in information about taxes. We already knew that the second installment of the city and county taxes was still to be paid. But we know from experience that homeowners in default have numerous problems. Unpaid taxes, unpaid alimony payments, child support, and a myriad other encumbrances are normal. The title officer at Bigland Title continued to search the county records and found more liens. Five certificates of Delinquency of Personal Property Tax and a State of California Franchise Tax Board Lien were on file.

The personal property taxes were not encumbrances against this property because they show a different address. While they would encumber the other personal property, they also encumber the individual. The Franchise Tax Board line (Figure 4.6) dated March 22, 1987, showed the address of 4206 Valley Avenue, which is the property that was being purchased. This particular lien is an encumbrance against the property as well as against the individual.

When you purchase from a seller prior to the Trustee's Sale, you purchase what the seller owes and what he owns. In this instance, the personal property taxes were a lien against the seller and the property. If the property has been sold at a Trustee's Sale, the liens for personal property would have been cleared from the property, so that the new owner would not be burdened, but they would still be part of the seller's personal debts.

It is important that you, as a buyer, research and understand the lien situation on any property you are buying. It is possible for the seller to have an encumbrance or lien against himself or herself personally that does not encumber the real estate. As always, the three-letter word is *ask*—ask the title officer, ask your attorney, ask your CPA, or you could make the big mistake of buying property with more liens than value.

SETTLEMENT

Settlement day with the seller is something the foreclosure buyer should consider carefully. At the time the Home Equity Purchase Agreement is signed, the costs of buying the property are largely unknown. The seller is likely to have a fixed notion of the sum to be paid for his equity and will tend to discount the subsequent costs. If the seller is prepared and kept informed of your findings, he will be prepared for the results.

For example, the Equity Purchase Agreement for the property requires that the buyer pay the seller $14,550. From this amount the contract states, on page

RECORDING REQUESTED BY

STATE OF CALIFORNIA
FRANCHISE TAX BOARD

87 67114

AND WHEN RECORDED MAIL TO:
FRANCHISE TAX BOARD
P O BOX 2952
SACRAMENTO CA 95812

RECORDED AT REQUEST OF
STATE OF CALIFORNIA

MARCH 27, 1987

AT 05:00 O'CLOCK PM
CONTRA COSTA COUNTY RECORDS
J. R. OLSSON
COUNTY RECORDER
FEE OFFICIAL
MAR 27 1987

———— SPACE ABOVE THIS LINE FOR RECORDER'S USE————

NOTICE OF STATE TAX LIEN

FILED WITH: CERTIFICATE NUMBER:

   COUNTY OF CONTRA COSTA   87083-003488

The Franchise Tax Board of the State of California hereby certifies that the following named taxpayer(s) is liable under Parts 10 or 11 of Division 2 of the Revenue and Taxation Code to the State Of California for amounts due and required to be paid by said taxpayer as follows:

Name of Taxpayer: Albert Abels

FTB Account Number: 556082746MIRE

Social Security Number: 556-08-2746(H)

Last Known Address: 4206 VALLEY RD   MARTINEZ   CA 94253

For Taxable Years: 1984

TAX	PENALTY	INTEREST	COLLECTION COSTS	PAYMENTS	TOTAL
1,760.00	594.00	167.01	9.00	1,802.96CR	727.09

Figure 4.6   Notice of State Tax Lien for Abels

two, Item 7, that the seller agrees to pay for any damages found by termite and roof inspections. The sellers will read and understand that paragraph but, unless they view the inspections or talk to the inspectors it will be difficult for them to accept the inspectors' reports. By suggesting that the sellers be on hand and available to review the inspectors' findings and observations, you will be more credible. If the seller knows the facts before you present the final settlement statement, his expectations will already have been adjusted. His knowledge that you are not taking advantage of him is especially important if you are to have a smooth transaction and his or her timely departure from the property.

Ready Termite Company Incorporated inspected the property (the report is reproduced as Figure 4.7) and was accompanied by the seller. The report was not a surprise because the sellers had received a similar report when they purchased the property. Most people have the termite damage repaired when they purchase property. However, this was not the case for this property.

If you purchase a home with known defects such as termite damage or roof leaks, you are considered an informed buyer in consenting to the purchase. Most buyers would require the seller to credit them with the amount of the repairs at the escrow or they would require the repairs be completed. Foreclosure buyers want the credit at the conclusion of the contract and then they will search for contractors or a handyman to perform the repairs at lower prices and by doing so improve their profit margins.

The seller was also available to discuss the roof repairs with Advanced Roofing Service (whose report is reproduced as Figure 4.8). Again the seller was not surprised as he had had experience in the roof repair trade. Together, these reports noted damage that would cost over $11,000 to repair. The final statement to the seller (Figure 4.9) shows that, when the termite, roofing repairs, back payments, and delinquent taxes are all paid, the seller actually owed us money.

You will notice charges for cleanup. Unfortunately, this seller just walked away and abandoned the house. It was full of trash and the front lawn looked like the city dump. In a situation such as this, it is recommended that you offer to pay the seller something to help him get started in a new location. For the sake of your business and your professional reputation, the money spent on cleanup would probably have been better spent on a couple of months' rent for the seller—payable, of course, when the property you are purchasing is left clean and vacant.

HOW DID WE SELL IT?

In selling the house, we kept three things in mind:

1. We had to know our buyers.
2. We had to make our advertising count.
3. We had to price the house to sell.

Knowing the Buyer

Ask yourself: Who does this house appeal to? Why would they buy this home? Where would they look for a bargain? Is this a bargain? If so, can we prove it?

Ready TERMITE CO.

2600 PACHECO BLVD.
MARTINEZ, CA 94653
(415) 223-3077

WORK AUTHORIZATION

Report No: ___15517___   Date: ___05-02-88___

You are hereby authorized to proceed with the work as specified in the report which is
dated: __04-27-88__ on the property at: __4206 VALLEY AVE., MARTINEZ__

If all work is not to be performed, please circle items to be completed.

        1A...$ 125.00
        1B...   150.00
        1C...   125.00
        2A...   1900.00
        2B...   1350.00
        2C...   1235.00
        2D...   125.00
        2F...   1475.00
        7A...   1475.00
        9A...   315.00
        _____   150.00...PERMIT & COORDINATION
                 $8425.00

Inspection Fee: _$150.00_____   Total Cost of Work:___$8,425.00_____.

It is agreed that funds to pay the costs of this agreement are to be released to
READY TERMITE CO., INC. upon filing a Notice of Completion with:
        ___owner___

READY TERMITE COMPANY, INC.

2600 Pacheco Blvd.
MARTINEZ, CA 94553
Phone 228-3077

STATEMENT

DATE 5-2-88

NUMBER 15517

TERMS: Due and payable within 10 days. A finance charge of 1-1/2% per month will
       be added to any past due balance

PLEASE DETACH AND RETURN WITH YOUR REMITTANCE

                                                        $_____

04-27-88	Inspection fee	$150.00

Figure 4.7   Ready Termite Work Statement

PROPOSAL

ADVANCED ROOFING SERVICE
1115 PLAZA DRIVE
MARTINEZ, CA 94553
CSL: 515344

No.

Date 4-27-88

Sheet No.

Proposal Submitted To:

Name	New Grouth Enterprises
Street	PO Box 5000-412
City	Danville
State	Ca.
Phone	837-2106

Work To Be Performed At:

Street 4206 Valley Av.
City Martinez,   State Ca.
Date of Plans   None
Architect

We hereby propose to furnish the materials and perform the labor necessary for the completion of

(1) Remove roofing at front porch only, Inspect for dryrot and repair. NOTE! repare not to exceed $750.00

(2) Install new Bri SP-4 membrane at front porch.

(3) Install new 20 year comp shingles over 15 lb. under layment (Color to be picked by owner) $1850.00

(4) leave jobsite clean and free of all roofing debra.

All material is guaranteed to be as specified, and the above work to be performed in accordance with the drawings and specifications submitted for above work and completed in a substantial workmanlike manner for the sum of
Dollars ($ 2600.00).

with payments to be made as follows: Payment in full on completion

Any alteration or deviation from above specifications involving extra costs, will be executed only upon written orders, and will become an extra charge over and above the estimate. All agreements contingent upon strikes, accidents or delays beyond our control. Owner to carry fire, tornado and other necessary insurance upon above work. Workmen's Compensation and Public Liability Insurance on above work to be taken out by
Roofing Contractor

Respectfully submitted

Per

Note—This proposal may be withdrawn by us if not accepted within 30 days.

ACCEPTANCE OF PROPOSAL

The above prices, specifications and conditions are satisfactory and are hereby accepted. You are authorized to do the work as specified. Payment will be made as outlined above.

Date

Signature

Figure 4.8 Roof Report

NEW GROWTH ENTERPRISES

TO: Albert Abels and Alice Abels

FROM: NEW GROWTH FINANCIAL   DATED: May 20, 1988

The following represents the breakdown of expenses which were
deducted from the net due seller per the Equity Purchase
Agreement dated April 14, 1988.

NEW DUE SELLER $14,550.00

LESS EXPENSES:

    Ready Termite Repairs   8,425.00
    Advanced Roofing Repairs   2,600.00
    Back Payments to Home Savings   2,225.93
    Clean-up   460.00
    Property Taxes   583.75
    Personal Property Tax Lien   148.93
    Tax Lien   802.44

        Total Expenses $15,246.05

NET DUE SELLER $ (696.05)

P.O. Box 5000   Suite 412   Danville, CA 94526   (415) 837-2106

Figure 4.9   Abels Final Statement from New Growth for Expenses

Advertising to Effect

Determine which newspaper the bargain hunter will read and advertise there—in local newspapers and penny savers. Write an ad that appeals to the buyer looking for a fixer-upper (see Figure 4.10).

Young couples and bargain hunters are the most logical prospects for fixer-upper houses. The young couples understand that profits can be and will be made by using so-called sweat equity. For those few who are willing to work and willing to clean up and fix up the problems of others, the properties that are in disrepair provide the place to start. Almost everyone has a relative, friend, or acquaintance who purchased a house, fixed it up, and sold it for a large profit. If you are a seller, the question is who will purchase your property? It will rarely be a wealthy investor and almost always will be a person who can work with his hands and has saved enough money for that first down payment. This same skillful person is willing to accept less than perfect just to get started in the world of real estate and homeownership. Another prospective buyer might be a handy person who understands home repair and how to do it economically.

Make up a flier to be delivered in the vicinity each Friday or Saturday before your Open House (see Figures 4.11 and 4.12). Fliers work. These fliers and the newspaper ads brought more than 35 people to the first Open House. Expect to distribute fliers on three or four Fridays and Saturdays. After all, most people have already planned the weekend by the time your first flier arrives. Repetition will pay off. Neighbors and their friends and relatives will buy your house, fixed up or not. So distribute numerous fliers. If, at each of your Open House functions, you take names and addresses of interested buyers looking for fixer-uppers, you will soon have a list of hundreds of interested buyers to whom you can send announcements of your next foreclosure bargain. If you are selling your own properties, you will save money on brokerage commissions. Put the property on the Multiple Listing Service if you are a broker or plan to hire a broker. The brokers don't expect you to pay full commission if you are paying for advertising and doing most of the work, but they have clients who they work hard to get. Don't chase them away by saying: no commission. Offer them one-third but settle on one-half of what is a normal or customary commission for your particular section of the country. If you do bargain, do not alienate the brokerage community. The brokers and agents will help you, of course; but they also want to get paid. Don't you?

Pricing the Property

Price the property to sell; forget top dollar. We hired a conservative appraiser. Her appraisal (Figure 4.13), as always, was conservative, between 8 and 10 percent below selling prices in the neighborhood. The Property Profile you receive from the title company will show selling prices in the neighborhood. From these, you can evaluate your appraisal. Our appraisal was conservative at $83,000 so we priced the house at $79,000. According to the Preliminary Title Report, comparable prices (one of our sources of information, included in the Property Profile, is reproduced as Figure 4.14) for Valley Avenue ranged from $68,000 to $89,000.

Sunday, May 15, 1988

724 Martinez

FORECLOSURE
OPEN SUNDAY 1–4
You'd have to steal this house to
get it for less. 4206 VALLEY AVE.
New Growth Financial
837-2106

Sunday, May 15, 1988

552-Martinez

FORECLOSURE
OPEN SUN 1–4 PM
You'd have to steal this
house to get it for less.
4206 Valley Ave. Drive by
then call 837-2106

Figure 4.10   Newspaper Ads for Examples of Foreclosed Properties

YOU WOULD HAVE TO

STEAL

THIS PROPERTY TO GET IT

CHEAPER

Drive by: 4206 Valley Avenue
Martinez, California
(East of 680)

Then call: 837-2106

Bargain Fixer-Upper

FORECLOSURE

New Growth Financial

Figure 4.11   News Flier for Direct Advertising for Foreclosure

SUPER BARGAIN FORECLOSURE

for SALE

4206 VALLEY DRIVE
MARTINEZ

OPEN HOUSE

Sunday, May 15th
1:00 p.m. – 4:00 p.m.
New Growth Financial: 837-2106

Figure 4.12   Another Flier for Foreclosure (Hand-Done)

Property Description & Analysis **UNIFORM RESIDENTIAL APPRAISAL REPORT** File No.

SUBJECT

Property Address	4206 Valley Avenue
City Martinez	County Contra Costa	State Ca.	Zip Code 94553
Legal Description	Please see preliminary title report; APN: 380-120-014-2
Owner/Occupant	owner	Map Reference 10-E2
Sale Price $ n/a	Date of Sale (5/88)
Loan charges/concessions to be paid by seller $ n/a
R.E. Taxes $ n/a	Tax Year 87/88	HOA $/Mo n/a
Lender/Client New Growth Enterprises
Danville, Ca.

Census Tract 3200.01

PROPERTY RIGHTS APPRAISED
- [x] Fee Simple
- [ ] Leasehold
- [ ] Condominium (HUD/VA)
- [ ] De Minimis PUD

LENDER DISCRETIONARY USE
Sale Price $
Date
Mortgage Amount $
Mortgage Type
Discount Points and Other Concessions
Paid by Seller $
Source

LOCATION [ ] Urban [x] Suburban [ ] Rural
BUILT UP [x] Over 75% [ ] 25-75% [ ] Under 25%
GROWTH RATE [ ] Rapid [ ] Stable

NEIGHBORHOOD ANALYSIS Good Avg. Fair Poor
Employment Stability [ ] [x] [ ] [ ]

SALES COMPARISON ANALYSIS

ITEM	SUBJECT	COMPARABLE NO. 1		COMPARABLE NO. 2		COMPARABLE NO. 3	
Address	4206 Valley Avenue	4276 Valley Avenue		4291 Irene Drive		4390 Cabrillo Drive	
Proximity to Subject		1 block		2 blocks		5 blocks	
Sales Price	$ n/a	$ 89,000		$ 82,000		$ 76,750	
Price/Gross Liv. Area	$ 66.08 ☑	$ 71.20 ☑		$ 63.08 ☑		$ 61.40 ☑	
Data Source	inspection	REDI/MLS 239566		REDI/MLS 260927		REDI/MLS 236847	
VALUE ADJUSTMENTS	DESCRIPTION	DESCRIPTION	+ (-) $ Adjustment	DESCRIPTION	+ (-) $ Adjustment	DESCRIPTION	+ (-) $ Adjustment
Sales or Financing Concessions		FHA		FHA		owner carry/ +assumption	
Date of Sale/Time	(5/88)	2/5/88		3/31/88		12/10/87	
Location	average	equal		equal		bks freeway	+4,000
Site/View	6,200/none	6000 /equal		6500 /equal		6200 /equal	
Design and Appeal	rambler	equal		equal		equal	
Quality of Construction	average	equal		equal		equal	
Age	35 years	33 years		33 years		36 years	
Condition	above ave.	good	-3,000	equal		good	-3,000
Above Grade Room Count	Total 6 : Bdrms 3 : Baths 1.5	Total 6 : Bdrms 3 : Baths 2	-1,000	Total 6 : Bdrms 3 : Baths 1	+1,000	Total 7 : Bdrms 3 : Baths 1	+1,000
Gross Living Area	1,256 Sq. Ft.	1,250 Sq. Ft.		1,300 Sq. Ft.	-1,000	1,250 Sq. Ft.	
Basement & Finished Rooms Below Grade	none	none		none		none	
Functional Utility	good	equal		equal		equal	
Heating/Cooling	wall/wall	equal		equal		equal	
Garage/Carport	1 garage	2 garage	-2,000	.5 garage	+1,000	0 garage	+2,000
Porches, Patio, Pools, etc.	patio porch	patio, fence porch		porch		porch	
Special Energy Efficient Items	insulation	equal		equal		equal	
Fireplace	0 fireplace	0 fireplace		wood stove	-1,000	0 fireplace	
Other (e.g. kitchen equip., remodeling)	built-in AEK	equal		equal		none	+3,000
Net Adj. (total)		[x] + [ ] - $	-6,000	[ ] + [x] - $	0	[x] + [ ] - $	7,000
Indicated Value of Subject		$	83,000	$	82,000	$	83,750

Comments on Sales Comparison: Comparable #1 best supports the indicated market value in size, quality, date of sale and location. Sale # 2 is most similar in condition and sale #3 is adjacent to the freeway on ramp for 680 freeway.

RECONCILIATION

INDICATED VALUE BY SALES COMPARISON APPROACH .... $ 83,000

INDICATED VALUE BY INCOME APPROACH (If Applicable) Estimated Market Rent $ n/a /Mo. x Gross Rent Multiplier n/a = $ n/a 0

This appraisal is made [x] "as is" [ ] subject to the repairs, alterations, inspections or conditions listed below [ ] completion per plans and specifications.

Comments and Conditions of Appraisal: These are the most comparable sales available in this area in this time frame. All sales have been confirmed closed.

Final Reconciliation: Market approach is considered the best indicator of present market value and the market indicates a value of $83,000. I am currently certified under the AIREA continuing education program. This appraisal was done in compliance with regulation R41C.

This appraisal is based upon the above requirements, the certification, contingent and limiting conditions, and Market Value definition that are stated in

[ ] FmHA, HUD &/or VA instructions.

[x] Freddie Mac Form 439 (Rev. 7/86)/Fannie Mae Form 1004B (Rev. 7/86) filed with client _____ 19___ [x] attached.

I (WE) ESTIMATE THE MARKET VALUE, AS DEFINED, OF THE SUBJECT PROPERTY AS OF April 26 19 88 to be $ 83,000

I (We) certify: that to the best of my (our) knowledge and belief the facts and data used herein are true and correct; that I (we) personally inspected the subject property, both inside and out, and have made an exterior inspection of all comparable sales cited in this report; and that I (we) have no undisclosed interest, present or prospective therein.

Appraiser(s) SIGNATURE _Jane B. Herwood RM_ NAME Jane B. Herwood RM

SIGNATURE (if applicable) NAME

[ ] Did [ ] Did Not Inspect Property

Figure 4.13   Residential Appraisal Report/Floor Plan

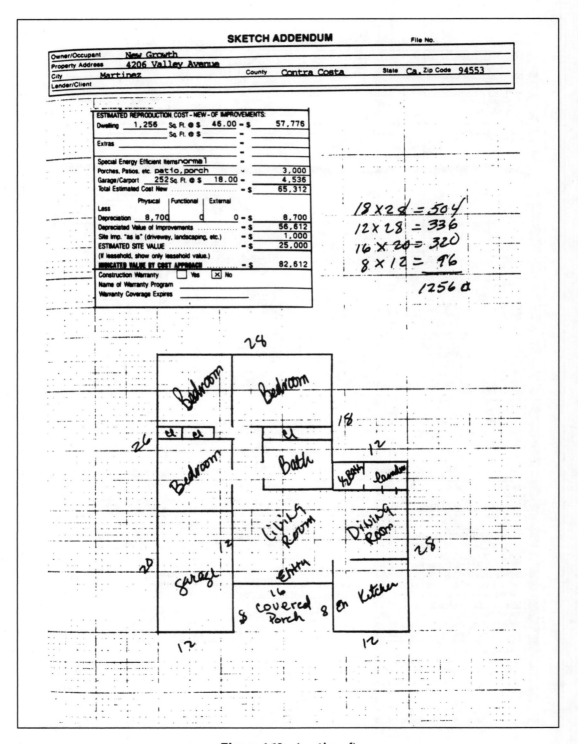

Figure 4.13 *(continued)*

TRW

— REAL ESTATE INFORMATION SERVICES —

CONTRA COSTA   1988-04   GRID--N 11   1-800-527-9663

* SALES - PARCEL SEQUENCE

ASSESSORS PARCEL NO. TRA / LEGAL DESCRIPTION	OWNER / MAILING ADDRESS / LOCATION ADDRESS	SELLER	LOT SZ / IMP SZ UNITS	ROOMS / BDRMS / BATHS	CN/YR POOL	TRNSFR / USE ZONE	DATE/NUMBER / LENDER / TTL CO	TFR AMT / LOAN AMT / ASSD VAL	IMPZ
380 113 014 0 76049 I VINE HILL MANOR LOT 126	PAMLAK, KRIS & KRISTINE 4165 VALLEY AVE., MARTINEZ CA 4165 VALLEY AVE MARTINEZ	ALLEN, CLAY	5,500 1080	6 4		10/02/87 11 R-6	14949 MARTIN P.STU N.AM	11,000 11,000 81,180	F D 51%
380 120 019 0 76049 I VINE HILL HOMESITES POR LOT 7	AZEVEDO, MANUEL 4216 VLY. AVE., MARTINEZ CA 4216 VALLEY AVE MARTINEZ	AZEVEDO, CAT 94553	14,168 1339	7 3	1.00	7/13/87 11 R-6	48904 1ST METROPOL FNDRS	30,000 30,000 68,088	F D 47%
380 120 037 3 76049 I POR RO LAS JUNTAS	CHRISTY, WAYNE & JUNE 4225 ARTHUR RD., MARTINEZ CA 4225 ARTHUR RD MARTINEZ	LLAMAS, MARI 94553	10,019 f180	5 2	2.00	6/25/87 11 R-6	35597 GUILD MTG WSTRN	106,000 100,700 28,137	F D 69%
380 120 038 0 76049 I POR RO LAS JUNTAS	NIVISON, RAY & TERESA 102 BRAMBLEWOOD LN, CONCORD CA 4219 ARTHUR RD MARTINEZ	RETTA, CHARL 94523	10,019 840	5 2		11/19/87 11 R-6	45163 HOME SAVINGS FNDRS	82,000 10,000 58,571	F O 51%
380 120 058 0 76049 I PARCEL MAP 22 PG 32 PCL B	MORECI +, DAVID 4276 VALLEY AVE, MARTINEZ CA 4276 VALLEY AVE MARTINEZ	MORGENSEN, E 94553	5,000 f038	6 3	2.00	2/05/88 11 R-6	20624 MEYER. MTG 1STAM	89,000 90,254 7,400	F F 54%
380 120 059 0 76049 I PARCEL MAP 22 PG 32 PCL C	ORR, CHERYL 565 CENTRAL AVE, MARTINEZ CA 565 CENTRAL AVE MARTINEZ	THOMAS, GARY 94553	5,000 f057	6 3	2.00	11/25/87 11 R-6	48918 MEYER. MTG FNDRS	7,500 77,850 2,936	F F 82%
380 131 006 0 76049 I *NEW* TRACT 2083 LOT 104	OLES, ALEXANDER AND MARRIET BOX 23467, PLEASANT HILL CA 4121 CABRILHO DR MARTINEZ	NINETE, ENRI 94523	5,220 935	5 3	1.00	2/19/88 11 R-6	28851 GREAT W. SV FNDRS	70,000 45,450 26,349	F D 63%
380 131 012 0 76049 I TRACT 2083 LOT 110	BOWLES, FREDERICK 401 GEORGIA ST., #145, VALLEJO CA 4155 CABRILHO DR MARTINEZ	HAM, DIANE 94590	5,670 935	5 3	1.00	12/01/87 11 R-6	51288 HAM, DIANE PLACR	11,500 8,445 46,628	F O 29%
380 131 012 0 76049 I TRACT 2083 LOT 110	HAM, DIANE 1828 ALMOND AVE., WALNUT CREEK CA 4155 CABRILHO DR MARTINEZ	RODERICK, CY 94596	5,670 935	5 3	1.00	12/02/87 11	52170 PLACR	7,000	F
380 131 017 0 76049 I VINE HILL GARDENS 1 LOT 27	WAGNER, ALLEN & LIA 4190 ARTHUR RD., MARTINEZ CA 4190 ARTHUR RD MARTINEZ	WAGNER, ALLE 94553	7,725 955	5 3		5/21/87 11 R-5	8609 N.AM MTG 1STAM	46,628 58,000 62,423	F F 61%
380 131 017 0 76049 I VINE HILL GARDENS 1 LOT 27	WAGNER, ALLEN 4275 ARTHUR RD, MARTINEZ CA 4190 ARTHUR RD MARTINEZ	WAGNER, LIA 94553	7,725 955	5 3	1.00	1/26/88 11	14070 AVOM REFINER	10,225 10,225 62,423	D F 61%
380 131 020 0 76049 I VINE HILL GARDENS 1 LOT 30	LOPEZ, JOSE 4160 ARTHUR RD., MARTINEZ CA 4160 ARTHUR RD MARTINEZ	HUD 94553	8,400 955	5 3	1.00	1/13/88 11 R-6	6694 MEDAL MTG N.AM	81,000 81,534 65,545	F F 44%
380 141 008 0 76049 I VINE HILL GARDENS 1 LOT 19	SPARMAN, WALTER AND LUCIENNE 4242 ARTHUR RD, MARTINEZ CA 4242 ARTHUR RD MARTINEZ	SPARMAN, WAL 94553	5,400 955	5 3	1.00	6/23/87 11 R-6	33179 BNFCL CALIF 1STAM	56,250 56,250 63,670	D F 45%
380 141 012 0 76049 I *NEW* VINE HILL GARDENS 1 LOT 15	MALL, TERRY AND RAMONA 4236 ARTHUR RD, MARTINEZ CA 4286 ARTHUR RD MARTINEZ	LACY, PHILLI 94553	5,400 955	5 3	1.00	2/19/88 11 R-6	28537 MEYER. MTG N.AM	75,500 76,793 35,480	F F 67%
380 141 020 0 76049 H VINE HILL GARDENS 2 LOT 42	HENNESSEE JULIA MA OUT OF COUNTY 4241 CABRILHO DR MARTINEZ	CARDENAS TIM	5,400 955	5 3	1.00	3/11/87 11	13499-363	13,000	P
380 141 021 0 76049 I *NEW* VINE HILL GARDENS 2 LOT 41	DE BONNEVILLE, DAVID & DUANNA 2301 W. SHELL. AVE, MARTINEZ CA 4235 CABRILHO DR MARTINEZ	DERKSEN, RON 94553	5,400 f207	6 3	1.00	3/03/88 11 R-6	36444 FNDRS	53,360 3,500	F F 57%
380 151 007 0 76049 I VINE HILL GARDENS 2 LOT 45	OLSON, ROY AND PAMELA 207 ELAINE DR, CONCORD CA 4370 CABRILHO DR MARTINEZ	BENTLEY, WAR 94523	5,400 955	5 3	1.00	8/06/87 11 R-6	67620 MEDAL MTG FN TY	64,770 78,500 69,785	F F 46%

Figure 4.14 TRW Breakdown of Property Profile in a Given Area (Martinez, CA)

The first offers came in at less than the asking price; however, after a few days of negotiation, we agreed to a selling price of $78,000 with a $3,000 brokerage commission. Not bad for a house we had owned for only four weeks.

Summarizing

The costs to purchase included curing the default on the first loan with Prosperity Savings, one month's mortgage payment, and fees for the appraisals and home inspections:

COST TO BUY

Prosperity Savings (to cure loan and penalties)	$7,225.93
Termite report	150.00
Roof report	100.00
Cleaning costs	460.00
Home inspection report	250.00
Appraisal fee	250.00
One monthly payment	452.00
TOTAL	8,887.93
Balance, on re-sale	19,542.31
PROFIT IN 42 DAYS	**$10,654.38**

= 5 =

Dealing in Foreclosures

The System Explained

In this chapter we give you a step-by-step guide to finding suitable property by following a system. We illustrate the procedures with a case history of a highly profitable purchase and re-sale of a house in Alameda, California. You will learn:

- How we found the property
- What we did step by step
- How the owner responded
- How we established the property's value
- What we found when we checked the Title Report
- What was revealed by the termite inspector's report
- What the roofing contractor revealed
- How we made a windfall profit when paying off the loan
- How we sold the property with minimum expense in a short period of time
- What the owners forgot to tell us
- How we treat our customers, so that they will give us those all-important testimonial letters.

LOCATING THE PROFIT MAKERS

Choosing the right neighborhood is not only a question of value and price but also of resale. Will the property be resold quickly? Is it too run down to rehabilitate economically? Is the neighborhood deteriorating or are property values rising? Will the home appeal to all buyers or only a select few? Is your objective to turn over the property quickly (make a quick sale) or do you plan to rehabilitate and then rent it and wait for appreciation? Is your philosophy that of a long-term holder or a short-term profit maker? By knowing your objective, you will select accordingly.

Select neighborhoods that produce profits. Most communities have affluent areas. If you plan to work the foreclosure market in these areas, you will succeed. However, proportionately fewer foreclosures are available in the country club or more wealthy sections of town. You will have a wider choice in the less moneyed areas.

Many communities have sections in which only minorities reside and, while they may not be as exclusive as the country club area, they are clean, the homes are well-kept, and the neighborhood desirable. Foreclosures purchased in these areas are very easy to sell because first-time home buyers start in these types of neighborhoods.

Middle-class neighborhoods between the two extremes provide most of the foreclosures. These foreclosures are caused by a number of different factors or problems. Divorce, sickness, death, changes in the economic conditions in the area all cause homeowners to miss payments and ultimately end up in foreclosure.

FIND DEFAULTING PROPERTY OWNERS BY SEARCHING RECORDS AND LISTINGS

Places to search include:

- County records
- Legal newspapers
- Subscription default services which check the county records daily or weekly
- Notices of Default (NOD), which are posted at the county court house or other public buildings.

CONTACT HOMEOWNERS

Methods could include: personal visits (knock on the door), telephone calls, door hangers, fliers, direct mail via postcards and letters that appeal to the owner by offering to help avert foreclosure.

OBTAIN FINANCIAL PROPERTY INFORMATION

Complete a *Property Evaluation Questionnaire* (Figure 5.1). If you follow the form as a checklist, ask all the questions and then think the situation through, you'll save yourself hundreds of hours of time spent driving and looking around. Each of the questions is important, so I suggest you get all the answers to your questions on the telephone *before* you visit the property.

Let's work our way through the form and figure out why we are asking each of the questions.

New Growth Financial

DATE: _____

ThBr _____

PROPERTY EVALUATION QUESTIONNAIRE

1. NAME OF OWNER: _____

2. PROPERTY ADDRESS: _____

   CITY _____ COUNTY _____

3. MAJOR CROSS STREET: _____

4. PHONE # (DAY) _____ (EVENING) _____

   BEST TIME TO CALL: _____

5. WHAT KIND OF PROPERTY IS IT? _____ AGE _____ SQ.FT. _____

6. #BEDROOMS _____ #BATHS _____ OTHER _____

   POOL (YES/NO)   GARAGE (1 2 3)

7. GENERAL CONDITION OF THE PROPERTY (DRAPES - CARPETS - PAINT)

   _____

   _____

8. HOW OLD IS THE ROOF _____

9. HAVE YOU HAD A RECENT TERMITE INSPECTION? YES/NO YEAR_____

10. HOW LONG HAVE YOU OWNED THE PROPERTY? _____

11. WHAT DID YOU PAY FOR THE PROPERTY? _____

12. HOW MUCH DO YOU OWE ON IT? _____

    1ST _____ 2ND _____ 3RD _____ OTHER _____

13. ARE THESE LOANS ASSUMABLE? (1ST) Y N (2ND) Y N (3RD) Y N

14. HOW MANY PAYMENTS ARE YOU BEHIND ____ TOTAL MOS. PMT: _____

15. AMOUNT TO CURE: _____

16. ARE YOU IN DEFAULT OR FORECLOSURE?   Y   N

17. DO YOU HAVE A TRUSTEE SALE DATE? _____

Figure 5.1   Property Evaluation Questionnaire

New Growth Financial

18.   HOW MUCH IS THE PROPERTY WORTH?_____

19.   HOW DO YOU KNOW THIS?_____

20.   IS THAT WHAT HOMES IN THE NEIGHBORHOOD ARE SELLING FOR? Y N

21.   DO YOU HAVE A RECENT APPRAISAL?   Y   N

22.   HAVE YOU HAD THE PROPERTY FOR SALE?   Y   N   HOW LONG?_____

      IF YES, DO YOU KNOW WHY IT HASN'T SOLD?_____

23.   HOW MUCH WILL YOU TAKE FOR THE PROPERTY?_____

APPOINTMENT: DATE_____TIME_____

NOTES/COMMENTS:_____

_____

_____

_____

_____

_____

_____

_____

_____

_____

_____

_____

_____

_____

_____

_____

Figure 5.1   *(continued)*

Where Is the Property Located?

Have you restricted your purchases to certain towns or locations? Do you know the street or neighborhood? Is it desirable? If so, why is it desirable?

What Kind of Property Is It?

Is it single family, duplex, apartment, farm, trailer park? Each is an opportunity for the knowledgeable buyer.

Description: Age, Size, and Improvements?

You will need these details in order to compare the property with others in the neighborhood to decide if you can make a profit on the deal. Too old, the house might not meet the current building codes; too young, the owner might not have enough equity to make it worth your while.

What Condition Is the Property In?

This is really subjective. Everyone has a different opinion of condition. It's probably wise to ask how old the carpets are and when the drapes were installed. In that way, you can compare your experience of their probable condition with what you are being told.

How Old Is the Roof?

Shake roofs will deteriorate rapidly after 10 years, so you should take that into account on your appraisal. You must pay professionals to look at the roof and evaluate it. Don't guess; this is a fatal mistake and it will prove costly. Sellers will generally assure you that the roof is in excellent condition. When you see spots on the ceilings, you'll be convinced otherwise.

Have You Had a Recent Termite Inspection?

Most termite reports are valid for only 90 days. Unless the homeowner has tried to sell the house, he probably does not have a recent report. Professional termite reports are as important as roof reports. Remember, *ask.* You'll save yourself a considerable amount of money if you ask a professional how to handle the termite work.

How Long Have You Had the Property? What Did You Pay for It?

The answers to these questions will tell you how much equity the owner is likely to have and also some idea of whether or not values in the neighborhood are appreciating.

How Much Do You Owe on It?

Many homeowners do not know what they owe. Before leaving your home or office, you must determine what they owe. Ask that the caller read the default notice to you. You need to know what is owed and what the selling prices are in the neighborhood so that you can decide if it is profitable to visit the property and make a deal with the owner.

Is the loan that is foreclosing a first, second, or third loan? This is an important question. You will find that owners will, from time to time, forget about one loan or another. When you buy from the owner, you buy what he owes and that includes *all* his loans on that property. The biggest mistake new buyers of distressed property make is to buy from the owner and then discover the existence of an additional Trust Deed that is senior to the one they bought. You must find out about *all* the loans and distinguish the senior loans from the junior loans. (See Chapter 3 for procedures to research thee loans.)

Are the Loans Assumable?

This consideration could be a deal breaker. If the loan is not assumable and the lender is hostile to your taking the loan, you may find that after you cure the default the lender takes foreclosure action against you. The suggested method is for you to take the loan "subject to," which simply means that you will pay the deficit and make the loan healthy and thereafter make the future payments as they come due. This is not a formal assumption and you are not taking on the responsibility or the liability for the payment of the loan.

How Much Will It Take to Cure the Default?

The lenders will welcome your payment to cure the loan. However, they have the rights, specified in the contract (Trust Deed), to accelerate the loan if the title is "alienated," that is, transferred. It is rare for the lenders to accelerate the loan, but they have these contractual rights and they have federal law to back them up. You will quickly find that most lenders will just accept payments. The few who even trouble to communicate with you will simply request that you assume the existing loan and pay them a fee for doing so. If they don't suggest an assumption, you should offer a small fee to do so. By small fee, I mean $1/2$ to 1 percent of the principal amount of the loan. Expect some brief negotiation as 1 percent is normal.

Are You Behind in Any Payments?

Of course they are or they wouldn't be calling you. But this is not a silly question. The *number* of payments in arrears is critical. If the owner has a Veterans Administration (VA) or Federal Housing Administration (FHA) loan, all of the equity could easily have been used up or have disappeared by the time you ask the question. Homes bought with FHA and VA loans are difficult to deal with because the VA and FHA react slowly when it comes to foreclosure. In many cases, the agencies do not start foreclosure proceedings until a year or more has transpired since the first default notice. If the homeowner has only a small equity, the interest on the loan together with late charges and foreclosure fees will have used it all up. In other words, the loan and the penalties and fees will exceed the retail value of the house.

Are You Only in Default or Is the Date of the Trustee's Sale Set?

Remember that the seller has three months to cure a default. Therefore, he or she might just be shopping around for a good deal. The motivated sellers are the homeowners who have been issued a Notice of Default (NOD). Under California law, the NOD, you will recall, is the first notice that the Trustor (homeowner) receives and it signals the start of the three-month reinstatement period during which, if the loan is made current, the foreclosure is cancelled. At the end of the three months, the lender will publish in a newspaper of general circulation a Notice of Trustee's Sale. This is what makes the homeowners motivated. If he doesn't sell his property before then, he will lose it all on the twenty-second day.

When Is Your Property Going Up for Sale?

Don't be surprised if the property is scheduled to be sold at the Trustee's Sale tomorrow morning. It's not unusual for some people to wait until the last minute. (See Chapter 6 for details on a 24-hour postponement.)

How Much Is the Property Worth?

The homeowner will either have no idea or will have an inflated idea of the value. For example, you could expect to be told that the house three doors away just sold for $XYZ. You will probably not be told that it was the best house on the block, that the seller financed it with a low-interest loan, and that the house you are discussing has two fewer bedrooms, no pool, and has never been painted, cleaned, or cared for.

Is That What Homes in the Neighborhood Are Selling For?

Having heard what the owner thinks his house is worth, you must ask this question. Most sellers will guess! As part of your homework before you go out to look at the property, *ask* brokers who know the area, *ask* for Multiple Listing Service (MLS) reports, *ask* appraisers, *ask* neighbors, *ask* the mailman, *ask* the merchants. Keep asking and you'll be successful.

Do You Have a Recent Appraisal?

In other words, what is the value of your home? This is a difficult question for most homeowners, for the same reason: They usually have an inflated idea of value.

Appraisals from brokers are fairly useful but I'd advise caution here. Most brokers appraise properties at about 10 percent above market value. If the seller does not have a professional appraisal provided by a Member of the Appraisers Institute (MAI), you can be assured that it is your job to determine the value.

Have You Had the Property for Sale?

Don't be surprised if they tell you it hasn't been for sale at all. (These are the people who are waiting for a miracle to come along and make their house payments.)

If it has been for sale, ask why it did not sell. Ask what the people who had looked at it had said about it. Find out what price the owners had been asking for it. Ask them what the realtor had told them.

How Much Will You Take for the Property?

After all the other questions, this one will be easy to answer. Don't be surprised when you are immediately challenged with "What will you give me?" or "As much as I can get." Be prepared for that kind of answer. Don't offend the caller. Just tell him that it is too early to evaluate the dollars and cents without visiting the property. This will lead you into the next question.

How Do I Get There? (Directions to the Property)

Make sure that you have the:

- Name
- Address (always get the nearest cross street)
- Telephone number (day and night).

Then make an appointment to visit the property and remember to note the date and time on your form. When you have hung up the telephone, check the address on the map and make a note of the relevant page. Also remember, when you make an appointment, to ask the owner to have all the loan documents available for your inspection. Your time is too valuable to waste waiting while the seller turns his attic upside down looking for pieces of paper. I can't stress enough how important it is to get the name, address, and telephone number. This information will be of value over and over again and without it, you'll waste more time than you can afford.

The record keeping is very simple in this business, but you'll be surprised how many times you'll refer back to this Property Evaluation Questionnaire. You'll also be surprised how many people call but do not set an appointment and then call again a few weeks later (as their time is running out) and don't realize they have already talked to you. It is always interesting to see if the information and motivation are the same on the subsequent call.

AFTER THE TELEPHONE INTERVIEW

Here are the key questions to ask yourself after you have completed the telephone interview. Make sure you can answer *every* question.

- Do you want property in this area?
- Will it meet code or the requirements of building permits?
- Do they owe the banks too much?
- Is it insurable?

- Is financing available?
- Are you wasting your time?
- Are the comparables easy to verify?
- Do you have different options, for instance, better property, better neighborhood?
- Will the house have dry rot?
- Can you buy it and sell it for a profit?

MEET THE OWNER

Establish a rapport. Tour the house and observe its good and bad points. Will it be marketable?

- Confirm the information you have already received and recorded on the Property Evaluation Questionnaire.
- Is the information the same as you received over the telephone? For example, the owners might have said that the roof does not leak but you notice stains on the bedroom ceiling.
- Determine if the owner really does own the property. (Review the Grant Deed.)
- Before leaving the office, remind the owner to have the Grant Deed available for review when you visit the property. Otherwise the search could take hours, while you sit and watch papers—everything from high school pictures to love notes from old friends—being dredged up out of shoe boxes and metal containers. The Grant Deed, along with the Notice of Default (NOD) and the Promissory Note, Mortgage, or Trust Deed, will usually be sufficient proof of ownership. Once your contract is effective, you will order a preliminary Title Report from the title company to confirm the information.

FIND OUT WHAT THE OWNER WANTS FOR THE PROPERTY; DETERMINE HIS EXPECTATIONS

Many sellers will be realistic about the value of their property. However, most owners will try to make you believe that it is higher than fair market value. A number of sources will provide information, including the Multiple Listing Service provided by real estate brokers, the Real Estate Data Inc. (REDI), and databanks, such as DAMAR and CMDC.

Multiple listing service

A listing is an authorization given by a homeowner to a broker to advertise and sell a house. The written listing agreement is taken by a member of a group of brokers organized so that each member of the group shares his or her listings with fellow members. The listings are usually made known by being compiled in a printed book that is subscribed to by each of the members. The book is called the MLS or Multiple Listing Service Book.

Before meeting the property owner, it is wise to check with local brokers and on homes for sale by owners to establish the values in the particular neighborhood. However, a quick review of values with your local broker will reveal the houses listed in the MLS book.

REDI

The Real Estate Data, Inc. provides assessors' information—plat maps, property characteristic information, the name and address of the current owner, and a litany of other information pertaining to the property.

DAMAR

This computer data bank provides current information taken from the assessor's roll and characteristics of the property. The computer read-out shows a name, address, property description, and comparable sales data. Such information saves buyers of distressed property hours of driving through neighborhoods looking for comparable properties. An example of the information provided by DAMAR is shown as Figure 5.2.

County assessors are required by state law to keep a list of all properties within the county and establish values for the properties so that the board of supervisors have accurate data on how much the tax receipts (revenue) will be for the coming years. With this knowledge, the supervisors direct the county administrators to budget expenditures. The list of real estate properties is generally referred to as the assessor's roll and it is updated regularly as property is bought and sold. Recently sold properties are very easy to assess as the assessment is a matter of reviewing the sales contract or simply having the seller and buyer advise the county of the sales price as part of the escrow procedures.

DAMAR purchases the county records data and then inputs the data into a mainframe computer. Subscribers then access the data.

In attempting to analyze a property, the investor is always concerned with paying too much. By using the DAMAR System and a Thomas Brothers *Map Book*, the investor simply selects the page and grid number of the applicable map and the DAMAR system responds with an Area Sales Analysis Profile. This data can then be compared with the price the investor expects to spend or negotiate.

This information is extremely valuable since it is detailed and can be restricted to a very small area. The data is excellent for any foreclosure buyer who is purchasing in a metropolitan area. The same data and maps are available, with even more detail, for other regions and cities. All types of properties are included: office buildings, industrial sites, single family homes, apartments, condominiums. Sales information and purchase dates are shown so it is clearly specific to the property you are researching. It is easy to get complete sales information and market value data on your home computer with a modem.

The DAMAR information is extensive but it is essential, whether you are researching a prospective purchase and performing an in-house appraisal prior to purchase or just becoming familiar with the neighborhood. Buyers at Trustee's Sales should be especially alert to the *Assessor's Parcel Number* (APN), which DAMAR will supply. This and the legal description, which is provided on the Notice of Trustee Sale, will define the property to be sold; the street address is not used.

```
++++++++++++++++++++++++
24 records found.


Command/Feature: pri

No. Page/Grd      Address        Date     Price    Area   $/SF   Rm Br Ba YB Sty P S

  1 11-B4   1320 WEBER ST      87/11  $195,000V  1,116 174.73   6  2 1  07 1
    11-B4   1324 BAY ST        87/11  $293,000V  1,970 148.73   8  4 1H 19 1    S Z

  3 11-B4   1320 WEBER ST      87/10  $195,000V  1,116 174.73   6  2 1  07 1
  4 11-B4   644 WESTLINE DR    87/09  $233,000F  2,298 101.39   8  4 3  65 2       V

  5 11-B4   1324 BAY ST        87/09* $293,000V  1,970 148.73   8  4 1H 19 1    S Z

  6 11-B4   1315 CAROLINE ST   87/08  $189,500F  2,538 $74.66   8  5 2  10 2
  7 11-B4   1320 WEBER ST      87/08  $195,000V  1,116 174.73   6  2 1  07 1
  8 11-B4
ALT-F10  HELP ' VT-100   ' FDX '  1200 E71 ' LOG CLOSED ' PRT ON  ' CR   ' CR
1317 9 ST         87/07  $140,000V  1,718 $81.49   6  3 1  99 2
  9 11-B4   1279 CAROLINE ST   87/07  $214,000V  1,374 155.74   6  3 2  35 1H
 10 11-B4   1109 CENTRAL AV    87/07  $171,500V  1,196 143.39   5  2 1  18 1       Z
 11 11-B4   1417 ST CHARLES    87/07  $225,000V  1,868 120.44   8  3 3  00 2       Z
 12 11-B4   1235 HAWTHORNE S   87/07  $470,000F  4,080 115.19   7  3 3H 50 2       V
 13 11-B4   1285 CAROLINE ST   87/03  $205,000F  1,720 119.18   5  2 2  20 2
 14 11-B4   920 CENTRAL AV     86/12* $125,000V  1,613 $77.49   5  2 2  20 1
 15 11-B4   1190 SHERMAN ST    86/11  $180,000V  1,444 124.65   6  3 2  37 1
 16 11-B4   652 WESTLINE DR    86/11  $227,500F  2,397 $94.91   7  4 3  64 2
 17 11-B4   1039 SAN ANTONIO   86/11  $180,000V  1,460 123.28   6  3 2  58 1
 18 11-B4        ST CHARLES    86/11  $250,000V  2,633 $94.94   9  4 2  26 2
 19 11-B4        PARU ST       86/11  $315,000V  2,460 128.04   9  3 2H 10 2     H
 20 11-B4        PORTOLA AV    86/10  $150,000F  1,492 100.53   6  3 1  35 1       B
 21 11-B4   017 SAN ANTONIO    86/08  $221,325V  2,304 $96.06   9  4 2  90 2
    11-B4   644 WESTLINE DR    87/09  $233,000F  2,298 101.39   8  4 3  65 2       V

  5 11-B4   1324 BAY ST        87/09* $293,000V  1,970 148.73   8  4 1H 19 1    S Z
```

COMPARABLE

Figure 5.2   DAMAR Report

CMDC

The California Market Data Cooperative is a databank or clearinghouse of appraisal data for the State of California. The data are obtained from public records, independent appraisers, lenders, and government appraisers. The data are available to any individual or investor who is willing to pay the annual fee of approximately $100 plus a monthly fee.

ESTABLISH THE LOAN AMOUNTS AND PAYMENTS THAT ARE IN ARREARS

It is especially important to establish the extent of the default since you will be the one to make payments and so stop the foreclosure process.

Know what you are buying! Property owners, under stressful conditions such as foreclosure, have a tendency to forget loans other than those being foreclosed. It might be the second trust deed that is foreclosing and the owner forgot to tell you about the first loan.

You certainly don't want to buy a property until you understand the lien situation. If you buy a pre-foreclosure property, you buy exactly what the owner owns. If you find that the owner has not told you about all the encumbrances, you could inadvertently buy an extra trust deed that would make the purchase unprofitable. Therefore, it is important to determine the encumbrances of all types, including taxes, bonds, judgment liens, assessments, and trust deeds (1st, 2nd, and 3rd). Remember, you purchase what the owner has committed to ownership. The wise foreclosure buyer reviews the loan documents, specifically seeking information about prepayment penalties, assumptions, and/or alienation clauses.

REVIEW THE EQUITY PURCHASE CONTRACT WITH THE SELLER

Use the Grant Deed to determine the Assessor's Parcel Number and obtain an accurate property description. Later you will compare this information with the preliminary Title Report to confirm that you are buying what you have contracted for and what you think you are buying.

List the loan balances you are buying. Determine the price you will pay the owner. (Negotiations are covered in Chapter 11.)

AVOID THE PITFALLS THAT MANY FORECLOSURE BUYERS IGNORE

Ask the owner about termite reports that might have been recently completed. If no report has been completed, ask the owner about known termite damage. In most circumstances, the owner will respond as if you accused him of living in a dirty house. Expect the owner to be very protective of his property and be aware that your questions may seem offensive. Use a tone of voice that is pleasant, not accusatory. It is your objective at this point to prepare the owner for the costs of repairing the termite damage if there is any. The contract that the author has used successfully specifically states that the seller will pay for damage found by termite and roof inspectors. Readers who use this or a similar clause in their equity purchase contracts will find that it saves thousands of dollars in unforeseen repair costs.

Loan documents should be reviewed in detail. Many loans are due on sale. If you are buying from the owner before the foreclosure sale, you should review the loan documents and determine if the loan has an alienation or acceleration clause. These are options that the lender may have written into the contract made with the owner from whom you are purchasing. Either of these clauses will allow the lenders to begin a foreclosure action against you if they become aware that you have purchased the property.

As the wise buyer, you should give this some thought prior to the purchase and determine alternatives. If, for example, the lenders are not getting paid and have started a foreclosure action, you might advise them that you will buy the property from the seller and then bring the payments up-to-date, provided that they agree, in writing, not to exercise their rights to accelerate the loan.

Alternatively, you could simply pay the back payments on the loan that is in arrears. The lender will then remove the property from the defaulted list or problem property list. This action will give you time to plan a strategy or even buy the property, fix it up, and re-sell it, before the lender becomes aware that the property has been sold to you. When the seller transfers the property to you by Grant Deed and your escrow office records the Grant Deed to establish your right of ownership in the property, the act of recording the deed will make it part of the public records. Some lenders subscribe to a service that investigates the records at the Recorder's Office and so may become aware that title has been transferred from the defaulting owner to you. What action the lender takes at this point varies. Lenders certainly have rights under the contract to take action. Some take action, some don't. If interest rates are rising rapidly and the loan you are curing and hoping to take (subject to) is a low-interest, long-term instrument, you should expect the lender to make some changes.

In the day-to-day world of hurry, hurry, most lenders are happy to receive payment on time and it has been the author's experience that the loans are rarely accelerated. This is not a rule, but it certainly is a win-win situation. The defaulting property owner is saving his credit rating; the lender is getting paid, which is what he contracted for in the first place; and you are benefiting by buying a property with very little actual cash.

In practice you will find that, although lenders will allow you to bring delinquent loans current, they will rarely allow you to pay off the loan, when you sell the property, without a prepayment penalty. Prepayment penalties vary in amounts and terms with each lender. It is not unusual to find prepayment penalties amounting to six months' interest. Private lenders, mortgage companies, and personal property lenders are especially severe in the written terms of their prepayment penalty clauses. In reviewing the updated contracts shown in this text you will notice the prepayment penalty is included in the seller's cost of sale.

A CASE STUDY

Gold in the City of Alameda

Now, we will take you behind the scenes of the successful purchase and resale of a house in Alameda, California, a city across the Bay from San Francisco. At the end of this chapter, you will find reproductions of all the documents pertaining to the various transactions required. Names are fictional.

How did we find the property? We subscribed to a reporting service called the Daily Default Infoservice that showed a defaulted property at 1054 Fair Oaks Avenue in the City of Alameda. Using the address shown on the Daily Default Infoservice, we sent the homeowner a series of letters (Figure 5.3).

By reviewing the Daily Default Infoservice report, the foreclosure buyer can determine loan date, original loan amount, delinquent date, and amount. This information is all valuable when and if the trustor/homeowner decides to respond to your letter of inquiry. If the seller telephones, and you are able to complete a Property Evaluation Questionnaire, the seller's information can be compared with the information already gleaned from the default listing, which was taken from information recorded at the county recorder's office.

Clyde Cutter received a number of letters suggesting that he contact our office for assistance. He did not respond until just before the Notice of Trustee's Sale (also known as a Foreclosure Auction) was posted on his property. A short time later, we became aware of the impending sale when the Daily Default Infoservice to which we subscribed showed it as scheduled. This notice (Figure 5.4) is an update of the notice we received earlier. The reader should note that the format of the report is much the same; however, the top line reads: "T/S 19852" (the T/S stands for Trustee's Sale). The loan date and number remain the same, but the dollar amount increases because it now includes back payments. The original loan amount was $78,542.77; with penalties and back payments, the amount due is now $87,908.69. The date and time of the Trustee's Sale is also noted on this announcement as is the location. Compare the details supplied in the Notice of Trustee's Sale (Figure 5.5) with the information provided by the Daily Default Infoservice or newspaper or whatever other source was used.

Clyde Cutter responded to the direct mail solicitation by returning the coupon that is part of the direct mail package sent to all defaulting homeowners. Upon receiving the coupon, we telephoned Clyde and completed a Property Evaluation Questionnaire. We then agreed to meet him. If Mr. Cutter had not responded to our mail solicitations, we might have tried to contact him by telephone or by knocking on his door. The combination of mail, telephone, and personal visits seems to be the most productive. Most homeowners receiving only letters offering to help just ignore the letters.

The negotiations to purchase the property were successful. Clyde Cutter entered into a Home Equity Purchase Contract (Figure 5.6). The original Grant Deed (Figure 5.7) drawn up when Clyde Cutter and Carrie Cutter purchased the property, was used to complete the Home Equity Purchase Contract because the property description in the Grant Deed is the only legal description. The Daily Default Infoservice is a private reporting service, and its reports are not accurate enough to be considered as legal documents. If a dispute were to arise on a particular property or parcel, the legal description and Assessor's Parcel Number given on the Grant Deed would be acceptable by a court; the description provided by the Daily Default Infoservice would not.

The Home Equity Purchase Contract differs from a standard Real Estate Purchase Contract in many ways. The Home Equity Purchase Contract contains many clauses that are required by the California Civil Code sections 1695 to 1695.14. The code specifies the size of the type and the language used in the contract. The intent of the code is to protect the seller of a foreclosure property.

New Growth Financial
"The Distressed Property Experts"
(415) 837-2106

Dear Homeowner,

Do you need a money miracle right now? Unlimited and fast sources of cash to end your money hassles are available. Let me help you! Would you like to have cash in 10 days or less?

With my easy to use program you can have thousands of dollars in just a few days.

You're not alone. At one tme or another, most of us have had legal hassles and money worries. I can really help you right now. We pay cash for houses and do so in 10 days or less. ▬▬▬▬

Of course, you are skeptical and I think I know why. Many of us, including myself, have been bitterly disappointed in the past with promises and little results.

WHAT RESULTS DID WE GET IN THE PAST

We have stopped the trustee sale process cold by talking with the lenders! This gives you time to make a deal. Time to locate a new home. Time to pack your possessions. Time to move.

This program really works. You'll receive cash or cashier's check within 10 days of our agreement. We take pride in the results we have produced for people like yourself. You will deal with the Vice President of our firm who has more than 10 years experience in solving real estate and people problems.

I know you may be skeptical. That simply shows your good common sense. The enclosed testimonial is proof from people who have put us to the test.

You have nothing to lose and so much to gain. Don't allow your home to be sold at PUBLIC AUCTION (trustee sale).

Call me at 837-2106.

(please turn to reverse side)

Figure 5.3   Introductory Letter from New Growth

Here are your options.

1. Put this letter in the wastebasket and perhaps miss your chance to get the cash you need to begin again.

2. Call 837-2106 and get fast relief from bill collectors and phone calls.

3. Do nothing and let indecision rob you of the equity in your home. Please don't let this happen.

CALL 837-2106 TODAY BEFORE IT IS TOO LATE!!!

****

OUR GUARANTEE TO YOU!!   be perfectly frank. If you are afraid someone will take advantage of you, let me relieve you of that anxiety. If you get a better written offer that is more beneficial than our proposal, I will cancel our contract. Yes! That is correct! We will release you from the contract if you get a better deal. You are the judge. Is that fair treatment? How can you lose? Stop procrastinating; indecision could cost you thousands of dollars if your property is sold at public auction (trustee sale).

****

Act now. Pick up the telephone and call Ted or Joe at 837-2106. Make us prove our claims. Allow us to help you now.

P.S. When you do pick up the telephone and call Joe or me, rest assured you are under no obligation and you won't get the hard sell. We really do want to help you.

P.S.S.

YOU need cash to solve your problem!

We have the cash you need!!!

Just pick up the telephone and dial 837-2106. Ask for Ted or Joe.

The CASH you need will be in your hands in TEN (10) DAYS.

Remember: If you take no action, your home will be sold at public auction and you will be evicted. That's the law. Make sure this doesn't happen to you.

© 1988 New Growth Financial.

Figure 5.3 *(continued)*

DAILY DEFAULT   INFOSERVICE   BOX 456   ANTIOCH   CA 94509 * 415/754-7039   F

INSTRUMENT NO.: DFLT-83481   RECORD DATE: 05/08/89 AP# 400-651-1   TAX ASSESSED VALUE: $139,000.00 : 1985

11-84

TRUSTOR: CLYDE CUTTER
PROP LOCALE: 1054 FAIR OAKS AVE., ALAMEDA, CA 94501
TRUSTEE: AIC TD CO.
ADDRESS: 3685 MT. DIABLO BL., LAFAYETTE, CA 94549
LENDER: PHONE: LN#:
PLACE OF SALE: ENTRANCE TO COUNTY COURTHOUSE, 1225 FALLON ST., OAKLAND, CA
ADD'L INFO.:

LOAN DATE: 6-9-86
BOOK-PAGE: 134089-
APROX MINM BID: $87,908.69
DATE OF SALE: 2-18-88
TIME OF SALE: 11 AM

RECORD DATE: 1-27-88   AP#: 501-814-96 TAX ASSESSED VALUE: $137,333: 1984

INSTRUMENT NO.: TS--19853

TRUSTOR: GREGORIO & MARJORIE POSADAS   SINCE SOLD TO:
PROP LOCALE: 37744 CARRIAGE CIR., FREMONT, CA 94536
TRUSTEE: AIC TD CO.
ADDRESS: 3685 MT. DIABLO BL., LAFAYETTE, CA 94549
LENDER: PHONE: LN#:
PLACE OF SALE: ENTRANCE TO COUNTY COURTHOUSE, 1225 FALLON ST., OAKLAND, CA
ADD'L INFO.:

LOAN DATE: 5-28-86
BOOK-PAGE: 122395
APROX MINM BID: $34,928.53
DATE OF SALE: 2-18-88
TIME OF SALE: 11 AM

88-A4

RECORD DATE: 1-27-88   AP#: 80-22-21   TAX ASSESSED VALUE: $75,000.00: 1983

INSTRUMENT NO.: TS-19654

TRUSTOR: LAURENCE MARTINEZ, ET AL   SINCE SOLD TO:
PROP LOCALE: 579 NEILSON ST., BERKELEY, CA 94707
TRUSTEE: AM-CAL SERVICE
ADDRESS: 390 S. ABEL ST., MILPITAS, CA 95035
LENDER: PHONE: LN#:
PLACE OF SALE: ENTRANCE TO COUNTY COURTHOUSE 39439 PASEO PADRE PARKWAY, FREMONT, CA
ADD'L INFO.:

LOAN DATE: 12-3-86
BOOK-PAGE: 303114-
APROX MINM BID: $41,212.55
DATE OF SALE: 2-24-88
TIME OF SALE: 10:30 AM

1-E4

TRUSTOR: JOHN WILEY, ET AL   SINCE SOLD TO:
PROP LOCALE: 3428 JORDAN RD., OAKLAND, CA 94602
TRUSTEE: CALIFORNIA RECONVEYANCE
ADDRESS: PO BOX 6200, NORTHRIDGE, CA 91328
LENDER: GREAT WESTERN BANK   PHONE: LN#:
PLACE OF SALE: CHICAGO TITLE 22320 FOOTHIL BL., HAYWARD, CA
ADD'L INFO.:

LOAN DATE: 12-27-84
BOOK-PAGE: 253737-
APROX MINM BID: $117,515.39
DATE OF SALE: 3-14-88
TIME OF SALE: 9 AM

10-D4

RECORD DATE: 1-26-88   AP# 531-34-65   TAX ASSESSED VALUE: N/A

INSTRUMENT NO.: TS-18393

Figure 5.4 Infoservice Listings for New Growth Clients

RECORDING REQUESTED BY

AND WHEN RECORDED MAIL TO

A.I.C. TRUST DEED SERVICES, INC.
3685 Mt Diablo Blvd., Suite 361
Lafayette, CA 94549

555659   87-09-31   SPACE ABOVE THIS LINE FOR RECORDER'S USE

Reference: 02-8709-0080

NOTICE OF TRUSTEE'S SALE

YOU ARE IN DEFAULT UNDER A DEED OF TRUST DATED 06/04/86 UNLESS YOU TAKE
ACTION TO PROTECT YOUR PROPERTY, IT MAY BE SOLD AT A PUBLIC SALE. IF YOU NEED
AN EXPLANATION OF THE NATURE OF THE PROCEEDINGS AGAINST YOU, YOU SHOULD
CONTACT A LAWYER.

On 02/18/88 at 11:00 A.M. A.I.C. T TRUST DEED SERVICES INC. as the duly
appointed Trustee under and pursuant to Deed of Trust, Recorded on 06/09/86 as Document no. 86-
134089 Book   Page   Of Official Records in the office of the Recorder of ALAMEDA
County, California.
executed by:
Clyde Cutter, as his sole and separate property

WILL SELL AT PUBLIC AUCTION TO THE HIGHEST BIDDER FOR CASH, (payable at time of sale
in lawful money of the United States) at ON THE STEPS TO THE
   COUNTY COURT HOUSE
   1225 FALLON STREET
   OAKLAND, CA
all right, title and interest conveyed to and now held by it under said Deed of Trust in the property situated
in said County, California, describing the land therein:
COMMENCING AT A POINT ON THE SOUTHERN LINE OF FAIR OAKS
AVENUE, FORMERLY LOUISA STREET, DISTANT THEREON 75 FEET
WESTERLY FROM THE POINT OF INTERSECTION THEREOF WITH THE
WESTERN LINE OF ST. CHARLES STREET, RUNNING THENCE WESTERLY
ALONG SAID LINE OF FAIR OAKS AVENUE 50 FEET; THENCE AT RIGHT
ANGLES SOUTHERLY 51.83 FEED; THENCE AT RIGHT ANGLES EASTERLY
50 FEET, AND THENCE AT RIGHT ANGLES NORTHERLY 51.83 FEET TO
THE POINT OF BEGINNING.

BEING A PORTION OF LOT NUMBER 1, AS SAID LOT IS DELINEATED AND
DESIGNATED UPON THAT CERTAIN MAP ENTITLED "MAP OF THE LANDS
OF THE TEUTONIA PARK AND HOMESTEAD ASSOCIATION AT ALAMEDA,
W.F. BOARDMAN, C. SUR.", FILED MARCH 10, 1877, IN THE OFFICE OF THE
COUNTY RECORDER OF ALAMEDA COUNTY.

APN: 73-393-61

PAGE ONE

Figure 5.5   Notice of Trustee's Sale for Clyde Cutter

The street address and other common designation, if any, of the real property described above is purported to be:

1054 FAIR OAKS AVENUE
ALAMEDA, CA 94501

The undersigned Trustee disclaims any liability for any incorrectness of the street address and other common designation, if any, shown herein.

Said saie will be made, but without convenant or warranty, expressed or implied, regarding title, possession, or encumbrances, to pay the remaining principal sum of the note(s) secured by said Deed of Trust, with interest thereon, as provided in said note(s), advances, if any, under the terms of the Deed of Trust, estimated fees, charges and expenses of the Trustee and of the trusts created by said Deed of Trust.

ESTIMATED TO BE; $87,908.69

The beneficiary under said Deed of Trust heretofore executed and delivered to the undersigned a written Declaration of Default and Demand for Sale, and a written Notice of Default and Election to Sell. The undersigned caused said Notice of Default and Election to Sell to be recorded in the county where the real property is located.

A.I.C. TRUST DEED SERVICES, INC.
SUBSTITUTED TRUSTEE

Date: 01/19/88

Publish: 01/28/88
         02/04/88
         02/11/88

Roger Smith

3685 MT. DIABLO BLVD., SUITE 361
LAFAYETTE, CA 94549
(415) 284-4644

Notice of Trustee's Sale

PAGE TWO

Figure 5.5 *(continued)*

HOME EQUITY PURCHASE CONTRACT

Alameda _____ California *Jan. 12* , 19 *88*

Lot 1 _____ Tract *Map of lands of the Teutonia Park & Homestead Assoc. of Alameda* Book _____ Page(s)_____

Address *1054 Fair Oaks Ave*   Ca *94501*

In consideration of the sum of $_____ receipt of which is hereby acknowledged by SELLER, the SELLER agrees to sell and the BUYER agrees to purchase the above decribed property for the sum of $_____ NET TO SELLER and to take title subject ONLY to existing encumbrances not in excess of:

1st TD $ *74,416^{49}* payable $ *1,046* per month _____% interest incl. TI _____

2nd TD$_____ payable $_____ per month _____% interest _____due date

3rd TD$_____ payable $_____ per month _____% interest _____due date

FULL PRICE $5,000.00

NOTICE REQUIRED BY CALIFORNIA LAW

UNTIL YOUR RIGHT TO CANCEL THIS CONTRACT HAS ENDED _____
OR ANYONE WORKING FOR *New Growth* _____ CANNOT ASK YOU TO SIGN ANY DEED OR ANY OTHER DOCUMENT.

We hereby agree to sell on the above conditions and terms.

BUYER *New Growth Ent.* _____ SELLER *Clyde Cutter* _____

BUYER *Ted Thomas V.P.* _____ SELLER_____

ADDRESS *185 Front Street* _____ ADDRESS _____

Danville _____ PHONE *837-2106* _____ PHONE_____

Figure 5.6   Home Equity Purchase Contract for Clyde Cutter

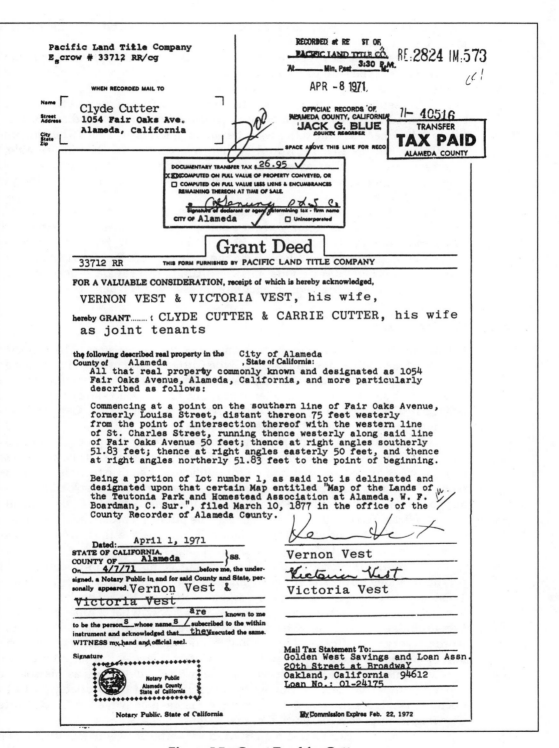

Figure 5.7 Grant Deed for Cutters

Violations by the purchaser are treated extremely harshly and, by some interpretations, even punitively.

Your state may have specific rules and regulations that protect the defaulting homeowner. Be sure to review and commit to memory exactly what requirements you must comply with to follow the law.

If the seller is pressured to sell his home before the Trustee's Sale, he will be motivated to get as much money as possible. In purchasing distressed real estate, it is wise to ask the seller what he wants in terms of cash. To our surprise, Mr. Cutter told us that he would be happy with $5,000. If you are able to accommodate the seller as easily, you are solving a problem in a win-win situation. Sophisticated negotiation techniques were not required in the purchase of this property.

The seller was well aware that his chances of receiving any money at the Trustee's Sale were very slim. Trustee's Sale proceeds are first distributed to the first lien holder and then to the lien holder who is next in priority. In this case the second in priority would have been the state tax lien. Rarely will sales at the Trustee's Sale (auction) provide sufficient funds to provide sellers with any money once the existing liens or encumbrances have been settled.

Caution—Caution—Caution

Let me illustrate the importance of checking the documents. The Notice of Trustee's Sale notifies the world that Clyde Cutter, as the owner of this sole and separate property, is in default. This ownership should be reflected on the Grant Deed unless some change has taken place. The Grant Deed shows Clyde Cutter and Carrie Cutter as joint tenants. Did a divorce take place? Does Carrie still own an interest in this property? We need to find out.

To find the answer, one must research the title for the property located at 1054 Fair Oaks Avenue in Alameda. In the County Recorder's Office all property records are recorded and maintained for public use. The title records in this case required research. This is a time-consuming endeavor and we took advantage of our good relationship with the local Bigland Title Company. Most title companies keep duplicate records that are the same as the public records. The title company employees refer to this as their titleplant or bank. To save time, we requested a *Property Profile* from the local Bigland Title Company office.

The profile is reproduced as Figure 5.8. A compilation of documents, the profile includes information pages, an assessor's map, a tract map, a Deed of Trust, a description of the property, and a Quitclaim Deed. This last document is exactly what we were looking for. We now know what happened between Carrie and Clyde Cutter. The Quitclaim Deed, dated January 29, 1979, is worded very specifically: "For valuable consideration, receipt of which is hereby acknowledged, Clyde and Carrie Cutter, his wife, as joint tenants, do hereby remiss, release, and forever quitclaim to Clyde Cutter as his sole and separate property . . . ," followed by a description of the property. With this document Carrie's interest in the property has been conveyed to Clyde Cutter. One might suppose a dissolution of marriage.

The Property Profile was requested shortly after the Home Equity Purchase Contract became valid. Bigland Title Company delivered the Profile in one day.

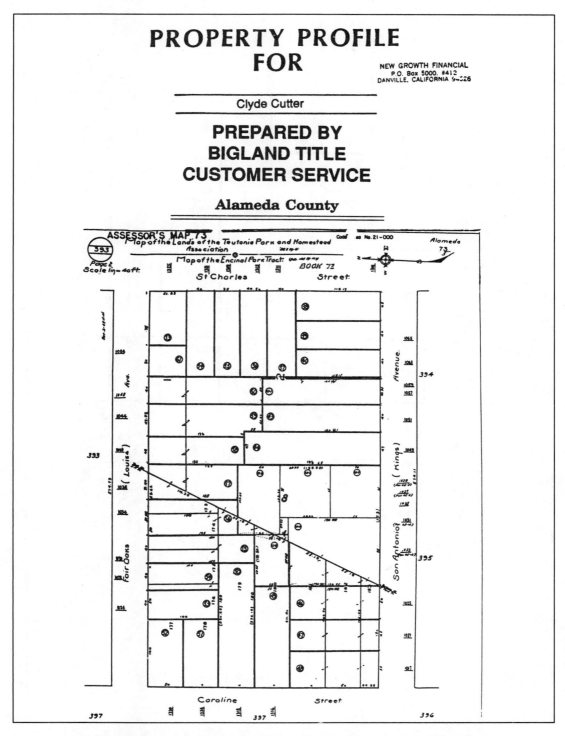

Figure 5.8   Property Profile for Cutter/Assessor's Map/Quitclaim Deed

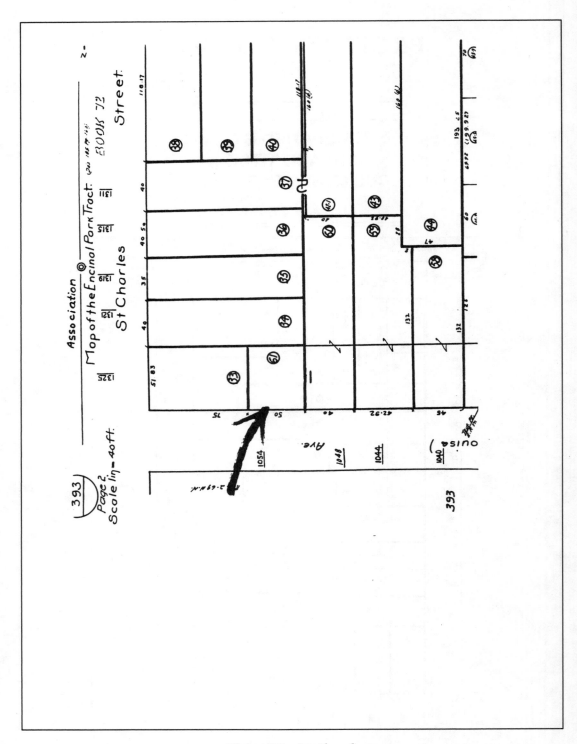

Figure 5.8 *(continued)*

RECORDING REQUESTED BY

AND WHEN RECORDED MAIL TO

Household Finance Corp.
2283 South Shore Center
Alameda, CA 94501
Attn: George

1101075

RECORDED at REQUEST OF **T-035249**
Title Insurance & Trust Co.
At 10:30 AM
FEB 26 1979
Official records of
ALAMEDA COUNTY, CALIFORNIA
RENE C. DAVIDSON
COUNTY RECORDER

SPACE ABOVE THIS LINE FOR RECORDER'S USE

LONG FORM DEED OF TRUST

CONTRACT RATE
OF
FINANCE CHARGE

On loans with Amount Financed over $10,000, the Annual Percentage Rate
of __15.201__ %
On loans with Amount Financed under $10,000:
1.48% per month on that part of the unpaid balance of Amount
Financed not exceeding $4,000, and 1.19% per month on any
part thereof exceeding $4,000.

Due Date of Final Installment of note secured hereby is __2-20-94__

This Deed of Trust, made this   twentieth day of   February 1979   , between
Clyde Cutter by quitclaim deed   , herein called Trustor, whose address is
1054 Fairoaks Avenue   Alameda   Ca   94501

HOUSEKEY FINANCIAL CORPORATION,

A CALIFORNIA CORPORATION, HEREIN   CALLED TRUSTEE, AND
HOUSEHOLD FINANCE CORPORATION OF CALIFORNIA, HEREIN CALLED
BENEFICIARY. WITNESSETH: THAT TRUSTOR IRREVOCABLY GRANTS, TRANSFERS
AND ASSIGNS TO TRUSTEE IN TRUST, WITH POWER OF SALE, THE PROPERTY IN
Alameda   County, CALIFORNIA, DESCRIBED AS:
see EXHIBIT "A"

PAGE TWO

In accordance with Section 2924b, Civil Code, request is hereby made by the undersigned TRUSTOR
that a copy of any Notice of Default and a copy of any Notice of Sale under Deed of Trust recorded
April 8, 1971 in Book __2824__ , Page __577__ , Official Records of __Alameda__ County,
California, as affecting above described property, executed by
__Clyde Cutter & Carrie Cutter, his wife__ as Trustor in which
__Sid Smith & Sallie Smith, his wife as joint tenants__ is named as Beneficiary,
and __Pacific Land Title Company__ as Trustee, be mailed to
__HOUSEHOLD FINANCE CORPORATION OF CALIFORNIA__ whose address is
__2283 South Shore Ctr. Alameda CA 94501__

Figure 5.8 *(continued)*

EXHIBIT "A"

1101075
PAGE 4

The land referred to herein is described as follows:

THE LAND REFERRED TO HEREIN IS SITUATED IN THE STATE OF CALIFORNIA, COUNTY OF ALAMEDA, CITY OF ALAMEDA, DESCRIBED AS FOLLOWS:

COMMENCING AT A POINT ON THE SOUTHERN LINE OF FAIR OAKS AVENUE, FORMERLY LOUISA STREET, DISTANT THEREON 75 FEET WESTERLY FROM THE POINT OF INTERSECTION THEREOF WITH THE WESTERN LINE OF ST. CHARLES STREET, RUNNING THENCE WESTERLY ALONG SAID LINE OF FAIR OAKS AVENUE 50 FEET; THENCE AT RIGHT ANGLES SOUTHERLY 51.83 FEET; THENCE AT RIGHT ANGLES EASTERLY 50 FEET, AND THENCE AT RIGHT ANGLES NORTHERLY 51.83 FEET TO THE POINT OF BEGINNING.

BEING A PORTION OF LOT NUMBER 1, AS SAID LOT IS DELINEATED AND DESIGNATED UPON THAT CERTAIN MAP ENTITLED "MAP OF THE LANDS OF THE TEUTONIA PARK AND HOMESTEAD ASSOCIATION AT ALAMEDA, W. F. BOARDMAN, C. SUR.", FILED MARCH 10, 1877 IN THE OFFICE OF THE COUNTY RECORDER OF ALAMEDA COUNTY.

A.P. NO.:   73-393-61

Figure 5.8 *(continued)*

Order No.

Escrow No.

Loan No.

WHEN RECORDED MAIL TO

DAVIS, CRAIG & YOUNG

Professional Corporations

P. O. Box 2426

1134 Ballena Boulevard

Alameda, CA 94501   *1101075*

RECORDED AT REQUEST OF

Title Insurance & Trust Co.

At 10:30 AM   **T-035248**

FEB 26 1979

OFFICIAL RECORDS OF

ALAMEDA COUNTY, CALIF

RENE C. DAVIDSON

COUNTY RECORDER

SPACE ABOVE THIS LINE FOR RECORDER'S USE

MAIL TAX STATEMENTS TO:

Clyde Cutter

1054 Fair Oaks Avenue

Alameda, CA 94501

DOCUMENTARY TRANSFER TAX $ ____ -0- ____

_____ COMPUTED ON FULL VALUE OF PROPERTY CONVEYED

_____ COMPUTED ON FULL VALUE LESS LIENS AND

ENCUMBRANCES REMAINING AT TIME OF SALE

DAVIS, CRAIG & YOUNG

H Theodore Craig 74

BY   H. THEODORE CRAIG III

QUITCLAIM DEED

FOR A VALUABLE CONSIDERATION, receipt of which is hereby acknowledged.

Clyde Cutter and Carrie Cutter, his wife, as joint tenants

do hereby REMISE, RELEASE AND FOREVER QUITCLAIM to

Clyde Cutter   as his sole and separate property

the real property in the City of Alameda State of California, described as County of Alameda

Figure 5.8 *(continued)*

Pitfalls

The difference in ownership was not the only discrepancy. The Deed of Trust that was included in the Property Profile showed an amount of $25,471.00, payable to Housekey Financial Corporation. This Deed of Trust did not correspond with the Notice of Trustee Sale. The loan number was different from that listed, the dollar amount was significantly smaller, and the loan date was seven years earlier than that of the Trust Deed that was being foreclosed upon.

Is this Deed of Trust senior to the one that is in foreclosure and scheduled for Trustee Sale? If it is senior in date, it is senior (or has priority) in right.

Or was the Daily Default Service wrong? Or was the Bigland Title office wrong? Or are there two loans on the property? A further check by Bigland Title Company verified the correct documents. What had happened? In preparing the Property Profile, Bigland Title Company had included the wrong Deed of Trust. We knew that the Deed of Trust mentioned in the Property Profile was not in foreclosure or set for Trustee's Sale, but there could have been a senior or prior lien to the Deed of Trust which was in foreclosure. First on file (recorded at the Recorder's office) is first in order of seniority.

By comparing the Daily Default Infoservice notice with the Deed of Trust issued in the Property Profile, we were made aware that the 1979 Trust Deed was not in foreclosure. The Daily Default Infoservice notice listed a different loan date (much later; 1986). It also revealed a significantly higher loan amount ($78,543), a different record date, and a different beneficiary or lender (Transamerica, not Housekey Financial Corp.).

Now the question is: Has this senior Deed of Trust been paid? If so, Bigland Title Company should be able to find a Reconveyance Deed. They were successful (Figure 5.9).

The lesson to be learned is: Know what you are purchasing and, if you are unsure, ask for help.

In determining which loan has priority it is important to understand that one of the methods the counties use in recording legal documents throughout the United States is a time-based system. The first person or company to record a document is first in right or priority. Therefore, if you filed a lien against a property on January 1, 1989, and someone else files (records at the County Recorder's Office) a lien on February 1, 1989, the first lien is the one filed on January 1, 1989, regardless of the dollar amounts of either lien. *First to record is first in right.* The biggest mistake a buyer can make is not to understand the lien situation on a property.

The property purchase became more interesting when, some weeks later, a preliminary title report was requested. The full report is not reproduced here, but the important pages are in Figure 5.10. One item in the report is especially interesting: The property carries a tax lien in favor of the State of California's Franchise Tax Board (Figure 5.11), the state agency that collects payroll taxes. This is an example of those items that owners tend to forget about. You, as a purchaser must do a thorough search of the records and deduct the costs of the liens from the proceeds of the purchase. If you don't, you will be the victim and pay for the mistake.

WHEN RECORDED PLEASE MAIL
THIS INSTRUMENT TO

    Clyde Cutter
    1054 Fairoaks Avenue
    Alameda, CA 94501

Order No. _____
Escrow No. 1101075

RECORDED AT REQUEST OF
Title Ins. & Trust
At 10:30 AM
AUG 19 1981

OFFICIAL RECORDS OF
ALAMEDA COUNTY, CALIFORNIA
RENE C. DAVIDSON
COUNTY RECORDER

Recon No.   E-005713

Full Reconveyance

HOUSEKEY FINANCIAL CORPORATION, a Corporation
duly appointed Trustee under the following described deed of trust

TRUSTOR   Clyde Cutter

Figure 5.9   Cutter Deed of Trust

RECORDING REQUESTED BY

AND WHEN RECORDED MAIL TO
Transamerica Financial Services
2361 Mariner Square Drive, Ste. 180
Alameda, CA 94501

Title Order No. _136790_ Escrow No. _____

RECORDED AT REQUEST OF
PIONEER TITLE COMPANY
At 8:30 AM
JUN 9 1986
OFFICIAL RECORDS OF
ALAMEDA COUNTY, CALIF
RENE C. DAVIDSON
COUNTY RECORDER

SPACE ABOVE THIS LINE FOR RECORDER'S USE

DEED OF TRUST AND ASSIGNMENT OF RENTS

LICENSE NO **985 0319**

DATE OF THIS DEED OF TRUST AND OF THE LOAN TRANSACTION		ACCOUNT NUMBER
June 4, 1986	June 9, 1986	403284

BENEFICIARY	TRUSTOR
TRANSAMERICA FINANCIAL SERVICES	Clyde Cutter, as his sole and separate
2831 Mariner Square Drive, Ste. 180	property
Alameda, CA 94501	NAME OF TRUSTEE Pioneer Title Insurance

THIS DEED OF TRUST SECURES FUTURE ADVANCES

Figure 5.9 *(continued)*

BIGLAND TITLE INSURANCE COMPANY
379 DIABLO ROAD, SUITE #102, DANVILLE, CA 94526
(415) 820-5700

PAGE 1
PRELIMINARY REPORT

Your No.: 86976
Order No.: 316826
Escrow Officer: Mary Jones
Title Officer: Mike Michaels
Property Address: 1054 Fair Oaks Avenue
Alameda, California

Dated as of FEBRUARY 8, 1988 at 7:30 A.M.

ORDER NO. 316826

PAGE 3
NOTICE OF TRUSTEE'S SALE UNDER THE TERMS OF SAID DEED OF TRUST

RECORDED	:	JANUARY 27, 1988, SERIES NO. 88-019852, OFFICIAL RECORDS
DATE OF SALE	:	02/18/88 AT 11:00 A.M.
NAME OF TRUSTEE	:	A.I.C TRUST DEED SERVICES INC.
ADDRESS	:	3685 MT. DIABLO BLVD., SUITE 361 LAFAYETTE, CA 94549
TELEPHONE	:	(415)284-4644

5. TAX LIEN IN FAVOR OF THE STATE OF CALIFORNIA, FRANCHISE TAX BOARD, WHOSE ADDRESS IS P.O. BOX 2952, SACRAMENTO, CA 95812.

AGAINST	:	CLYDE CUTTER
CERTIFICATE NO.	:	87252-003250
ACCOUNT NO.	:	547604144EHLE
AMOUNT	:	$2.035.80
RECORDED	:	SEPTEMBER 14, 1987, SERIES NO. 87-253981,OFFICIAL RECORDS

6. ANY POSSIBLE INVALIDITY OF TITLE OR EFFECT THEREON, BY REASON OF EXERCISE OF ANY RIGHTS OF RESCISSION OR CANCELLATION, OR OTHERWISE, OR ASSERTION OF ANY RIGHTS PURSUANT TO CHAPTERS 655, 819 1015 AND 1029, STATUTES OF 1979, CALIFORNIA STATUTES, ENACTED FOR THE PROTECTION OF RESIDENTIAL PROPERTY OWNERS IN FORECLOSURE AS SET FORTH IN SAID STATUTES.

NOTE: ACCORDING TO THE PUBLIC RECORDS, NO DEED CONVEYING THE PROPERTY DESCRIBED IN THIS REPORT HAS BEEN RECORDED WITHIN A PERIOD OF SIX MONTHS PRIOR TO THE DATE OF THIS REPORT, EXCEPT AS SHOWN HEREIN:

TITLE OF THE VESTEE WAS ACQUIRED BY DEED RECORDED FEBRUARY 1, 1988, SERIES NO. 88-028659, OFFICIAL RECORDS.

Figure 5.10 Cutter Preliminary Report

RECORDING REQUESTED BY

STATE OF CALIFORNIA
FRANCHISE TAX BOARD

AND WHEN RECORDED MAIL TO:
FRANCHISE TAX BOARD
P O BOX 2952
SACRAMENTO CA 95812

87-253981

'87 SEP 14 AM 8 30

RECORDED IN OFFICIAL RECORDS
OF ALAMEDA COUNTY, CALIF
D. R. DAVIDSON
COUNTY RECORDER

SPACE ABOVE THIS LINE FOR RECORDER'S USE——

NOTICE OF STATE TAX LIEN

FILED WITH:

COUNTY OF ALAMEDA

CERTIFICATE NUMBER:

87252-003250

The Franchise Tax Board of the State of California hereby certifies that the following named taxpayer(s) is liable under Parts 10 or 11 od Division 2 of the Revenue and Taxation Code to the State Of California for amounts due and required to be paid by said taxpayer as follows:

Name of Taxpayer: Clyde Cutter

FTB Account Number: 547604144EHLE

Social Security Number: 547-60-4144(H)

Last Known Address: 762 ATLANTIC AVENUE   ALAMEDA CA 94501

For Taxable Years: 1985

TAX	PENALTY	INTEREST	COLLECTION COSTS	PAYMENTS	TOTAL
1,212.00	606.00	208.80	9.00	0.00	2,035.80

Figure 5.11   Notice of Tax Lien

Independent Inspections

In the course of the purchase negotiations, the seller explained that the roof had been replaced 10 years ago. We obtained the roof report (Figure 5.12). According to Walnut Creek Roofing Company, the roof would need only minor repairs for an estimated cost of $350. The inspection fee was another $100.

The termite report was a real shocker! Rose Exterminator Company is a very reliable exterminating service; they are very detailed and thorough. This is exactly what you, as a buyer of distressed real estate, want. The report is too long to reproduce in full (see Figure 5.13). However, the total amount required to repair the damage was $42,644.00!

After the termite report and the roof report were reviewed, it was time to decide whether this would be a profitable purchase or whether the property should be conveyed back to Clyde Cutter. So, we had next to determine how much the property was likely to be worth on the market. The professional appraiser's report (Figure 5.14) showed a value of $120,500. Knowing that this appraiser's estimates were conservative, we decided that the value of the property was at least $130,000.

We telephoned real estate brokers who were listing properties in the immediate area (six to ten blocks). Asking prices ranged from $150,000 to $300,000. This information was not really useful as the homes are not similar; some are huge Victorians, up to 4,000 square feet; while others were 1,000-square-feet traditional homes. Open houses in the area provided a better evaluation. We toured homes that were similar to our foreclosure purchase to compare prices and amenities. For comparable houses, the asking prices ranged from $160,000 to $180,000, which made this foreclosure property look like a good buy.

A final check using the DAMAR computer databank confirmed our findings. The DAMAR Area Sales Analysis Profile that we requested for the city of Alameda, California, is reproduced as Figure 5.15. The DAMAR computer check of properties sold in the relevant grid of the Thomas Brothers map showed the lowest price to be $189,000 and the highest to be $293,000. This property was definitely a good buy.

(If the decision had gone the other way and we wished to convey [deed] the property back to Clyde, the time and cost would be minimal. The County Recorder would charge transfer taxes at the rate of $1.10 per $1,000 of the purchase price and the nominal recording fees.)

Now We Own It; Let's Get It Sold

Price is always important when it comes to sales. But even more important than price is knowledge of the market. The people who live in the Country Club areas rarely, if ever, buy fixer-upper or foreclosure houses. Young eager beavers, real estate agents, opportunity seekers, and trade workers all know that this is the way to make bucks fast. Sweat equity is what they like to call it.

Advertise and appeal to the people who are looking for this type of property. If you put your ad in the Bridge Club newsletter you are wasting money and effort. ASK! Find out where the fixer-upper people look for the bargains. Don't underestimate your buyer. The bargain hunters and fixer-upper people know

WALNUT CREEK Roofing Company

Mailing Address: P.O. Box 396
Walnut Creek, Calif. 94596
Phone: 934-4842

License No. 360240   ROOFING — GUTTERS — DOWNSPOUTS   Date ___2-8-88___

Cust. Phone ___837-2106___

I 425

REQUESTING AGENT ___Nancy Patterson—New Growth___   SELLER _____

AGENT'S ADDRESS ___P. O. Box 5000 Suite 412, Dan.___   PURCHASER _____

TITLE COMPANY ___N/A___   EXCROW NO. ___N/A___

ADDRESS OF INSPECTION ___1054 Fair Oaks Dr., Alemeda___

☐ INTERIOR INSPECTION   ☒ EXTERIOR INSPECTION
☐ EVIDENCE OF ROOF LEAKS   ☐ DRY ROT
☐ DETACHED BUILDINGS INSPECTED   ☐ COMPOSITION SHINGLES
☐ WOOD SHAKE   ☐ WOOD SHINGLES
☐ CLAY TILE   ☐ CONCRETE TILE
☒ BUILT UP ROOF (type) _____   ☐ GUTTER INSPECTED

APPROXIMATE AGE OF ROOF _____
APPROXIMATE LIFE EXPECTANCY _____
CONDITION OF ROOF   FAIR____ GOOD____ OTHER____

PROBLEMS TO BE CORRECTED

1 ☐ METAL EDGING   8 ☐ PARAPET WALL COVERINGS
2 ☐ CHIMNEY FLASHINGS   9 ☐ VALLEYS DETERIORATED
3 ☐ FELT EXPOSURE   10 ☐ BROKEN TILE
4 ☐ DEBRIS ON ROOF   11 ☐ MISSING SHINGLES
5 ☐ SHRUBS OR TREE OVER ROOF   12 ☐ IMPROPERLY INSTALLED ROOF
6 ☐ HIP 2ND RIDGE DETERIORATED   13 ☐ AIR CONDITIONER
7 ☐ ROOF NEED TO BE REPLACED   14 ☒ OTHER

COST TO REPAIR $___350.00___   COST TO REPLACE $_____   INSPECTION FEE $___100.00___

REMARKS _____
        PLEASE SEE ATTACHED REPORT
_____
_____
_____
_____
_____
_____
_____

INSPECTED BY: Pat Crowe

"Repairs are not guaranteed." Complete re-roofing is guaranteed for three years. Specifications for re-roofing furnished upon request. Work will only be performed after notification of funds in escrow, unless other arrangements have been made to the satisfaction of WALNUT CREEK ROOFING COMPANY

Figure 5.12   Walnut Creek Roof Report

Patterson
Page 2
February 8, 1988

RE: 1054 Fair Oaks Dr., Alemeda

This home has a Ten Year type, Built-Up roof on it. Following are the
results of my inpspection.

14 a. The top of the walls need to be cleaned down and resealed.

14 b. The stucco walls have lost their watertightness and need to be
resealed and caulked.

The cost to do the above work would be $350.00.

We do not inspect any projections above or below the roof line. Such
as gutters, windows, chimneys, walls, skylights, heating or air
conditioning and take no liability for their condition. Nor do we
inspect solar panels or the roof underneath unless easily accessible.

Figure 5.12   *(continued)*

ROSE EXTERMINATOR CO.
Since 1860
WISE PROTECTION

America's Oldest Exterminating Service

HOME OFFICE: 626 POTRERO AVENUE • SAN FRANCISCO 94110 • (415) 647-2323

WESTERN DIVISION OFFICES

ALBUQUERQUE, NEW MEXICO—(505) 266-5888   LOS ANGELES, CALIFORNIA—(800) 662-7673
DENVER, COLORADO—(303) 534-0014   PHOENIX, ARIZONA—(602) 242-2583
LAS VEGAS, NEVADA—(702) 876-0780   SACRAMENTO, CALIFORNIA—(916) 383-7673

Consult Your Local Telephone Directory for Branch Office Nearest You

AUTHORIZATION AGREEMENT

PROPERTY ADDRESS   1054 FAIR OAKS AVE., ALAMEDA

ROSE EXTERMINATOR COMPANY is hereby authorized to perform the work as recommended in our STANDARD INSPECTION REPORT FORM dated   1-25 , 1988 . Charges to perform the work are itemized below. Where required by ordinance or statute, Client shall be responsible for providing or installing acceptable smoke detection devices.

ITEM #1=$600.00, #3=$16,900.00, #4=$12,800.00, #5=$630.00, #6=$2,121.00, #7+$3,218.00, #9+$900.00, #10=$850.00, #11=$1,610.00, #12=$300.00, #14=$65.00, #15+$1,950.00, #18+$400.00, #19=$300.00

TOTAL $42,644.00

Figure 5.13   Exterminator Report for 1054 Fair Oaks, Alameda

Valuation Section   **UNIFORM RESIDENTIAL APPRAISAL REPORT**   File No. _____

Purpose of Appraisal is to estimate Market Value as defi___ the Certification & Statement of Limiting Conditions.

COST APPROACH

BUILDING SKETCH (SHOW GROSS LIVING AREA ABOVE GRADE)
If for Freddie Mac or Fannie Mae, show only square foot calculations and cost approach comments in this space

See attached sketch

No obsolescence noted.

Land to improvement ratio is normal for the area.

Land value by abstraction.

ESTIMATED REPRODUCTION COST - NEW - OF IMPROVEMENTS:

Dwelling 1,162 Sq. Ft. @ $ 50.00 = $		58,100
Sq. Ft. @ $ =		
Extras basement =		1,500
=		
Special Energy Efficient Items normal =		
Porches, Patios, etc. patio =		2,500
Garage/Carport 192 Sq. Ft. @ $ 16.00 =		3,072
Total Estimated Cost New .... = $		65,172

	Physical	Functional	External		
Less					
Depreciation	27,200	0	0	= $	27,200
Depreciated Value of Improvements .... = $					37,972
Site Imp. "as is" (driveway, landscaping, etc.) = $					2,500
ESTIMATED SITE VALUE .... = $					80,000
(If leasehold, show only leasehold value.)					
INDICATED VALUE BY COST APPROACH .... = $					120,472

(Not Required by Freddie Mac and Fannie Mae)
Does property conform to applicable HUD/VA property standards? ☐ Yes ☐ No
If No, explain: _____

Construction Warranty ☐ Yes ☒ No
Name of Warranty Program _____
Warranty Coverage Expires _____

SALES COMPARISON ANALYSIS

The undersigned has recited three recent sales of properties most similar and proximate to subject and has considered these in the market analysis. The description includes a dollar adjustment, reflecting market reaction to those items of significant variation between the subject and comparable properties. If a significant item in the comparable property is superior to, or more favorable than, the subject property, a minus (−) adjustment is made, thus reducing the indicated value of subject; if a significant item in the comparable is inferior to, or less favorable than, the subject property, a plus (+) adjustment is made, thus increasing the indicated value of the subject.

ITEM	SUBJECT	COMPARABLE NO. 1		COMPARABLE NO. 2		COMPARABLE NO. 3	
Address	1054 Fair Oaks Drive	1521 Minturn Street		1117 Pacific Avenue		1310 Santa Clara Avenue	
Proximity to Subject		1/2 mile		3 blocks		9 blocks	
Sales Price	$n/a	$ 128,000		$ 125,000		$ 124,000	
Price/Gross Liv. Area	$ 103.70 ☑	$ 100.00 ☑		$ 100.40 ☑		$ 122.05 ☑	
Data Source	Inspection	CMDC/REDI		CMDC/REDI		CMDC/REDI	
VALUE ADJUSTMENTS	DESCRIPTION	DESCRIPTION	+ (−) $ Adjustment	DESCRIPTION	+ (−) $ Adjustment	DESCRIPTION	+ (−) $ Adjustment
Sales or Financing Concessions		new conv.		new conv.		new conv.	
Date of Sale/Time	(1/88)	10/27/87		8/31/87		10/30/87	
Location	good	equal		equal		equal	
Site/View	2,591.5/none	3256 /equal		2025 /equal		2875 /equal	
Design and Appeal	split level	equal		equal		equal	
Quality of Construction	average	equal		equal		equal	
Age	50 years	51 years		57 years		76 years	+2,000
Condition	fair	average	−3,000	average	−3,000	good	−6,000
Above Grade Room Count	Total 5 / Bdrms 2 / Baths 1	Total 6 / Bdrms 2 / Baths 1.5	−1,500	Total 4 / Bdrms 2 / Baths 1		Total 5 / Bdrms 2 / Baths 2	−3,000
Gross Living Area	1,162 Sq. Ft.	1,280 Sq. Ft.	−3,000	1,245 Sq. Ft.	−2,100	1,016 Sq. Ft.	+3,800
Basement & Finished Rooms Below Grade	100 sq.ft. unfinished	equal		none	+1,000	none	+1,000
Functional Utility	good	equal		equal		equal	
Heating/Cooling	floor	equal		equal		equal	
Garage/Carport	1 garage	1 garage		1 garage		0 garage	+1,500
Porches, Patio, Pools, etc.	patio porch	fence porch		patio porch		patio,fence porch	−1,000
Special Energy Efficient Items	insulation	equal		equal		equal	
Fireplace(s)	1 fireplace	0 fireplace	+500	1 fireplace	−500	1 fireplace	−500
Other (e.g. kitchen equip., remodeling)	range	equal		equal		equal	
Net Adj. (total)		☐ + ☒ − $	−7,000	☐ + ☒ − $	−4,600	☐ + ☒ − $	−2,200
Indicated Value of Subject		$ 121,000		$ 120,400		$ 121,800	

Comments on Sales Comparison: Comparable #2 best supports the indicated market value in size and location. Sale #1 is slightly out of area but a recent sale of similar size. Sale #3 is a smaller unit in superior condition. An adjustment of $500 was used for fireplace/doesn't work

INDICATED VALUE BY SALES COMPARISON APPROACH .... $ 120,500

INDICATED VALUE BY INCOME APPROACH (If Applicable) Estimated Market Rent $ */a /Mo. x Gross Rent Multiplier n/a = $ 0

This appraisal is made ☒ "as is" ☐ subject to the repairs, alterations, inspections or conditions listed below ☐ completion per plans and specifications.

Comments and Conditions of Appraisal: These are the most comparable sales available in this area in this time frame. All sales have been confirmed closed.

RECONCILIATION

Final Reconciliation: Market approach is considered the best indicator of present market value and the market indicates a value of $120,500. I am currently certified under the AIREA continuing education program. This appraisal was done in compliance with regulation R41C.

This appraisal is based upon the above requirements, the certification, contingent and limiting conditions, and Market Value definition that are stated in

☐ FmHA, HUD &/or VA instructions.
☒ Freddie Mac Form 439 (Rev. 7/86)/Fannie Mae Form 1004B (Rev. 7/86) filed with client _____ 19___ ☒ attached.

I (WE) ESTIMATE THE MARKET VALUE, AS DEFINED, OF THE SUBJECT PROPERTY AS OF January 25 1988 to be $ 120,500

I (We) certify: that to the best of my (our) knowledge and belief the facts and data used herein are true and correct; that I (we) personally inspected the subject property, both inside and out, and have made an exterior inspection of all comparable sales cited in this report; and that I (we) have no undisclosed interest, present or prospective therein.

Appraiser(s) SIGNATURE _Jane B. Harwood RM_   Review Appraiser SIGNATURE _____ ☐ Did ☐ Did Not Inspect Property
NAME Jane B. Harwood RM   (if applicable) NAME

Freddie Mac Form 70 10/86 /19Ch.   AB   Forms and Worms Inc.® 315 Whitney Ave., New Haven, CT 06511 1(800) 243-4545   Item #130960   Fannie Mae Form 1004 10/86

Figure 5.14 Residential Appraisal Report for 1054 Fair Oaks

```
                    D A M A R C O R P O R A T I O N
                    Real Estate Information Systems
-----------------------------------------------------------------------
                              A S A P   Report
                         Area Sales Analysis Profile

County: ALAMEDA CA                    Page/Grid: 11-B4
        Total Sales                        88
        Total Resales                       6
        Total New Home Sales (sold within one
          year of construction)

        Average Living Area Size         2047
        Average Year Built               1928
        Average Lot Area                 5807
        Average Number of Rooms          7.05
        Average Number of Bedrooms       3.21
        Average Number of Baths          1.86

        Pool = 1%   View = 8%   Central Air =      Waterfront = 6%   Floodzone-

Price Range (1986 only)   $111,000 to    $367,500   Predominant Value   $238,500
Age Range (entire sample)   15 yrs to      83 yrs   Predominant Age       67 yrs
```

AREA SALES ANALYSIS PROFILE (ASAP) PROGRAM

Please press <RETURN> to continue or enter one of the following:
            OPTION - to select another database
            HELP   - for more information
            LOG   - to log-off

Current ASAP is available for the following counties:

CALIFORNIA		GEORGIA	ARIZONA
1. Alameda	7. San Bernardino	13. De Kalb	17. Maricopa
2. Contra Costa	8. San Diego	14. Fulton	
3. Los Angeles	9. San Francisco		ILLINOIS
4. Orange	10. San Mateo	TEXAS	18. Chicagoland
5. Riverside	11. Santa Clara	15. Dallas	
6. Sacramento	12. Ventura	16. Harris	

Enter corresponding number for desired county: 1

Enter grid(s):
  - Maximum 16 grids; do not enter the word GRID.
  - If more than one grid, separate with commas.
  - For assistance enter <HELP>

Enter grid(s):   11-b4

You have requested an ASAP Report for:

11-B4   ALAMEDA CA

Press <RETURN> to continue or
Enter <NEW> to change your profile.

There are a total of 88 in the selected profile area.
Do you want to PRINT the ASAP report <Y> or <N> y

Figure 5.15   DAMAR Report for Same Address

Distribution of Sales (in Thousands of $) for 1986:

21- 30	31- 40	41- 50	51- 60	61- 70	71- 80	81-100	101-125	126-150
							14%	4%

151-175	176-200	201-225	226-250	251-275	276-300	301-350	351-400	401-450
14%	14%	19%	9%	4%		14%	4%	

451-500	501-600	601-700	701-800	801-900	901-1000	>1000

Type Loan for 1986:

Conventional	FHA	VA	Assumable	Creative	Other
38%				28%	

Living Area in Square Feet (entire sample):

200- 400	401- 600	601- 800	801-1000	1001-1200	1201-1500	1501-1750
		2%	6%	5%	23%	11%

1751-2000	2001-2500	2501-3000	3001-3500	3501-4000	4001-5000	over 5000
7%	17%	9%	5%	2%	7%	

Year built:	Pre-1900	01-20	21-30	31-40	41-50	51-60	61-70	71-80	81-90
		38%	25%	22%	1%	3%	6%	1%	

A V E R A G E S A L E S D A T A (B y Y e a r)

Year	Total Sales	Average Price	Average Cashdown	Average Loan	Living Area	$ Per Sq Ft	Median Price
1986	9	$202,480	43%	$110,050	2,073	$ 97.67	$180,000
1985	12	$223,125	14%	$150,612	2,212	$100.85	$212,000
1984	6	$301,500		$207,000	2,860	$105.41	$399,000
1983	3	$143,333		$112,691	1,738	$ 82.47	$130,000
1982	2	$222,500	52%	$ 52,500	3,143	$ 70.79	$315,000
1981	2	$168,500	54%	$ 96,000	2,108	$ 79.93	$230,000
1980	6	$157,900	24%	$119,816	2,415	$ 65.36	$175,000
1979	16	$104,843	26%	$ 80,426	1,531	$ 68.43	$105,500
1978	15	$106,573	26%	$ 78,533	2,092	$ 50.94	$112,000
1977	17	$ 84,570	26%	$ 62,152	1,863	$ 45,38	$75,000

DAMAR Corporation (c) 1988   Real Estate Information Systems   (800) 873-2627

Figure 5.15   *(continued)*

values. The research we did before buying showed that comparable houses were selling at prices of between $150,000 and $300,000.

Read the advertisements. Who do they appeal to? Think about your offer. Don't ask more than the market price or you will hold the property forever. Remember: You make your money by buying, not by selling. Anyone can sell a property provided it is priced right.

Look at your competition. Your price can be higher than theirs—if you have more to offer. Determine for yourself before you advertise, the best points of your property:

- Is it price?
- Is it location?
- Is it size?
- Is it a bargain?
- Is the financing special?
- Is it the best property in the neighborhood?
- Is it the last of a model?

The answers to these questions will help you to define yours as USP (Unique Selling Property) or a USA (Unique Selling Attraction). Without these attributes, you'll have a tough time selling and competing in the market. Don't be an also-ran. Be different and your house will sell quickly. If you don't have a bargain or if you fixed it up yourself and want top dollar, write your ad to appeal to the white-collar workers who play golf and tennis all weekend.

The Alameda Journal is delivered to every house in the city of Alameda every Friday. It is where people look for real estate bargains. The small ad we ran caused a crowd to form in front of 1054 Fair Oaks Avenue. The bargain hunters noticed the asking price $137,500 and pounced on the first person with the access key.

The property was sold on the first day on which it was held open for inspection. Bargain hunters recognized that the asking price was significantly below the neighborhood values and the profit potential was extremely high. The buyers lived in the city of Alameda and knew who the competition was. In order to pre-empt other offers and not miss this opportunity, they offered more than the asking price to make sure that *they* would be the new owners.

The price was later reduced to $136,900 when the financial institution advised the buyer that a prepayment penalty was due. We were unable to avoid giving the discount in this case but our subsequent contracts require that the seller (yes, the person we buy from), must pay the prepayment penalty.

Bigland Title Company carried out the final escrow and the seller's instructions for the disposition of the purchase price are reproduced in Figure 5.16. You will note that the State of California Franchise Tax Board was paid in escrow. The fee was deducted from the seller's profit. The fact that we had to do a fair amount of research to unearth it in the first place should bring home to the buyers of foreclosure or distressed property the importance of determining the lien status of the property.

The final check from Bigland Title Company was in the amount of $56,940.22. Not bad when one considers it only cost $12,599.72 to cure (bring

SELLER'S INSTRUCTIONS

BIGLAND TITLE

379 Diablo Rd., #102, Danville, CA 94526
ESCROW OFFICER Judi Johnson
ENCLOSED ARE THE FOLLOWING: _____
_____ Deed in favor of Stier, et al

DATE February 26, 1988
ESCROW NUMBER 86976
PROPERTY ADDRESS 1054 Fair Oaks Ave.
Alameda, CA

Which you may deliver and/or record when you have collected for me the sum of $ 136,900.00 as follows:
LESS A _____ DEED OF TRUST FOR $_____ IN FAVOR OF _____
_____

ESTIMATED STATEMENT	DEBITS	CREDITS
PURCHASE PRICE		
RECEIVED FROM BUYER OUTSIDE OF ESCROW		
DEPOSITS TO ESCROW $ BROKER $		
DEED OF TRUST FIRST SECOND		
DEMAND OF: TRANSAMERICA FINANCIAL SERVICES	76,794.70	
LOAN TRUST FUND BALANCE		
Federal express charges for payoff check	30.00	
PRO RATE FIRE INS. PREM. $ FOR YR PD TO		
PRO RATE REINT @ $ FR TO		
PRO RATE COUNTY TAXES FOR 1/2 YR $221.99 PD TO 7/1/88		135.30
TAXES PAID both installments 87/88 + penalties	466.17	
Tax sale No. 404109 86/87	531.02	
COMMISSION NONE		
Pay Franchise Tax Board (est)	2,148.94	
COUNTY TRANSFER TAX		
3 R REPORT - REFUND TO		
NOTARY FEE	20.00	
RECONVEYANCE FEE		
RECORDING FEE (est)	20.00	
Drawing documents	50.00	
Title insurance premium (owners)	564.80	
Credit for title insurance binder issued in 86956		530.55
ESTIMATED BALANCE TO: (X) SELLER ( ) BIGLAND TITLE CO.	56,940.22	
TOTALS	$137,565.85	$137,565.85

These instructions are effective until revoked by written demand on you by the undersigned or any one of them. I hereby agree to pay all my propert costs and fees, including any adjustments, and authorizxze you to deduct same from funds due me and remit balance to NEW GROWTH ENTERPRISES
c/o_____ NEW GROWTH ENTERPRISES, a California Corporation
received _____,19 _____ Time _____ BY: ___ *Ted Thomas* _____
BIGLAND TITLE   TED THOMAS, Vice President

Figure 5.16   Seller's Instructions Inclusive of Escrow

current) the defaulted loan from Transamerica Financial Services. In the six-week holding period, two monthly payments were required; the only additional funding requirements were for a termite inspection, a roof inspection, a home inspection, the appraisal fee, and advertising. These fees and payments came to less than $4,000.00.

Settlement

On moving day, we presented Clyde Cutter with a check for $1,000 and he was pleased to accept it. Contractually we did not owe him any money as the termite report showed that more than $42,000 of repairs were needed, a sum far in excess of the $5,000 we had agreed to pay for Clyde Cutter's equity. However, if Clyde was in effect penniless, which he was, and we didn't give him money to move from the premises, how would we get him to leave? The alternatives that the buyer of foreclosure or distressed property has in this situation are either to pay the previous owners to leave and give them a check when they have vacated the property, or to pay the legal costs of removing them. To have an attorney draw the papers and evict Clyde would take time; the required court order would take more time. Of course, the sheriff would ultimately evict Clyde if it were necessary, but it's much easier to be generous, pay the homeowner to leave, and avoid the legal hassle. But time your payment carefully: Do not pay the home-owner until he has actually removed all of his belongings from the property and has given you the key.

6

Buying in the Preforeclosure Market

What Are the Legal Requirements?

In this chapter you will learn:

- About the three distressed-property markets
- What a foreclosure is
- How to analyze the numbers before the sale to make *big profits*
- The requirements of the California Civil Code Sections pertaining to Home Equity Purchasing Foreclosure consultants and mortgage consultants
- Advantages and disadvantages of buying before the Trustee's Sale
- The secret of getting a postponement for that desperate seller who calls hours before the Trustee's Sale.

THE MARKET

The foreclosure market in California may be divided into three separate steps, depending on time when the distressed property is for sale. Each step has its advantages and disadvantages. Some buyers specialize in one step; others will consider purchases at any of the stages, depending on the conditions applicable to the particular property. The first stage, called preforeclosure, lasts from the time a lender begins foreclosure proceedings until the property goes on the block at a Trustee's Sale; the second stage is the Trustee's Sale itself; the third stage is after the Trustee's Sale, when the property, having received no bids, reverts back to the lender and is referred to as Real Estate Owned (REO). At each stage, you will be buying from a different seller, so you must tailor your approach accordingly. During preforeclosure, you are buying from the property owner who is unable to pay the loan; at the Trustee's Sale you are buying from the Trustee (who is acting on behalf of the lender); REO you are buying from the bank or savings and loan association that made the original loan on the property. After

165

reading this book, you will understand all the steps in the series, but you'll have to decide for yourself which you prefer. The author likes to work in all three because each offers different advantages.

PREFORECLOSURE: THE PROS AND CONS OF BUYING BEFORE THE TRUSTEE'S SALE

The principal advantage is in the seller's motivation. Usually the property owner would rather sell than be foreclosed upon. However, while owners are motivated to sell, they must be contacted and at times this can prove difficult. Most property owners have been delinquent (in default) for a period of time so they have been the recipients of numerous telephone calls from the lender and, in many cases, from collection agencies as well. Don't expect one telephone call to work. You need to knock on the door.

If you can reach the owner before the foreclosure sale and help solve his or her difficulties, you'll find a motivated seller. Sellers are under severe stress so don't expect them to welcome your first call. Persistence will, however, build a small amount of trust that will open the door to negotiation.

This method of purchase is especially lucrative. One must follow and adhere to the *Foreclosure Consultants Law* without fail. The law is simple and straightforward. The California law appears to be one of the toughest in the country. This, like any other body of law, is rapidly changing and you should consult an attorney who is versed in this segment of real estate law as it applies to your particular state or area. (Similar laws apply in other states and it is important that you become familiar with them.) This law is very specific and violators may be prosecuted and penalized. The penalties for violators appear to be excessive from the standpoint of someone who really is helping the troubled homeowner who, without the foreclosure buyer, will lose his home and receive no money. The Foreclosure Consultants Law was written to protect the homeowner and is, nevertheless, a good law. It's advantageous to understand the law because, once you learn it and use the proper legal contracts, the competition will be lessened. As with any law, if you learn to live within its boundaries you will not be penalized.

There are other good points about buying before the sale. You are helping the owner, and your help will be appreciated by the motivated seller who is wise enough to sell and save some dollars to take care of his family. Owners would prefer some money before the sale to nothing at the Trustee's Sale.

The main advantage of buying before the Trustee's Sale is that you get to view the inside of the home and are able to discuss and observe any damage that might require your attention and repair before you re-sell the property. This is an advantage that the buyer at the Trustee's Sale doesn't enjoy.

An additional advantage in purchasing before the Trustee's Sale is that you will have time to review the market and appraise the property. Real estate brokers use the Multiple Listing Service (MLS) almost exclusively to find and evaluate property. The MLS is an excellent tool for comparing local values and prices and comparing neighborhoods and various sections of cities and town. The foreclosure market has no MLS. Foreclosures notices are listed in the legal newspaper, posted at the county court house, or published by one of the services that lists Trustee's Sales, defaults, and REO.

If you follow the contract provisions and appraisal techniques that are provided in this book, you will not buy a bad property.

For example, when you buy before the Trustee's Sale, you are able to hire a professional to perform a termite inspection. If the home has termite damage, you can further negotiate with the owner for a lower purchase price and if the owner refuses, you have a right to cancel the contract. You have only wasted time and not spent your money.

The advantage for you is that you will need less cash to buy from the owner than you would to buy at the Trustee's Sale. Following is an example of the cash outlay for a typical purchase.

House value	$100,000
Loan in default	$60,000
Past-due payments	$4,000
Foreclosure trustee's fees	$1,000
Total	$65,000

Let's assume that you negotiate and sign an Equity Purchase Agreement to pay the owner $5,000 in cash. Then you pay the back payments of $4,000 plus the foreclosure fees of $1,000 and assume the loan. For a cash outlay of $10,000, you have assumed $60,000 of debt and have a house with a market value of $100,000, that is, you have bought the house for 70 percent of its value. An excellent purchase.

This should also be a profitable purchase. Even if you had paid more and owned the house for $80,000, you would have made a great deal that may be better than any you might have made at the Trustee's Sale because you don't have any competitive bidders.

The biggest advantage, however, is that you have used only $10,000 of your cash. If you had purchased the property at the Trustee's Sale, you would have spent a minimum of $65,000 (the amount of the loan and fees and back payments) in cash. Having to put down so little cash, you have the ability to purchase many more distressed properties before the sale, than you would have if you had been obliged to put the full $65,000 down to buy at the Trustee's Sale. The objective is to gain profit as soon as possible. The ability to purchase numerous properties accelerates your chances of making large profits.

UNDERSTANDING THE LOAN DOCUMENTS

Preforeclosure property may be characterized as one of two types, depending on the type of documentation by which the loan was granted. The loan document will be either a Deed of Trust (Trust Deed) or a Mortgage. The legal requirements for foreclosing on delinquent loans are different depending on which document is used in your state.

THE DEED OF TRUST AS A SECURITY DOCUMENT

A Deed of Trust is a contract by which title to a property is conveyed to a Trustee as security for the repayment of a loan. This contract involves three parties. The

Trustor is the owner who borrows from the lender, or creditor, who is called the *Beneficiary.* In order to control the property during the period of the obligation, "bare legal" title is held by the *Trustee* designated in the Deed of Trust.

If the borrower does not meet the obligations of the promissory note, the lender may initiate foreclosure. If the security document is a Deed of Trust, foreclosure may be sought through a Trustee's Sale. If the security document is a Mortgage, foreclosure becomes a court action and the property will be disposed of at a Judicial Sale.

If foreclosure is sought as a Trust Deed, the beneficiary (the lender) sends a Declaration of Default to the Trustee who is then instructed to record a Notice of Default in the county in which the property is located. The foreclosure clock starts running when the Notice is recorded and the owner has three months in which to make the loan current. This is called the *reinstatement period.* At the end of this period, the Notice of Sale is recorded and published once a week for the following three weeks. At the end of this publication period, the Trustee's Sale is held at the location set by the Trustee. The successful bidder or the beneficiary receiving the property at the Trustee's Sale receives a Trustee's Deed. Foreclosure using a Trust Deed normally takes about four months or 111 days.

THE FORECLOSURE OF A MORTGAGE VERSUS A TRUST DEED

It is important to recognize several differences in the foreclosure processes for Deeds of Trust and for Mortgages. First, the original owner of a Trust Deed retains no rights after the Trustee's Sale, that is, there is no equity right of redemption as there is with a foreclosure mortgage. Conversely, nor does the original borrower have any further obligations to the lender, who may not pursue the borrower for any deficiency between the amount of money obtained at the Trustee's Sale and the amount owing to the lender. However, if the property is foreclosed as a mortgage and the debt is not a purchase money installment, the beneficiary may pursue the borrower for the difference between the amount owed and the amount collected.

A mortgage is a contract by which property in the form of real estate is *hypothecated* (pledged without delivery of title) for the repayment of a loan. This means that the mortgage could very well qualify as the security document for the promissory note offered by the borrower. The mortgage, however, has a number of features that affect the usefulness of the document as a security device should the borrower fail to meet the obligations of the promissory note. In order to understand those features, we must examine the mortgage in some detail.

A mortgage requires interaction between two parties, the borrower (the mortgagor) and the lender (the mortgagee). When the mortgagor borrows money using a mortgage, he does not relinquish title to the property even temporarily although not all of the obligations of the promissory note have been met. When the borrower defaults, the lender who expects payment must foreclose judicially, by court action. Judicial foreclosure is instituted by the mortgagee's filing a lawsuit to foreclose. The mortgagor retains the right to reinstate the obligation up to the point of the court decree. This procedure could easily take the mortgagee a year or more. Further complicating the situation is the mortgagor's right of redemption in many states. Different states have different laws regarding mortgage and Trust Deed foreclosures. Review these facts with your attorney and title company. Even when the mortgagee has successfully foreclosed on the property by a judicial action, the property owner in many states is further protected and allowed a right of redemption as a matter of state law. The right may last a very short time, one month, or as long as one year. Under the right of redemption rules, the homeowner who lost the home at the foreclosure auction is allowed to redeem the property by paying the auction sale price plus interest to the new buyer and then taking control of the property. Because state laws vary, ask the trustee or your attorney about the details.

THE BASIC STEPS OF PREFORECLOSURE BUYING

Let's briefly review the methods by which you can help defaulting homeowners solve their problems and receive a substantial reward for doing so.

After you have located a potential seller, you must make contact by telephone, by direct mail, or by knocking on the door. Your success rate will improve dramatically if you pursue all three approaches simultaneously. Then you must investigate the seller's problems. When you have found out what he needs, negotiate a purchase of his equity and, finally, sing the Equity Purchase Agreement. Remember, all the parties who signed the original deed, the Grant Deed, must sign the Equity Purchase Agreement, unless an original interest has been disposed of.

PITFALLS OF THE PREFORECLOSURE MARKET

You must be cautious and especially alert when dealing with owners who will waste your time and make you think they are going to sell to you. They will invite other foreclosure buyers to bid on your contract. When a person is in default, he or she receives mail from other foreclosure buyers and from lenders who want to lend out even more money. Expect the owners to be pursuing several alternatives. If they are not happy with your proposal, they will look until the final hour. Plan on this and keep solving their problems or you may lose your prospective bargain.

Buying before the sale is easier for you if the owner is running out of time. As you recall from the review of the foreclosure period, the homeowner has 90 days to cure the default (bring the payments current) before the start of the 21-day publication period and final Trustee's Sale. If you contact the owners immediately after the default notice is issued, they probably won't be motivated to sell. After all, 90 days plus 21 days is almost four months and the miracle they have been waiting for will certainly arrive in that time.

The really motivated sellers will answer your telephone inquiries, letters, and house calls about four to six weeks before the Trustee's Sale, when they realize that the foreclosure clock is running down. Think about the problems of the owner at this point: no money, no place to go, and no alternatives.

But don't believe that, in purchasing the equity, you have solved the owner's problems. Even if you have made a deal with the owner and he or she has nowhere to go and very little money, the problem will soon become yours. The owner will not move. Plan ahead for this contingency. Be sure the sellers understand that you will pay them only when they have left the premises and removed all of their personal possessions. And, even with such an understanding, don't expect each of the homeowners that you deal with to give you the keys and then walk away with your check. Remember, you must be a problem solver. People pay for solutions. The homeowner will need help with moving, garage sales, transferring the utilities, and a great deal of understanding. If you intend to succeed again and again you'll need to establish a positive attitude and handle the homeowner's problems.

If you do otherwise, it will be a costly mistake. Possession of the property might require that you evict the former owner. If the owner is not receiving enough money to move and get re-established, I'd suggest you pay for the move and the initial costs of renting an apartment. This cost is insignificant when compared to the time and effort of an eviction. The dollar costs will add up rapidly in the eviction process with the attorney fees, mortgage payments, property taxes, filing fees, insurance, and property damage. The owner may become hostile and could damage the property as a result. If the owner is irrational, you should probably walk away from the deal. The foreclosure marketplace is full of opportunities that make sense. Owners who try to take advantage of your good intentions will use up your time and money. Forget them and keep moving.

AUTOMATIC POSTPONEMENT

There is another type of transaction you may be inclined to walk away from, even though the seller is motivated to the point of desperation. What about the seller who contacts you one day before the sale? If you normally purchase property in California and use a Home Equity Purchase Agreement, Section 1695 of the Civil Code requires that you allow the owner a five-day right of rescission. But you don't have five days. The Civil Code in California also allows the home equity purchaser to buy the property just before it goes on the auctioneer's block. For example, even if a property is scheduled to be sold at 10:00 A.M., the law allows you to buy it at 8:00 A.M. Remember the regularly recurring theme of this book: Do your homework.

If you purchase before the Trustee's Sale, you must know what you are purchasing. You have very little time to do a thorough title search, but you *must* find out about the existence of any encumbrances or liens on the property. Don't simply shrug your shoulders and tell the owner that you can't help him.

Get a postponement. Section 2924g (6)(1) of the Civil Code in California allows the trustor (the owner) to be granted a 24-hour postponement of the sale. Check the rules that apply in your state. First have a Home Equity Purchase Agreement signed and agreed to by all parties. Then have the seller sign the Request for Automatic Postponement (see Figure 6.1). Do not simply give the Automatic Postponement document to the seller and then expect him or her to show up to sign the contract. Many sellers won't. They will get the postponement and then go shop for a better deal. This is desperation!

You need the one-day postponement to review the records at the County Recorder's Office. Then you will be knowledgeable enough to purchase the property with its known liens and encumbrances. Don't let the seller hurry you into giving him or her any cash until you are sure of the condition of title.

**Request for Automatic Postponement by Trustor
Pursuant to California Civil Code Section 2924g(c)(1)**

I/we, _____, being the trustor(s) under that deed of trust having as security property located at _____, City of _____, State of California hereby request the one-time, one business day postponement of the trustee's sale currently scheduled for _____ A.M/P.M., _____, 198___, pursuant to California Civil Code Section 2924g(c)(1) to obtain cash sufficient to satisfy the obligation secured by said deed of trust and/or bid at the sale of said property.   The   source   from   which   the   funds   are   being   obtained   is   as   follows:

_____ _____

_____.

Date: _____, 197____

_____
Trustor

_____
Trustor

Figure 6.1   Request for Automatic Postponement by Trustor

APPENDIX: CALIFORNIA CIVIL CODE FORECLOSURE LAW

judgment adjust the equities between the parties. *(Added by Stats.1961, c. 589, § 3. Amended by Stats.1971, c. 244, § 1.)*

Cross References

Purchaser's lien for amount paid, see § 3050.
Transfer of obligations, see § 1457 et seq.

§ 1693. Effect upon relief of delay in notice of rescission or in restoration of benefits

When relief based upon rescission is claimed in an action or proceeding, such relief shall not be denied because of delay in giving notice of rescission unless such delay has been substantially prejudicial to the other party.

A party who has received benefits by reason of a contract that is subject to rescission and who in an action or proceeding seeks relief based upon rescission shall not be denied relief because of a delay in restoring or in tendering restoration of such benefits before judgment unless such delay has been substantially prejudicial to the other party; but the court may make a tender of restoration a condition of its judgment. *(Added by Stats.1961, c. 589, § 4.)*

Cross References

Notice of rescission, see § 1691.

CHAPTER 2.5. HOME EQUITY SALES CONTRACTS

Section

§ 1695. Legislative findings and declarations

(a) The Legislature finds and declares that homeowners whose residences are in foreclosure have been subjected to fraud, deception, and unfair dealing by home equity purchasers. The recent rapid escalation of home values, particularly in the urban areas, has resulted in a significant increase in home equities which are usually the greatest financial asset held by the homeowners of this state. During the time period between the commencement of foreclosure proceedings and the scheduled foreclosure sale date, homeowners in financial distress,

especially the poor, elderly, and financially unsophisticated, are vulnerable to the importunities of equity purchasers who induce homeowners to sell their homes for a small fraction of their fair market values through the use of schemes which often involve oral and written misrepresentations, deceit, intimidation, and other unreasonable commercial practices.

(b) The Legislature declares that it is the express policy of the state to preserve and guard the precious asset of home equity, and the social as well as the economic value of homeownership.

(c) The Legislature further finds that equity purchasers have a significant impact upon the economy and well-being of this state and its local communities, and therefore the provisions of this chapter are necessary to promote the public welfare.

(d) The intent and purposes of this chapter are the following:

(1) To provide each homeowner with information necessary to make an informed and intelligent decision regarding the sale of his or her home to an equity purchaser; to require that the sales agreement be expressed in writing; to safeguard the public against deceit and financial hardship; to insure, foster, and encourage fair dealing in the sale and purchase of homes in foreclosure; to prohibit representations that tend to mislead; to prohibit or restrict unfair contract terms; to afford homeowners a reasonable and meaningful opportunity to rescind sales to equity purchasers; and to preserve and protect home equities for the homeowners of this state.

(2) This chapter shall be liberally construed to effectuate this intent and to achieve these purposes. *(Added by Stats.1979, c. 1029, § 1.)*

§ 1695.1. Definitions

The following definitions apply to this chapter:

(a) "Equity purchaser" means any person who acquires title to any residence in foreclosure, except a person who acquires such title as follows:

(1) For the purpose of using such property as a personal residence.

(2) By a deed in lieu of foreclosure of any voluntary lien or encumbrance of record.

(3) By a deed from a trustee acting under the power of sale contained in a deed of trust or mortgage at a foreclosure sale conducted pursuant to Article 1 (commencing with Section 2920) of Chapter 2 of Title 14 of Part 4 of Division 3.

(4) At any sale of property authorized by statute.

(5) By order or judgment of any court.

(6) From a spouse, blood relative, or blood relative of a spouse.

(b) "Residence in foreclosure" and "residential real property in foreclosure" means residential real property consisting of one- to four-family dwelling units, one of which the owner occupies as his or her principal place of residence, and against which there is an outstanding notice of default, recorded pursuant to Article 1 (commencing with Section 2920) of Chapter 2 of Title 14 of Part 4 of Division 3.

(c) "Equity seller" means any seller of a residence in foreclosure.

(d) "Business day" means any calendar day except Sunday, or the following business holidays: New Year's Day, Washington's Birthday, Memorial Day, Independence Day, Labor Day, Columbus Day, Veterans' Day, Thanksgiving Day, and Christmas Day.

(e) "Contract" means any offer or any contract, agreement, or arrangement, or any term thereof, between an equity purchaser and equity seller incident to the sale of a residence in foreclosure.

(f) "Property owner" means the record title owner of the residential real property in foreclosure at the time the notice of default was recorded. *(Added by Stats.1979, c. 1029, § 1. Amended by Stats.1980, c. 423, § 4.)*

§ 1695.2. Written contract; size of type; language; signature and date

Every contract shall be written in letters of a size equal to 10-point bold type, in the same language principally used by the equity purchaser and equity seller to negotiate the sale of the residence in foreclosure and shall be fully completed and signed and dated by the equity seller and equity purchaser prior to the execution of any instrument of conveyance of the residence in foreclosure. *(Added by Stats.1979, c. 1029, § 1.)*

Cross References

Failure to comply with this section, right of cancellation, see § 1695.5.
Requirements of this section to be provided by equity purchaser, see § 1695.6.

1695.3. Contents; survival of contract

Every contract shall contain the entire agreement of ιe parties and shall include the following terms:

(a) The name, business address, and the telephone umber of the equity purchaser.

(b) The address of the residence in foreclosure.

(c) The total consideration to be given by the equity purchaser in connection with or incident to the sale.

(d) A complete description of the terms of payment or other consideration including, but not limited to, any services of any nature which the equity purchaser represents he will perform for the equity seller before or after the sale.

(e) The time at which possession is to be transferred to the equity purchaser.

(f) The terms of any rental agreement.

(g) A notice of cancellation as provided in subdivision (b) of Section 1695.5.

(h) The following notice in at least 14-point boldface type, if the contract is printed or in capital letters if the contract is typed, and completed with the name of the equity purchaser, immediately above the statement required by Section 1695.5(a):

"NOTICE REQUIRED BY CALIFORNIA LAW

Until your right to cancel this contract has ended,

_____

(Name)

or anyone working for_____

(Name)

CANNOT ask you to sign or have you sign any deed or any other document."

The contract required by this section shall survive delivery of any instrument of conveyance of the residence in foreclosure, and shall have no effect on persons other than the parties to the contract. *(Added by Stats.1979, c. 1029, § 1. Amended by Stats.1980, c. 423, § 5.)*

Cross References

Failure to comply with this section, right of cancellation, see § 1695.5.
Requirements of this section to be provided by equity purchaser, see § 1695.6.

§ 1695.4. Right of cancellation; time and manner of exercise

(a) In addition to any other right of rescission, the equity seller has the right to cancel any contract with an equity purchaser until midnight of the fifth business day following the day on which the equity seller signs any contract or until 8 a.m. on the day scheduled for the sale of the property pursuant to a power of sale conferred in a deed of trust, whichever occurs first.

(b) Cancellation occurs when the equity seller personally delivers written notice of cancellation to the address specified in the contract or sends a telegram indicating cancellation to that address.

(c) A notice of cancellation given by the equity seller need not take the particular form as provided with the contract and, however expressed, is effective if it indicates the intention of the equity seller not to be bound by the contract. *(Added by Stats.1979, c. 1029, § 1.)*

Cross References

Return of original contract and other documents upon cancellation, see § 1695.6.

§ 1695.5. Right of cancellation; notice of right; form

(a) The contract shall contain in immediate proximity to the space reserved for the equity seller's signature a conspicuous statement in a size equal to at least 12-point bold type, if the contract is printed or in capital letters if the contract is typed as follows: "You may cancel this contract for the sale of your house without any penalty or obligation at any time before _____

(Date and time of day)

See the attached notice of cancellation form for an explanation of this right." The equity purchaser shall accurately enter the date and time of day on which the rescission right ends.

(b) The contract shall be accompanied by a completed form in duplicate, captioned "notice of cancellation" in a size equal to 12-point bold type, if the contract is printed or in capital letters if the contract is typed, followed by a space in which the equity purchaser shall enter the date on which the equity seller executes any contract. This form shall be attached to the contract, shall be easily detachable, and shall contain in type of at least 10-point, if the contract is printed or in capital letters if the contract is typed, the following statement written in the same language as used in the contract:

"NOTICE OF CANCELLATION

_____

(Enter date contract signed)

You may cancel this contract for the sale of your house, without any penalty or obligation, at any time before _____.

(Enter date and time of day)

To cancel this transaction, personally deliver a signed and dated copy of this cancellation notice, or send a telegram _____,

(Name of purchaser)

at _____

(Street address of purchaser's place of business)

NOT LATER THAN _____

(Enter date and time of day)

I hereby cancel this transaction _____.

(Date)

_____"

(Seller's signature)

(c) The equity purchaser shall provide the equity seller with a copy of the contract and the attached notice of cancellation. _(Added by Stats.1979, c. 1029, § 1. Amended by Stats.1980, c. 423, § 6.)_

Cross References

Mortgage foreclosure consultants, owner's right to cancel contract with consultant until midnight of "third business day" as defined by provision of this section, see § 2945.2.

Requirements of this section to be provided by equity purchaser, see § 1695.6.

Return of original contract and other documents upon cancellation, see § 1695.6.

§ 1695.6. Contract requirements; responsibility of equity purchaser; prohibited transactions; bona fide purchasers and encumbrancers; cancellation; return of original documents; untrue or misleading statements; encumbrances

(a) The contract as required by Sections 1695.2, 1695.3, and 1695.5, shall be provided and completed in conformity with those sections by the equity purchaser.

(b) Until the time within which the equity seller may cancel the transaction has fully elapsed, the equity purchaser shall not do any of the following:

(1) Accept from any equity seller an execution of, or induce any equity seller to execute, any instrument of conveyance of any interest in the residence in foreclosure.

(2) Record with the county recorder any document, including, but not limited to, any instrument of conveyance, signed by the equity seller.

(3) Transfer or encumber or purport to transfer or encumber any interest in the residence in foreclosure to any third party, provided no grant of any interest or encumbrance shall be defeated or affected as against a bona fide purchaser or encumbrancer for value and without notice of a violation of this chapter, and knowledge on the part of any such person or entity that the property was "residential real property in foreclosure" shall not constitute notice of a violation of this chapter. This section shall not be deemed to abrogate any duty of inquiry which exists as to rights or interests of persons in possession of the residential real property in foreclosure.

(4) Pay the equity seller any consideration.

(c) Within 10 days following receipt of a notice of cancellation given in accordance with Sections 1695.4 and 1695.5, the equity purchaser shall return without condition any original contract and any other documents signed by the equity seller.

(d) An equity purchaser shall make no untrue or misleading statements regarding the value of the residence in foreclosure, the amount of proceeds the equity seller will receive after a foreclosure sale, any contract term, the equity seller's rights or obligations incident to or arising out of the sale transaction, the nature of any document which the equity purchaser induces the equity seller to sign, or any other untrue or misleading statement concerning the sale of the residence in foreclosure to the equity purchaser.

(e) Whenever any equity purchaser purports to hold title as a result of any transaction in which the equity seller grants the residence in foreclosure by any instrument which purports to be an absolute conveyance and reserves or is given by the equity purchaser an option to repurchase such residence, the equity purchaser shall not cause any encumbrance or encumbrances to be placed on such property or grant any interest in such property to any other person without the written consent of the equity seller. _(Added by Stats.1979, c. 1029, § 1. Amended by Stats.1980, c. 423, § 7.)_

Cross References

Transfer or encumbrance of interest to third party by equity purchaser, treble damages, see § 1695.7.

Violations of this section or practice of fraud or deceit by equity purchaser, civil and criminal sanctions, see §§ 1695.7, 1695.8.

§ 1695.7. Violations by equity purchaser; civil actions; actual damages; equitable relief; attorneys' fees and costs; exemplary damages

An equity seller may bring an action for the recovery of damages or other equitable relief against an equity purchaser for a violation of any subdivision of Section 1695.6 or Section 1695.13. The equity seller shall recover actual damages plus reasonable attorneys' fees and costs. In addition, the court shall award exemplary damages or equitable relief, or both, if the court deems

§ 1695.7 CONTRACT 228 Div. 3

such award proper, but in any event shall award exemplary damages in an amount not less than three times the equity seller's actual damages for any violation of paragraph (3) of subdivision (b) of Section 1695.6 or Section 1695.13. Any action brought pursuant to this section shall be commenced within four years after the date of the alleged violation. *(Added by Stats.1979, c. 1029, § 1. Amended by Stats.1980, c. 423, § 8.)*

§ 1695.8. Violations by equity purchaser; criminal penalties

Any equity purchaser who violates any subdivision of Section 1695.6 or who engages in any practice which would operate as a fraud or deceit upon an equity seller shall, upon conviction, be punished by a fine of not more than ten thousand dollars ($10,000), by imprisonment in the county jail for not more than one year, or in the state prison, or by both that fine and imprisonment for each violation. *(Added by Stats.1979, c. 1029, § 1. Amended by Stats. 1985, c. 270, § 1.)*

§ 1695.9. Nonexclusivity of chapter

The provisions of this chapter are not exclusive and are in addition to any other requirements, rights, remedies, and penalties provided by law. *(Added by Stats.1979, c. 1029, § 1.)*

§ 1695.10. Waiver

Any waiver of the provisions of this chapter shall be void and unenforceable as contrary to the public policy. *(Added by Stats.1979, c. 1029, § 1.)*

§ 1695.11. Severability

If any provision of this chapter, or if any application thereof to any person or circumstance is held unconstitutional, the remainder of this chapter and the application of its provisions to other persons and circumstances shall not be affected thereby. *(Added by Stats.1979, c. 1029, § 1.)*

§ 1695.12. Absolute conveyance with repurchase option deemed loan transaction; rights of bona fide purchasers or encumbrancers

In any transaction in which an equity seller purports to grant a residence in foreclosure to an equity purchaser by any instrument which appears to be an absolute conveyance and reserves to himself or herself or is given by the equity purchaser an option to repurchase, such transaction shall create a presumption affecting the burden of proof, which may be overcome by clear and convincing evidence to the contrary that the transaction is a loan transaction, and the purported absolute conveyance is a mortgage; however, such presumption shall not apply to a bona fide purchaser or encumbrancer for value without notice of a violation of this chapter, and knowledge on the part of any such person or entity that the property was "residential real property in foreclosure" shall not constitute notice of a violation of this chapter. This section shall not be deemed to abrogate any duty of inquiry which exists as to rights or interests of persons in possession of the residential real property in foreclosure.

(Added by Stats.1979, c. 1029, § 1. Amended by Stats.1980, c. 423, § 9.)

§ 1695.13. Prohibited acts

It is unlawful for any person to initiate, enter into, negotiate, or consummate any transaction involving residential real property in foreclosure, as defined in Section 1695.1, if such person, by the terms of such transaction, takes unconscionable advantage of the property owner in foreclosure. *(Added by Stats.1980, c. 423, § 10.)*

Cross References

Exempt persons and firms, see Business and Professions Code § 10133.1.

§ 1695.14. Rescission

(a) In any transaction involving residential real property in foreclosure, as defined in Section 1695.1, which is in violation of Section 1695.13 is voidable and the transaction may be rescinded by the property owner within two years of the date of the recordation of the conveyance of the residential real property in foreclosure.

(b) Such rescission shall be effected by giving written notice as provided in Section 1691 to the equity purchaser and his successor in interest, if the successor is not a bona fide purchaser or encumbrancer for value as set forth in subdivision (c), and by recording such notice with the county recorder of the county in which the property is located, within two years of the date of the recordation of the conveyance to the equity purchaser. The notice of rescission shall contain the names of the property owner and the name of the equity purchaser in addition to any successor in interest holding record title to the real property and shall particularly describe such real property. The equity purchaser and his successor in interest if the successor is not a bona fide purchaser or encumbrancer for value as set forth in subdivision (c), shall have 20 days after the delivery of the notice in which to reconvey title to the property free and clear of encumbrances created subsequent to the rescinded transaction. Upon failure to reconvey title within such time, the rescinding party may bring an action to enforce the rescission and for cancellation of the deed.

(c) The provisions of this section shall not affect the interest of a bona fide purchaser or encumbrancer for value if such purchase or encumbrance occurred prior to the recordation of the notice of rescission pursuant to subdivision (b). Knowledge that the property was residential real property in foreclosure shall not impair the status of such persons or entities as bona fide purchasers or encumbrancers for value. This subdivision shall not be deemed to abrogate any duty of inquiry which exists as to rights or interests of persons in possession of the residential real property in foreclosure.

(d) In any action brought to enforce a rescission pursuant to this section, the prevailing party shall be entitled to costs and reasonable attorneys fees.

(e) The remedies provided by this section shall be in addition to any other remedies provided by law. *(Added by Stats.1980, c. 423, § 11.)*

7

How to Sell
Your Properties

And Tips on Successful Negotiating

In this chapter you will learn:

- Techniques and insights on how to sell your bargain property
- How to give your property a certain look that will favorably impress the toughest buyer
- What it really takes to be a marketing genius
- The double benefits of offering free help to charities
- How to use three checklists to fill the house with prospective buyers
- Insider information and strategies for selling and keeping revenues
- How to negotiate those successful deals.

Ask yourself if you are really excited about the property you are dealing with. If you aren't, it will probably be reflected in your efforts and in your earnings. I refuse to take on projects or certain properties if the possibilities do not excite me. From experience, I know, that my lack of enthusiasm will be reflected in the outcome of the project.

Figure 7.1 is a checklist of all the procedures and preparations that have to be made in selling a house. Make sure that these are completed before you put the property on the market.

CREATING THE MARKET

Maximum profits are a result of multiple sales. Follow up your sales program with other products to the same buyer and buyer's families or friends. In other words, try to sell your foreclosures or fixer-uppers to all the people who are associated with your prospects. Virtually everyone wants to own real estate especially when you are selling it at very attractive prices.

CHECKLIST: BEFORE YOU SELL	
ITEM TO BE COMPLETED	**DATE COMPLETED**
Home is in excellent repair/looks good	
Have a realistic sales price — check the comparables	
Have five financing programs done — S & L's, Banks, Mortgage Brokers	
Have a Mortgage Broker walk the property	
Prepare my notebook with information about schools, shops, commute routes, etc.	
Purchase my front yard sign	
Contact my home warranty agent	
Prepare my flier	
Have fliers printed	
Prepare my advertising budget	
Prepare my advertisement	
Establish the dates they will first run	
Contact the title or escrow company	
The date I will become more flexible if my house has not sold as quickly as I want	
The date I MUST move on	

© 1988 New Growth Financial

Figure 7.1   Checklist for Points before Sale

Encourage your buyers to bring their families and friends to your Open House or to your showings. Contact these buyers later with short newsletters, personal telephone calls, and fliers. Let them know that you remember them and keep them informed of your next purchase.

Past experience has taught that the customer who buys one rental or investment property will invariably buy another. For you, this makes for added earnings and profits. Remember, multiple sales is the answer. GM does it. Toyota does it. All the successful companies do it. The big names in real estate include Donald Trump, Malcolm Forbes, Gerald Hines, Tramell Crow, and Craig Hall. All of those tycoons of real estate, at one time or another, have been involved in distressed real estate.

Continually improve your follow-up to these customers and you will increase your sales each year. You will be amazed at how quickly you can establish a waiting list of buyers for your foreclosure properties.

People with common real estate interests will flock to you to purchase your foreclosure properties. They will give you valuable insight into what type of bargains they are looking for. Think about it! The clients (the buyers) telling you what they want you to buy. Yes! Telling you exactly what they want and what needs you can satisfy for them.

Most businesses are founded on the basis of solving people's problems and satisfying needs. If you become the source of bargain fixer-uppers and foreclosure properties, these hungry real estate investors will keep your telephone very busy. Your success will come from adopting a strategy that is unique rather than one that is used by all your competitors. Be yourself; be an individual.

Read the newspaper and take notice of the advertising that pertains to the markets in which you plan to buy and sell. Make a special effort to find the real estate classes given by others. Drop by and observe what they do. You will soon realize you have a big advantage because you have a totally different and unique product.

The whole market place wants fixer-uppers. Bargains! Bargains! Bargains! These are the money-makers you can profit from without waiting for inflation. You will be making money the old fashioned way; earning it with your newly gained expertise. Doctors, attorneys, bankers, accountants, real estate brokers have one thing they all recommend: fixer-uppers.

You will become financially independent by solving the problems and filling the needs of the people who want fixer-uppers. Once you become the established source of good deals and fixer-uppers, the real estate brokers will telephone you because they will recognize the good deals for their clients. This will increase your repeat business. Just as it has done for Domino's Pizza, McDonalds, Ford and all the rest, the multiple sale will carry you to success.

Listen to your clients. They will tell you what types of property they want. Listen to the bankers and the executives from the Savings & Loan Associations. They will tell you what they have to sell. It is possible to tailor-make your transactions to fit the needs of both the banker and the buyers.

Everyone wants a home to live in. Most bankers have financed homes for borrowers. The problem is: Many people cannot afford what they buy, or they get divorced, or they go bankrupt. The banker gets the property back. He has two problems. He gets no interest payment on his loan and the property itself starts to deteriorate—the lawns don't look good, the house is dirty. But the banker doesn't do business in the real estate market for homes. He does business in the money market. It is time for you to solve the problem by purchasing the property dirt cheap and selling it to any one of these hundreds of buyers who are searching for a bargain to fix up.

Your market research is to listen to your customers; they will tell you what they want. Go get it for them!! In most cases, the bargain purchaser is looking for a home to fix up and live in or a fixer-upper to rent or possibly sell. Do yourself and your customers a favor. Find the sellers of distressed property, the banks, the savings and loan associations, the homeowners. Locate all the sources. Then, when you have bought a likely looking property, advertise your fixer-upper in the local newspaper. In a short time, you'll have a waiting list of prospective purchasers. Everyone needs a place to live. Older properties require rehabilitation. Some properties need only simple improvements, such as paint, landscaping, or new appliances. These properties can bring in dollars quickly for that one person with vision and the willingness to perform the work. Sweat equity is not a joke. It is the way thousands of your friends and relatives started. Most foreclosure and distressed properties look a little run-down. With sweat equity invested in clean-up, paint, and a little creativity, these properties can be turned into solid gold.

Foreclosure buyers avoid paying too much and they avoid the overpriced properties because they buy wholesale. You are unique because you are buying at the bottom of the price range and then performing the fix-up. You won't be trapped by that villain, the negative cash flow.

Motivation plus action equals success. Before you make the wholesale purchase, whether it is at the Trustee's Sale, an REO from the bank, or a preforeclosure property from the owner, be sure you have a plan and know how you are going to sell the property. In other words, don't wait until you own it to think about selling it. Do your homework. Go out into the marketplace and ask questions of the brokers, the buyers, and your friends and relatives. Ask them what they want to buy. Then you'll know what will sell, the property price to pay, and where to concentrate your selling efforts. Find out who can afford your properties. Then interview them in depth. Find out what they want and need. Your sales efforts will be easy when you sell what the customer wants.

Attend Open Houses given by real estate brokers and builders in the neighborhood. These people will give you valuable information that you can add to your market research. Real estate brokers also know about distressed properties you can follow up on. In talking with these outside sources, attempt to develop your personality so that you have a good rapport, be friendly and likable. You'll find that people will give you more information. Remember, most people like to tell you what they know.

ADVERTISING TO BEST ADVANTAGE

Nobody will know what you have for sale until you tell them. You have an audience out there—everybody wants a bargain. Some advertising is free; some you have to pay for. Part of your homework will be to know how much it is going to cost you to re-sell the foreclosed property you just bought. Telephone your local newspaper and the large metropolitan newspapers in the immediate area and request a rate card. The rate card tells you what you get for how much and how to tell the paper what you want to say. These prices will change, but the information is always available.

Bargain-hunters are not going to be persuaded by glowing descriptions. They *know* that it won't look like a million dollars; they *know* a bargain when they see one—and hear your price. Telling them that it is a foreclosure property will tell them all they want to know about the probable condition; telling them that it's a bargain is telling them something they want to hear.

The Basics of Classified Ads

First of all you must get the reader's attention. Secondly, you show the readers what's in it for them. In other words, what is the advantage to them. People don't believe you. You must prove it in your advertisement as much as possible. The most difficult thing to do is to persuade people to take advantage of your offer. So try to solve a problem you know they have. Finally, ask for the purchase. If you don't request action from them, most people will sit back and do nothing.

When you advertise, remember that you are not alone on the page of classified advertisements. Surveys have shown that the average newspaper reader spends only 15 minutes a day reading the newspaper. Keep that statistic in mind when you write your advertisement. You must get the reader's attention by writing a headline that will have some appeal.

Most real estate buyers want a bargain or a piece of real estate that gives them an advantage over other buyers. So try to capture the reader's attention with a headline that offers a reward: more money, less work, something to make life easier. The reader must gain something. Think about how you can increase the reader's financial status, social standing, emotional security, or well being. Or take the opposite approach and point out that in buying your product, the readers will avoid risks, losses, worries, mistakes, or some undesirable condition. Think about telling them how quickly and easily you will perform or get the job completed, closing escrow, for instance.

Readers like to real headlines that start with *"How To"* followed by an explanation of something that will make life easier or richer for them. Some readers may notice headlines that ask a question and require them to read further to get the possible answer.

If you target your advertising to specific markets and types of buyers, your success rate will improve. Don't advertise to the world, pick your customer and pick the media. Foreclosures and fixer-uppers usually appeal to a certain audience. Think about that audience. What will get the attention of those particular readers? Maybe words such as Bargain, Foreclosure, Money-Saver, Make a Fortune? You will think about all those insecure buyers that don't want to or may not know how to fix up a property.

Remember, readers are thinking about themselves, not about your property. So how are you going to benefit the reader? Will you save them money? You will hit the bull's eye when you show in your advertisement how your property will benefit them. You will have their attention. Tell them your property is bigger, smaller, better located, and best available. Tell them why your property is the best.

Tell them what benefit it will confer on them. The more the advertisement shows the reader the benefits and advantages, the more response you can expect.

Start with a Good Headline

Gold Coast is a special area within the City of Alameda—use it in the headline. Local residents know this to be a prestigious and wealthy area with expensive homes. Most homes in the Gold Coast area are very expensive and are maintained to the highest standards. The headline is the attention getter because anyone looking in Alameda knows this is an expensive part of town and fixer-uppers are hard to find.

The Body of the Ad

The body of the ad explains the basics of the property. The real benefit comes at the end: $137,500—an unheard of price! We have appealed to the greed of each and every real estate broker and investor. Properties in this neighborhood showed asking prices ranging from $190,000 to $350,000. This advertisement attracted more than 60 people to an Open House. Three offers were received within two hours of the opening. One offer was ultimately accepted and the transaction was completed. The details of that transaction are described in Chapter 5.

Each reader will find a benefit that appeals to everyone: money saver, prestige, chance to strike it rich, a handyman special, work that can be done on weekends and nights, low price and a great neighborhood. In summary, the headline is the most important, followed by the appeal to the reader's interest, followed by the benefit. What makes your house the best? Answer that question and you will sell the house. In this case, it was the price.

Placement and Layout

Think about how your advertisement will look in the newspaper. Don't get fancy, you are not winning an art prize. You are trying to get the reader's attention so that he or she will stop and read about the benefits you are offering.

Spend time leafing through the classified ads and see how other advertisers write and display their ads. Try to decide what advertisements appeal to you. Remember, don't copy. Find your own style and try to be different. Your ad should contrast with those of the competition.

After you write your ad, read it out loud and say to yourself, "So what?" That is what the reader is asking himself. Answer the "so what?" What benefits and advantages will the reader gain by purchasing your foreclosure? It is difficult to sell your products if you don't offer reasons to buy them. Try to answer the questions in your ad: how?, why?, and how quickly or easily the foreclosure home will make the reader's life better.

OPEN HOUSE

The Open House is important. The prospective buyers are probably going to perform the repairs on your house; they need to see it before they even think about the price. And you need to see them. You only need one buyer for this house, but you plan to have more properties and holding a weekend or Sunday Open House is how you'll meet prospective buyers and acquire names to add to your waiting list.

Figures 7.2 and 7.3 are checklists of action to be taken before you show a property. Figure 7.2 is a rundown of chores that need to be completed to make that all-important first impression a favorable one. What the brokers call "curb-appeal" is one of the major selling points of a house, even a fixer-upper. It's much easier for a potential buyer to look favorably on what needs to be fixed-up if the exterior at least looks neat and tidy. Figure 7.3 is a list of housekeeping chores that need to be done before every Open House, even if you just did them last week.

Fliers give you a good way to get the word out. Figures 7.4 and 7.5 are examples of fliers used to advertise foreclosure property. These fliers were delivered to every house for five to seven blocks around the house we were selling, every weekend for *five* weeks, until the house was sold.

ORIGINAL SALES CHANNELS

Think of other sales channels that are different from the normal ones to sell your properties. How about sending a brochure with the details of your offering to all the brokers in your area? Explain that you are an expert in distressed property and you want to work with them. They are probably looking for good properties for their investor clients or maybe their first-time buyers.

Think about local associations of doctors, lawyers, accountants, or community groups. Send them a flier and a short PR piece about your fixer-upper. You'll be pleasantly surprised at the calls you receive.

Church and fraternal groups are always looking for new items, bargains, and money-making ideas for their newsletters and their congregations. For you their interest is advertising. Think about donating a percentage of your profit or even a set fee, if one of the members buys your fixer-upper. Consider paying a small fee for each member who walks through the house. Think about the exposure. Maybe the newspaper will cover the event. Of course, serve coffee and cookies to everyone.

Boy Scouts, Girl Scouts, will be happy to help. The list goes on and on.

With just a small amount of motivation and creativity, you'll get exposure you can't believe and you'll save thousands of dollars by not paying large brokerage commissions. The big plus is you will be helping your community while you help yourself. Don't delay! Get started! It is fascinating, as are the people you'll meet in the exciting world of real estate.

FREE ADVERTISING

How do you get the free advertising and publicity that will put you on the road to riches? Give somebody something for nothing—you'll be repaid!

Take a black and white picture of your distressed property. Send it, first class, to all the local brokers and real estate agents. They will automatically reproduce this glossy photo as photocopies and send it to all of their clients. Of

IMPRESS THE TOUGHEST BUYERS

Exterior Inspection

		Yes	No	Comment
1.	Curb clearly marked?			
2.	Lawn green?			
3.	Shrubs and trees pruned?			
4.	Exterior bugs sprayed?			
5.	Eaves freshly painted?			
6.	Side yard debris stacked?			
7.	All animal leavings cleaned?			
8.	Shrubs cleared from heating unit?			
9.	Garage cleaned; items away?			
10.	Front door cleaned?			
11.	Outside windows cleaned?			
12.	Childrens' toys put away?			

You Only Get One Chance To Make A First Impression

Figure 7.2   Checklist for Property Points (Positive Sale Points)

HOUSEKEEPING CHECKLIST

Interior Walk-Thru

		Yes	No
1.	All cobwebs cleaned?		
2.	All light fixtures cleaned?		
3.	Oven cleaned?		
4.	Drip pans on stove cleaned?		
5.	Sink sanitized?		
6.	Under the sink organized?		
7.	Linen closet organized?		
8.	Coat closet organized?		
9.	Toilet bowl flush installed?		
10.	All mildew killed?		
11.	Fixtures spotless with shine?		
12.	Inside windows cleaned?		
13.	All drapes and curtains cleaned?		
14.	Refrigerator door car polished?		
15.	Washer and dryer car polished?		

© 1988 New Growth Financial

Figure 7.3   Housekeeping Checklist

YOU WOULD HAVE TO

STEAL

THIS PROPERTY TO GET IT

CHEAPER

Drive by: 4206 Valley Avenue
Martinez, California
(East of 680)

Then call: 837-2106

Bargain Fixer-Upper

FORECLOSURE

New Growth Financial

Figure 7.4   Representative Flier for 4206 Valley Avenue, Martinez, CA

FOR SALE
LARGE FAMILY HOME

OPEN HOUSE SUNDAY 1 p.m. - 5 p.m.

- NEW PAINT
- NEW CARPET
- 1450 SQUARE FEET
- 4 BEDROOMS
- 2 BATHS

- FIREPLACE
- DISHWASHER
- 2 CAR GARAGE
- FAMILY ROOM
- AIR CONDITIONING

LOCATED IN QUIET, RESIDENTIAL NEIGHBORHOOD
EASY ACCESS TO FREEWAY
LOOKS LIKE NEW

PRICE: $169,500

9829 BROADMOOR DRIVE, SAN RAMON
CONTACT GLEN ROSE 939-1131

Figure 7.5   Open House Flier for San Ramon Property

course, they will want a commission on the sale but you can agree to paying only half their normal commission. They will be more than happy to work with you.

Send the picture to all the local churches and fraternity organizations. Don't forget the local magazines and flea market newspapers. Tell them you will pay them a sizable fee if the picture is used and you sell the property as a result. The newspapers may need filler for a particular issue and they may use the picture of your house. You can always set aside a given portion of your price to be donated in the name of the paper to a local charity. If the paper runs your picture, be sure to tell the editor your results.

Each time someone buys and fixes up a property or you buy and fix up or do any major improvements, be sure to write a short public relation (PR) piece to send to all the newspapers, magazines, and local organizations. If your skills are not in the area of PR and copywriting, hire someone, a professional, to do this for you. The importance of PR cannot be overstated. People want to know about neighborhood improvements and news. The newspapers recognize this and will give you free PR if you are creative and what you submit is newsworthy.

Find a particular reason that your property is special and interesting. Newspapers, local magazines and newsletters are all searching for interesting stories. If you issue a PR release each time you purchase a fixer-upper in a certain area, you'll soon become known as the good guy who helps the community and the local charities and neighborhoods will promote you as a helper.

The formula for success is: repeat business to the same clients. This requires name recognition. If you sell them once you will sell them again. It is exciting to hear the telephone ring without large advertising costs. PR programs that are well thought out will create a constant flow of new clients looking for fixer-uppers. This is a win-win solution. You are solving problems in your business and you will get richer for doing so.

People pay for solutions. The clients always want to know what is in it for them. Answer that question and you solve the problem.

How about this suggestion? Buy a distressed property and then sell it to a *local* investment buyer or possibly a new homeowner. Then pass on half of the profit to the local YMCA, Red Cross, or your favorite charity. The newspapers would love a story like that. The headline might read "LOCAL DISTRESSED-PROPERTY EXPERT PASSES ALONG PROFIT TO THE BALTIMORE YMCA." The Better Business Bureau, the Board of Realtors, and the Chamber of Commerce will all get behind your efforts.

Think about being called the expert. Think about the exposure to new clients who want fixer-uppers. Then you can tell them about your list of other distressed properties on which they, in turn, can make money by fixing and selling. It is a win-win situation for everyone. The charity benefits and you are perceived as the expert at solving problems. That is the way to make your fortune. Not in selling, but in solving.

How about a buy-back guarantee? The rehabilitated property will be worth more money. You could guarantee a price at which you would repurchase or buy back the property within one year. Another win-win situation. You sell your property and the buyer does not have to worry about taking a loss on the deal.

The customers who are satisfied buyers will sell the future clients if you can just get them to participate. Offer them a bonus for each client they bring.

Ask them for testimonial letters. Or better yet, offer a donation to their favorite charity in their own name. One of the fundamental human needs is for recognition. Show your clients recognition by doing something they appreciate. Get them recognition, get their names in the newspaper, sponsor something in their names. Everyone wants this type of publicity. The success formula again: Selling the same customer again and again.

Effective customer relations and PR can put you way ahead of any competition. If you are motivated to succeed, put some of those secrets you've read in this chapter to work. It could change your life.

8

Trustee's/Sheriff's Sales

How to Buy at Auction

In this chapter you will learn:

- The advantages and disadvantages of buying at a Trustee's/Sheriff's Sale
- Who is qualified to buy
- How to read Notices of Default (NODs) and Notices of Trustee's Sales
- How to analyze the numbers before the sale to ensure that you make a big profit
- The requirements of a Judicial Sale proceeding
- The principles of bankruptcy law and how it affects distressed property.

The best known market for distressed property is the Trustee's/Sheriff's Sale, which is held at the end of the foreclosure period when the defaulting owner has been unable to cure the default. The property is auctioned and if no one bids on it, it reverts to the lender. Rarely are there enough proceeds remaining from the bidding for the hapless owner to collect.

A Judicial Sale/Sheriff's Sale is held for similar reasons (nonpayment of a loan), but because it is a judicial procedure, it requires the participation of the court, and is more cumbersome, expensive, and time consuming.

Had the defaulting owner declared bankruptcy (also a legal procedure) and then still not been able to cure the default, the property could be sold for the benefit of the creditors at a Sheriff's Sale. Once again, the effect on the owner is probably the same: the owner receives little if any of the proceeds.

JUDICIAL SALES

Judicial foreclosure differs from a foreclosure under a Deed of Trust in that a court process is involved and different instruments (documents) are signed by the borrower/mortgagors, and the lender/mortgagee.

Some states use mortgages as the security instruments to secure a loan on

189

residential property. The mortgage is simply a document signed by a borrower who hypothecates (pledges) his property as security. In the event of default or nonpayment, the lender will file suit in court requesting permission to sell the property to recover the debt. If the lender's suit prevails, the court will authorize the lender to evict the borrower, reclaim, and ultimately sell the property, and finally recover the funds loaned. This process is called a judicial foreclosure. The process is cumbersome because it requires attorneys and court dates with their associated delays and extra costs. It could take a lender as long as one year to collect its principal.

In comparison, the Deed of Trust system is much simpler and because it is a matter of established law, and so does not require a court to adjudicate. Therefore, the system is referred to as a nonjudicial foreclosure. For example, when a homeowner signs a Deed of Trust, he is called the trustor and the party loaning the funds is called the beneficiary. Up to this point, the relationship is similar to that between a mortgagee (lender) and a mortgagor (borrower). However, under the Deed of Trust system, the trustor (homeowner) pledges (hypothecates) his home as security and gives a trustee, who is an independent third party, the right to sell the home at auction in the event of default or nonpayment. The beneficiary is required only to advise the Trustee of lack of payment or default. The trustee will then issue a NOD (Notice of Default) and the remaining process, a matter of law, is pretty much automatic and does not get jammed up in the court system.

SHERIFF'S/JUDICIAL'S SALES: ADVANTAGES AND DISADVANTAGES

The Trustee's/Sheriff's Sale is the auction process everyone has read about. Sales are conducted in the highly populated counties almost daily. If the property has a value above the loan amount outstanding, this is a great opportunity. The sales are listed in the legal newspapers and posted at the county courthouse and other public places. Check your state and county for the exact publication requirements.

Buying at this juncture has some advantages. One is that the Foreclosure Consultants Law does not apply, another is that you receive a deed from the trustee, a Trustee Deed. In your state, this might be a Sheriff's Deed or a Certificate of Title. The disadvantage is that the property is not accessible before the auction. In most instances, you are unable to check the roof, hire a termite inspector, or evaluate the structure or the foundation. Bid accordingly, or you'll pay the price later.

Figure 8.1 shows a Notice of Default (NOD), the legal document that alerts the owner and the public that the lender has begun the foreclosure proceeding, which, in fact, begins on the date on which the NOD is recorded. It lists the owner's indebtedness to date. But be aware that the sum of money mentioned in the default notice refers only to the particular Deed of Trust/Mortgage on which the lender has elected to foreclose, and this amount may well be only part of what is owed on the property. You must determine what other debt the property is carrying before you can calculate its probable worth to you.

Figure 8.2 shows a Notice of Trustee's Sale, which is published about a month before the scheduled sale. Check your state and county for the exact publication

125 12th Street   Suite #111
Oakland, Ca. 94607
(415)444-2682

T.S. No. _____ 5072

SPACE ABOVE THIS LINE FOR RECORDER'S USE

Notice of Default

IMPORTANT NOTICE

IF YOUR PROPERTY IS IN FORECLOSURE BECAUSE YOU ARE BEHIND IN YOUR PAYMENTS, IT MAY BE SOLD WITHOUT ANY COURT ACTION, and you may have the legal right to bring your account in good standing by paying all of your past due payments plus permitted costs and expenses within the time permitted by law for reinstatement of your account, which is normally five business days prior to the date set for the sale of your property. No sale date may be set until three months from the date this notice of default was recorded (which date of recordation appears on this notice).

This amount is $ _____ 2,074.95 _____ as of _____ March 9, 1990 _____, and will increase until your account becomes current. You may not have to pay the entire unpaid portion of your account, even though full payment was demanded, but you must pay the amount stated above.

However, you and your beneficiary or mortgagee may mutually agree in writing prior to the time the notice of sale is posted (which may not be earlier than the end of the three-month period stated above) to, among other things, (1) provide additional time in which to cure the default by transfer of the property or otherwise: or (2) establish a schedule of payments in order to cure your default; or both (1) and (2).

Following the expiration of the time period referred to in the first paragraph of this notice, unless the obligation being foreclosed upon or a separate written agreement between you and your creditor permits a longer period, you have only the legal right to stop the sale of your property by paying the entire amount demanded by your creditor.

To find out the amount you must pay, or to arrange for payment to stop the foreclosure, or if your property is in foreclosure for any other reason, contact: _____ **BARBARA GOODMAN, c/o California Trust**
NAME OF BENEFICIARY OR MORTGAGE

Deeds Inc., 125 – 12th Street, #111, Oakland, CA 94607 415/444-2682
MAILING ADDRESS.   TELEPHONE

If you have any questions, you should contact a lawyer or the government agency which may have insured your loan.

Notwithstanding the fact that your property is in foreclosure, you may offer your property for sale, provided the sale is concluded prior to the conclusion of the foreclosure. Remember, **YOU MAY LOSE LEGAL RIGHTS IF YOU DO NOT TAKE PROMPT ACTION.**

The undersigned hereby gives notice of a breach of the obligation for which the following Deed of or transfer in trust was given:

Trustor: **MIETTA JONES, also known as TOMMIETTA JONES, a single woman**
Trustee: **PLACER TITLE COMPANY**
Dated: **03/01/89**   Recorded: **03/08/89**   as Doc. No.   **89-063487**
in Book   Page   of Official Records of the County of   **ALAMEDA**
State of California, and notice of intention to sell or cause the property subject to said deed of or transfer in trust to be sold to satisfy said obligation. All sums secured by said deed of trust have been and are declared by the beneficiary to be and are immediately due and payable, by reason of said breaches.

NATURE OF BREACH: **Failure to pay installment of interest which became due 12/15/89.**

Figure 8.1   Notice of Default

NOTICE OF TRUSTEE SALE

LN No.: _____

TS No.: __90-1602__

NOTICE

YOU ARE IN DEFAULT UNDER A DEED OF TRUST DATED __SEPTEMBER 18, 1990__
UNLESS YOU TAKE ACTION TO PROTECT YOUR PROPERTY, IT MAY BE SOLD AT A PUBLIC SALE.
IF YOU NEED AN EXPLANATION OF THE NATURE OF THE PROCEEDING AGAINST YOU, YOU SHOULD
CONTACT A LAWYER.

NOTICE is hereby given that on __TUESDAY__ , the __9th__ /day of __APRIL__ 19__91__
at the hour of __10:00 A.M.__ at the MAIN STREET ENTRANCE TO THE CITY HALL,
__1666 NORTH MAIN STREET,__

in the City of __WALNUT CREEK,__ County of __CONTRA COSTA__ California.
CALIFORNIA LOAN SERVICING, INC, a California corporation as Trustee, will sell at public auction to the

highest bidder, for cash, in lawful money of the United States, all payable at the time of the sale, the follow-

ing described real property, situated in the City of __CONCORD__

County of __CONTRA COSTA__ State of California, and described as follows:

PARCEL "C" AS SAID PARCEL IS SHOWN ON PARCEL MAP FILED JULY 3, 1973
IN BOOK 28 OF PARCEL MAPS, PAGE 44, CONTRA COSTA COUNTY RECORDS.

     APN: 147-322-009

The Street address and other common designation, if any, of the real property described above is purported

to be: __1675 DAVID AVENUE, CONCORD, CA,__

The undersigned disclaims any liability for any incorrectness of the Street address or other common designa-

tion, if any, show herein.

     Said sale will/be made, but without warranty, express or implied, regarding title, possession, or encum-

brances, to pay the remaining principal sum of the note(s) secured by said Deed of Trust, with interest

thereon, as provided in said note(s), advances, if any, under the terms of the Deed of Trust, fees, charges

and expenses of the Trustee and of the trusts created by said Deed of Trust in the amount of approx-

imately $ __132,143.25__ pursuant to the power of sale conferred in that certain

Deed of Trust Executed by __CLINTON MATHIS WALKER AND JACQUELINE RUTH WALKER,__

__HIS WIFE AS JOINT TENANTS__ as Trustors, to

__NORTHWESTERN TITLE COMPANY OF ALAMEDA COUNTY,__
__a corporation,__ As Trustee,

for the benefit and security of __HERBERT R. MEYER, TRUSTEE MEYER FAMILY__
__TRUST UTD 1/1/76__

Dated, __Sep. 18, 1990__, and Recorded __Oct. 01, 1990__ Instr. No. __90-205132__
Book __16155__ Page __802__ . Official Records of the County of __CONTRA COSTA__

Figure 8.2   Trustee Notice

requirements. Again, the indebtedness to date is noted, but again, that is only as much as has accumulated on the foreclosing Deed of Trust/Mortgage.

The Trustee's/Sheriff's Sale is very businesslike and no emotions are involved. If other bidders are competing, learn from them. Grade yourself and judge your knowledge of values and your overall understanding of the market. Compare yourself with the competition. Don't let other professional bidders intimidate you. They will be worrying about you as much as you are worrying about them. Do your homework, know the resale value of the property you are bidding on, and don't get excited. Set a maximum bid and stop when the crier (auctioneer) reaches that amount. It is okay to lose the deal; I can assure you there will be more distressed property available.

Rarely will you find first-time buyers bidding at a Trustee's/Sheriff's Sale. It would be unusual to see an amateur who does not understand real estate values and the associated liabilities of buying and bidding at such a sale. That isn't to say that the sale is closed to the public; it's not. From time to time, an amateur will buy at the sale and drive the price higher than a professional like yourself (after reading this book) would consider reasonable. The amateur will get stung by paying too much. Don't worry about him. He won't be back until he has recovered his loss.

WHO'S MOTIVATED?

The major reason for bidding at the Trustee's/Sheriff's Sale is that the profit potential is very high. Foreclosure sales are outside the regular real estate market, so no laws of supply and demand prevail. Real estate brokers do not represent the sellers or the buyers in this market; even the sellers do not represent themselves. No one is trying to get the best possible price for the property. Real estate brokers and agents are not pushing for commissions and trying to drive the prices up. The bidders at the Trustee's/Sheriff's Sale are other foreclosure buyers, all of whom are trying to buy for as little as possible.

The competitive bidding process of any auction is difficult to predict. You can be assured that, if the real estate market is hot (high demand) and homes are selling fast (in less than 30 days), you'll find a lot of bidders at Trustee's/Sheriff's Sales. If the property is a bargain, which is what we are looking for, you should expect competition from other bargain hunters. If they are professionals, they will know values and not raise their bids above the value at which they can make a profit.

You should make a step-by-step analysis of your costs before you buy at a Trustee's/Sheriff's Sale.

WHAT ABOUT THE REDEMPTION PERIOD?

Redemption (the right to buy back the property even after it has been auctioned) applies after the public auction in some states. However, for REO and VA and HUD property, the redemption period will already have expired. You should review the status of judicial and nonjudicial auctions in all the states in which you want to purchase property (see Figure 8.3).

SAN BERNARDINO COUNTY

TRUSTEE SALES

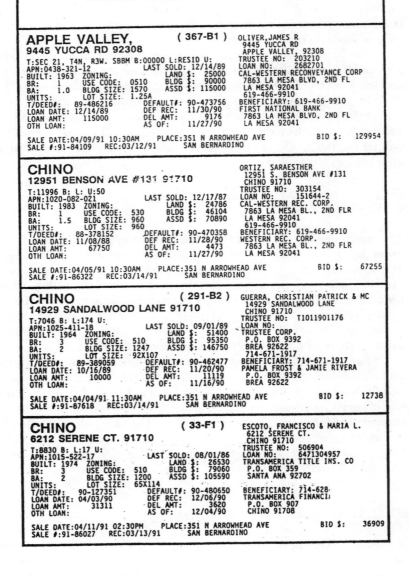

APPLE VALLEY, (367-B1)
9445 YUCCA RD 92308

```
T:SEC 21, T4N, R3W. SBBM B:00000 L:RESID U:
APN:0438-321-12          LAST SOLD: 12/14/89
BUILT: 1963  ZONING:          LAND $:   25000
BR:     1    USE CODE: 0510   BLDG $:   90000
BA:    1.0   BLDG SIZE: 1570  ASSD $:  115000
UNITS:       LOT SIZE: 1.25A
T/DEED#:  89-486216     DEFAULT#: 90-473756
LOAN DATE: 12/14/89     DEF REC:  11/30/90
LOAN AMT:    115000     DEL AMT:     9176
OTH LOAN:               AS OF:    11/27/90

SALE DATE:04/09/91 10:30AM  PLACE:351 N ARROWHEAD AVE
SALE #:91-84109   REC:03/12/91    SAN BERNARDINO
```

OLIVER,JAMES R
9445 YUCCA RD
APPLE VALLEY, 92308
TRUSTEE NO: 203210
LOAN NO: 2682701
CAL-WESTERN RECONVEYANCE CORP
7863 LA MESA BLVD, 2ND FL
LA MESA 92041
619-466-9910
BENEFICIARY: 619-466-9910
FIRST NATIONAL BANK
7863 LA MESA BLVD, 2ND FL
LA MESA 92041

BID $: 129954

CHINO
12951 BENSON AVE #131 91710

```
T:11996 B: L: U:50
APN:1020-082-021        LAST SOLD: 12/17/87
BUILT: 1983  ZONING:          LAND $:   24786
BR:     1    USE CODE: 530    BLDG $:   46104
BA:    1.5   BLDG SIZE: 960   ASSD $:   70890
UNITS:       LOT SIZE: 960
T/DEED#:  88-378152     DEFAULT#: 90-470358
LOAN DATE: 11/08/88     DEF REC:  11/28/90
LOAN AMT:    67750      DEL AMT:     4473
OTH LOAN:               AS OF:    11/27/90

SALE DATE:04/05/91 10:30AM  PLACE:351 N ARROWHEAD AVE
SALE #:91-86322   REC:03/14/91    SAN BERNARDINO
```

ORTIZ, SARAESTHER
12951 S. BENSON AVE #131
CHINO 91710
TRUSTEE NO: 303154
LOAN NO: 151644-2
CAL-WESTERN REC. CORP.
7863 LA MESA BL., 2ND FLR
LA MESA 92041
619-466-9910
BENEFICIARY: 619-466-9910
WESTERN REC. CORP.
7863 LA MESA BL., 2ND FLR
LA MESA 92041

BID $:   67255

CHINO (291-B2)
14929 SANDALWOOD LANE 91710

```
T:7046 B: L:174 U:
APN:1025-411-18         LAST SOLD: 09/01/89
BUILT: 1964  ZONING:          LAND $:   51400
BR:     3    USE CODE: 510    BLDG $:   95350
BA:     2    BLDG SIZE: 1247  ASSD $:  146750
UNITS:       LOT SIZE: 92X107
T/DEED#:  89-389059     DEFAULT#: 90-462477
LOAN DATE: 10/16/89     DEF REC:  11/20/90
LOAN AMT:    10000      DEL AMT:    11119
OTH LOAN:               AS OF:    11/16/90

SALE DATE:04/04/91 11:30AM  PLACE:351 N ARROWHEAD AVE
SALE #:91-87618   REC:03/14/91    SAN BERNARDINO
```

GUERRA, CHRISTIAN PATRICK & MC
14929 SANDALWOOD LANE
CHINO 91710
TRUSTEE NO: T1011901176
LOAN NO:
TRUSTEE CORP.
P.O. BOX 9392
BREA 92622
714-671-1917
BENEFICIARY: 714-671-1917
PAMELA FROST & JAMIE RIVERA
P.O. BOX 9392
BREA 92622

BID $:   12738

CHINO (33-F1)
6212 SERENE CT. 91710

```
T:8830 B: L:17 U:
APN:1015-522-17         LAST SOLD: 08/01/86
BUILT: 1974  ZONING:          LAND $:   26530
BR:     3    USE CODE: 510    BLDG $:   79060
BA:     2    BLDG SIZE: 1200  ASSD $:  105590
UNITS:       LOT SIZE: 65X114
T/DEED#:  90-127351     DEFAULT#: 90-480650
LOAN DATE: 04/03/90     DEF REC:  12/06/90
LOAN AMT:    31311      DEL AMT:     3620
OTH LOAN:               AS OF:    12/04/90

SALE DATE:04/11/91 02:30PM  PLACE:351 N ARROWHEAD AVE
SALE #:91-86027   REC:03/13/91    SAN BERNARDINO
```

ESCOTO, FRANCISCO & MARIA L.
6212 SERENE CT.
CHINO 91710
TRUSTEE NO: 506904
LOAN NO: 6471304957
TRANSAMERICA TITLE INS. CO
P.O. BOX 359
SANTA ANA 92702
BENEFICIARY: 714-628-
TRANSAMERICA FINANCI/
P.O. BOX 907
CHINO 91708

BID $:   36909

Figure 8.3 Notice of Trustee Sales in San Bernardino County

The rules governing the redemption period are different from state to state and for different types (residential/farm) property. First determine the rules for your state and then learn the exceptions to the rules, if any. It is possible to purchase at the auction (which may be called a Sheriff's Sale in your state) and find that the homeowner who loses the property at the sale has as long as a year in which to redeem the property. This is a business risk that you must evaluate prior to bidding at the auction sale. From a practical standpoint, you must consider the fact that the party redeeming the property will be required to pay cash plus an interest rate of return on your investment. This requirement tends to reduce the likelihood of most redemptions.

In other states, such as California, the sale is final and the homeowner (trustor) has no right of redemption. However, procedures vary from state to state, so check the codes and statutes for your state.

BANKRUPTCY

Bankruptcy law and probate law are complicated and the details are beyond the scope of this book, but a brief outline will suffice as an introduction. A person or business may file for bankruptcy at any federal bankruptcy court, and in doing so must report all assets and liabilities as well as income. Immediately upon receipt of the bankruptcy filing, an automatic stay goes into effect, stopping all creditors from enforcing collection actions and usually preventing lawsuits until the Stay is lifted. Thus, bankruptcy temporarily stops the foreclosure process and any property involved may not be sold until the bankruptcy court lifts the stay.

The federal bankruptcy code is administered by courts and the trustees, and the federal system in most cases takes precedence over the state court system. The sections of the bankruptcy code that buyers of distressed property should concern themselves will include Chapter 7, which results in a liquidation of debt, and the more commonly used Chapters 11 and 13, which enable corporations and individuals, respectively, to attempt to reorganize and pay off the debt.

Chapter 7

Chapter 7 is commonly used when an individual or a business has liabilities that exceed assets and there is little possibility that the debtor will be able to pay the debts even if the payments are postponed to a future date. The estate (the assets) are assigned to a Trustee in Bankruptcy who will sell them. The proceeds are then distributed to the creditors on a pro rata basis. Taxes are always paid first unless a court order prevents their payment. Then wages are paid and, finally, unsecured liens. The holders of secured liens, for example, real estate loans, must look to their security (the property itself) for a return of their investment.

Chapter 11

Chapter 11 consists of that section of the code that applies to the reorganization of businesses. If a business is attempting to continue to function, the management require relief from creditors in order to operate at all. The business will file for a

Chapter 11 (reorganization) bankruptcy. Creditors may or may not appoint a creditors' committee. A committee, if formed, has the responsibility to assist the court and management with the reorganization of the debtor's commitment, including the reduction of wage and labor costs and release from union contracts. Continental Airlines provides a good example of Chapter 11 bankruptcy. The company abrogated the union contract, was therefore able to reduce labor costs significantly, and so survived. If successful, Chapter 11 companies will pay creditors over a period of time. If not, the creditors' committee and management will develop a plan to liquidate the assets and distribute the proceeds to the creditors.

Chapter 13

Chapter 13 is for individuals who hope to work out a repayment program. Individuals can find themselves in various difficulties, such as those caused by a death in the family, divorce, medical expenses, and loss of work for extended periods. Bills accumulate rapidly. If the individual is employed steadily, but needs time to make payments to creditors, a repayment plan is permitted under Chapter 13 protection. The bankruptcy court will, as in all bankruptcies, require reports of progress and will issue guidance. The bankrupt individual must be capable of paying current debts on secured loans in addition to paying the agreed (possibly compromised) debts on past due bills. If the bankrupt individual is still unable to meet his or her commitments, the court will require that the assets be liquidated and the assets divided among the creditors.

What Should a Foreclosure Buyer Be Cautious of Regarding Bankruptcies?

If you plan to buy before the Trustee's or Sheriff's Sale or at the sale itself, find out if the seller is in bankruptcy. If the homeowner has filed for protection under Chapter 13 of the bankruptcy code, and many of them have, you as a preforeclosure buyer cannot purchase the home without court approval. The sellers don't always realize this fact, or possibly they may forget to mention it to you. This oversight can waste your time and money because the work that you perform and any money you pay the seller will disappear; the court will more than likely rule that the creditors have first rights on the debtor's equity in the home anyway. As always—*ask* the seller about bankruptcy.

If the property is in bankruptcy, the lender will request from the court a relief of stay in order to sell the property at an auction sale. Lenders usually plead that their equity is in jeopardy and that the security is marginal or deteriorating. If the court approves, and it usually does, the lender will receive permission to foreclose and sell at a Trustee's/Sheriff's Sale. If the lender is granted a relief of stay by the court, the only alternatives for the trustor/homeowner is to pay cash for the loan delinquency (which is unrealistic if one is in bankruptcy) or allow the sale to proceed and accept the associated loss of equity, if equity is available.

Can Bankruptcy Cause Trouble after the Trustee's Sale?

Be aware that the bankruptcy laws are federal, not state, laws. If the real estate has been sold prior to a Trustee's or Sheriff's Sale under a state law, the sale can be set aside under the federal bankruptcy law if, in the court's opinion the property was sold for substantially less than its fair market value or if some other unreasonable action occurred. Creditors can petition the court to make such a ruling if they suspect unfairness or think they can increase the settlement from the ultimate distribution of funds.

But don't pass up property that comes on the market as a probable bankruptcy sale. The potential to make a lot of money is there for that motivated person who is willing to learn about the gray or unknown areas of the law.

TRUSTEE'S/SHERIFF'S SALES

In your search for the bargain purchases, attend at least four or five actual auctions (Trustee's/Sheriff's Sales). There are several reasons for attending an actual auction:

1. You have plenty of cash and want a bargain property, you don't have time to follow all the other methods in this book.
2. The current debt is too high and if purchased before the auction there wouldn't be any profit potential. For example, the 1st and 2nd loan amount to more than the property is worth. After the auction, the second is extinguished.
3. The seller won't sell before the auction . . . doesn't make sense but it happens every day.
4. The seller has disappeared and can't be located.

Auctions present opportunities, but also have traps. That's why you should attend numerous auctions before making a bid and then only after thorough research. Here's some of the things you can expect.

1. The auction is relatively quick and sometimes only two or three minutes and it's over. Don't be late or you'll miss your chance to bid.
2. Many more people will attend than bid. Expect to see small groups but most of them are spectators. Expect the auctioneer to verify everyone's qualifications before the auction. Most auctioneers will request identification and a certified check or cash up to the amount you intend to bid. Without verification, you don't know who you are bidding against, and if he or she is qualified to raise the price and cause you to bid higher than you have planned.
3. Bidding may start at a strange level, therefore, you should know what is owned so there won't be any surprises. The bid could be for a second mortgage above a first. Know what you are buying! Don't bid up a second mortgage without knowing exactly what is due on the first. Don't forget about taxes and other liens that may have a superior position to the lien which you are bidding on. Research the title and the encumbrances or don't be a player. You could end up bankrupt by taking on more debt than you can handle.

4. If you are the high bidder on a second, you can take over the first loan. If the bank is the high bidder on the second loan they can substitute you as the new owner at a later date. Go to the sale and make a deal with the bank later and you won't need to use all your cash.

Expect one of three events to occur at the Trustee's/Sheriff's Sale:

1. The sale is postponed. (This happens more often than not.)
2. The bank is high bidder and gets the property back. In the all-cash states, the bank gets the property as much as 95 percent of the time. In the states that don't require all cash, the bank still gets the property most of the time up to 75 percent.
3. A private investor/purchaser like yourself is the high bidder and ends up with the bargain purchase. After the sale it's OK to make a deal with this person because they may be willing to give you a bargain just to turn the profit quickly. Think about that, you could do the same with other bidders?

PROBLEMS

If the homeowner is still in the house and you're the successful bidder at the Trustee/Sheriff Sale it will be your responsibility to remove the occupant. The legal process to remove the occupant physically from a house you acquire at a Trustee/Sheriff's Sale can take months. Meanwhile, you are responsible from the date of the sale for principal, interest, taxes, and insurance payments.

The law is written to protect tenants, even those who don't pay their debts. The judge most likely doesn't own any rentals, and is not and never has been a landlord. The judge assumes you are a slumlord, and you are evil and gouging poor people for rent so you can get wealthy from the rent you charge.

A good research book regarding evictions is *The Landlord Law Book,* by Nolo Press. Rules of the Trustee's/Sheriff's Sales differ from state to state. In some states, cash is needed the day of the auction and it varies from 10 percent to 100 percent of the sale price. The rules vary so it is imperative that you review the rules with your local sheriff and attorney. For example, in some states if you bid and win, then change your mind after placing a deposit, you can forfeit your deposit and be held libel.

WHAT TO DO BEFORE ATTENDING A TRUSTEE'S/SHERIFF'S SALE

Verify before attending the auction:

- Sale/Auction has not been postponed
- The banks or lenders bidding instructions to the auctioneer. Bankers sometimes will take their loss on the property at the sale; if that's the case, don't bid above the price they will get for it. You can probably buy the property after the sale for less than the minimum sale price to the public.

- Cash deposit requirements
- Cash required and when it is due
- Type of payment required, that is, cashier's check, certified check, or money order
- Don't make the check payable to an institution, make it payable to yourself. Then you can endorse it over to the auctioneer. Otherwise, you may not be able to cash the checks or put them back in your account since they are made payable to an outsider.

Obtain your local foreclosure procedures and bidding instructions from your sheriff's office or clerk of the court. Your county may or may not provide written procedures. In the rare case where they do not you'll need to research the rules or have an attorney review them with you.

Steps before the Trustee's/Sheriff's Sales

Determine market value using comps, comparables, appraisals, computer sources, DAMAR and DATAQUICK, title company property profiles and drivebys.

Establish your maximum bid and stick with it. Some bidders get caught up in the excitement and forget the objective is not to win the bidding but to get a good deal.

Last minute cancellations occur quite frequently. Telephone on the day of the auction to verify time, place, and minimum bid. The auctions are frequently cancelled or postponed because the sellers file for bankruptcy to prevent or delay the sale. Another reason for postponement could be that an investor such as yourself has put up the money to stop the foreclosure.

At the auction, qualify the other bidders. Only qualified bidders, with certified funds, are supposed to bid. If the auctioneer doesn't qualify the bidders you could be bidding against yourself because the other party does not have any money.

Determine your cash needs. Will you need all the cash or will it only require a deposit. How much of a deposit? When will you have to come up with the remaining balance? Hours? Days? Weeks? This is all very important information. If you default, will you lose your deposit? Upon re-auction can you be held responsible for any deficiencies between your original bid and the new bid?

What are your intentions for the property? Fix-up, sell in the retail market, or a quick turn around? Fast bucks or the last bucks?

What will you do if the property is auctioned at the sale to the lender? You could write a letter and tell them you observed the Trustee/Sheriff Sale and you want an appointment to discuss the possible purchase of the property. At this point, the property is an REO, and will end up on the new persons desk. He won't even know that he was the high bidder, since the paper work will take days or maybe weeks to reach him or her. You might end up with a realtor at this point or possibly the institutional lender will have a staff member handle the situation. In either case, you want to make an offer and you already probably know more about the questioned property than the lender.

As we have stated earlier in the chapter, foreclosure laws of each state are involved and sometimes complicated. In most states, there is a variety of methods in which a lender may foreclose. Real Estate law firms are the experts in the liquidation laws and will provide the specific information regarding the statutes in your state.

Readers should understand the concepts of power of sale foreclosure and a judicial foreclosure and in a few states the strict methods of foreclosure. The various methods are dictated by the state laws. The method of foreclosure is further dictated by the language of the security instrument.

POWER OF SALE FORECLOSURE

This is the most common method of foreclosure. It is used primarily in the western and southern states. The law in these states allows the borrower to waive the right to a court proceeding in the event of a default. This waiver or provision is included in the language of the security instrument (loan document). The instrument's language must specify the notice period and terms under which the foreclosure sale may occur. Each state's statutes provide for minimum period of notice to prevent abuses by the lenders.

In most power of sale states, the most common security instrument (loan document) is a deed of trust/trust deed. The trust deed is a three-party instrument. The parties involved include the Trustor (borrower), the Trustee (independent third party) and the Beneficiary (lender). The Trustee holds title to the property for the benefit of the Trustor borrower. This right to hold title is granted to the Trustee in the language of the trust deed. The trustee also hold the title to the property for the benefit of the beneficiary. Again, this is outlined in the language of the trust deed. The trustee's only legal rights are to act as a fiduciary and only execute the responsibility that is granted in the trust deed instrument.

If the Trustor borrower defaults, the Trustee is given the right (empowered) to serve notice in the required manner to the Trustor. This is usually accomplished at the request of the lender (beneficiary). The trustee must act as a fiduciary, that is, person of trust, and only act within the confines of specific state statutes.

Assuming default by the Trustor/borrower, the Trustee is empowered to serve the notice of default. Again, this is usually at the request of the lender and was authorized by the signing of the trust deed by the Trustor at the time of the initial borrowing. The notice is in a legal form which is published in the newspaper. The state statutes will allow for the exact details of publication and exposure to the public. Following the specific notice periods and publication, the property may be sold at a public auction.

Power of sale foreclosure, in most cases, is faster and less expensive than other methods of foreclosure. Although there are cases where a lender may want to foreclose via the judicial method. Your attorney will be your adviser. An example of a judicial foreclosure would be if a deficiency judgment is desirable and not obtainable under the power of sale method.

JUDICIAL FORECLOSURE

The judicial foreclosure is the second most common method of foreclosure. The judicial foreclosure proceeding takes place in the county where the property is located. The process takes place in the court room or other place designated by the judge.

Judicial foreclosure states use a mortgage which is a two-party instrument. The parties involved are the mortgagee/lender and the mortgagor/borrower.

The judicial action is different from state to state and specified in the state's statutes. The following similarities are common to most states that use the judicial foreclosure process.

The above summary is incomplete and the reader should be aware that this simplified analysis is compiled for instruction purposes. Many of the states will require more steps for this to be a completed process.

Step 1—Filing the Complaint

This is the initial step. The complaint is filed in the county in which the property is located and names all parties that may have an interest in the property. The attorney will usually file a lis pendens at the same time that the complaint is filed. The filing of the lis pendens will put the world on notice of filing litigation. The complaint will describe the nature of the default and parties involved.

When the complaint is filed, a summons is placed with the sheriff or processor for service upon all the named defendants (homeowners). The homeowners will have a specified time depending on the state laws to answer the complaint. This time will be specified in the state statutes.

Step 2—Entry of Decree of Judgment

This is the next step in the legal process. The complaint will set a time and place where the parties will come together before a judge to present their arguments. In most cases, the mortgagor (homeowner) will not appear and will be defaulted. If that is the case, the court will grant the mortgagee lender a judgment which will join (merge the terms of the note into the judgment and cut off the mortgagor's right to reinstate the note by paying the delinquent payments. The judgment will set the total debt including all fee, principal, interest and allowable advances. The judgment will also order the property sold at auction in the event the total debt is not paid.

Step 3—Notice of Foreclosure Sale

This step will let the world know that the property is going to be sold at a public auction. The announcement of the foreclosure sale will be given in a manner prescribed by the state law. This will alert all possible bidders of the pending sale so the highest possible price may be obtained through competitive bidding. This is fine in theory but the real world is . . . often only the lender will tender a bid.

Step 4—The Foreclosure Sale

The sale is held following the required notice period if the judgment amount is not paid. The sale is held at a public auction under the direction of the court. The lender is allowed to bid up the established debt without additional payment. The successful bidder will become the owner of the property, upon payment subject to redemption rights of the mortgagor if any.

Redemption Period

In some states, the law allows the mortgagor to recover the property, that is, redeem by paying the bid amount, plus interest to the successful bidder for a period after the foreclosure sale. Redemption periods are usually allowed in the agriculture states and may be extended by state law. Possession rights of the property during the redemption period vary. Review your state law for the correct timing.

Note: This short discussion is intended as a sample and is not to be used in lieu of proper counsel with an attorney in your state who is aware of the state laws that apply to the area in which you intend to purchase distressed properties.

Vermont and Connecticut have laws that allow the use of a strict foreclosure.

In this type of foreclosure, there is actually not sale of the property at an auction, as in the trust deed states. The court provides the homeowner with protection for a limited period of time. Then the creditors are given what is called a law day to bid for the property. All lien holders are given time to bid on the property and cure the loan. If none of the lien holders bid successfully and pay the 1st mortgage holder his back payments and fees due, the property will finally go to the first mortgage holder. This process can take many months and payments and penalties will be accruing.

Distressed property buyers should be alert that this type of foreclosure allows the alert buyer an opportunity to mail letters and contact the seller for a long period of time and offer to purchase his interest.

This summary is incomplete and the reader should be aware that this is a *simplified* analysis. Many states will require additional steps and procedures. Your legal counsel is your best adviser in these matters.

=9=

Real Estate
Owned (REO)

Wholesale Real Estate from the
Banks and Other Lenders

Real Estate Owned (REO) is the real estate used as collateral for loans that have foreclosed. The ownership of the property itself has reverted to the bank, insurance company, or individual lender. In this chapter, you will learn:

- How REO sales take place
- How to buy from the banks
- Who holds the REO
- Where the best deals are
- How to buy at IRS sales
- How to buy at state tax sales
- The details of the judicial foreclosure sale process.

THE PROCESS OF SELLING REO

REO have advantages and disadvantages for the foreclosure buyers. The big advantage in buying REO from the bank is that the lender has the ability to restructure the loan with favorable terms, lower interest rates, and long payment schedules. It is also possible to negotiate low down payments of approximately 5 to 10 percent, and bargain for a waiver of points and fees. There is a good possibility that the lender will even offer a discounted purchase price. But none of these advantages is guaranteed. The disadvantage is that if no member of the public bids at the Trustee's/Sheriff's Sale, the lender may have lent too much on the property or the property might be losing value for some other reason.

The foreclosure action is a result of a borrower's defaulting on a loan that was secured by real estate. Usually, a lender has lent money to the owner of a property and the property is used as security to assure the lender that the loan will be repaid. If the lender does not receive payments as promised and agreed, the lender has the authority, given when the borrower signs the trust deed or mortgage, to foreclose under the contract. In California, the buyer signs a deed of trust and a promissory note. In other states, the relevant document may be called a mortgage and promissory note.

The deed of trust (mortgage) contains a provision that requires the beneficiary (the lender) to deliver the note and deed of trust to an independent third party called a Trustee. The Trustee holds the deed of trust and note until it is paid in full. If the property owner does not pay as agreed, the beneficiary (lender) will advise the Trustee (the third party) to sell the property to the highest bidder at a Trustee's Sale and then repay the loan with the proceeds from the sale. The Trustee will advertise the property for sale in a legal newspaper and possibly in other papers of general circulation (examples shown in Chapter 8). Notices of Trustee's/Sheriff's Sales are also posted on bulletin boards in county and public buildings.

If the Trustee announces the auction (Trustee's Sale) to sell the property and no one shows up to make a competitive bid, the lender automatically bids for the property at the minimum price that the announcement advertised as the sale price. In common terms, that is referred to as "the lender bids in." The astute buyer contacts the lender after the sale and starts negotiations. If the lender is foreclosing on a property with more equity than the mortgage value, for example, a $100,000 mortgage and a $200,000 sale value, the foreclosure buyer should expect very little cooperation from the lenders. The lender knows that this type of sale will attract a crowd to the Trustee's/Sheriff's Sale. In other circumstances, the lender will be motivated to sell the property. However, being motivated does not mean that the lender will give you the property. The bank officer you talk with will be obligated to sell for the highest price possible. After all, he works for the bank, and stockholders really frown on his giving money away.

Expect no favors and don't believe everything you read in the newspapers about financial institutions going broke and just crying to rid themselves of REO. They do indeed have too many REO, but the mandate of the institutions is to make the stockholders rich—not you. If you approach the lender with a win-win attitude, you'll open the door. REO can be a gold mine, but like all mining, will take some effort and time. Remember: Bank officers are being evaluated by their superiors every day, not to mention by the bank board and the FDIC. In the negotiations, you therefore become a real opponent. Don't become obnoxious. Work at building rapport and a long-term relationship will develop. And keep in mind the negotiation techniques discussed in Chapter 6.

Who Holds REO?

Almost anyone who lends money and secures it with real estate could end up with an REO. Banks, savings and loan institutions, and insurance companies have most of the property in this category. However, let's not forget the federal government: Federal Housing Authority (FHA) and Veterans Administration (VA) foreclosures are not unusual. Together the VA and HUD/FHA foreclose on more than 40,000 homes and apartment properties each year. Even individuals who sell their property can end up with REO when the new buyers neglect to pay.

To find REO, look in the local and legal newspapers for the announcements of the Trustee's/Sheriff's Sales and subscribe to a commercial service that provides information on defaults. Contact the note holders, local and regional banks, savings and loan associations, personal property lenders (such as Morris Plan and Beneficial Finance Corporation), real estate brokers who specialize in REO, over-extended builders and developers, private owners, and credit unions.

None of these lenders is in the real estate business. Their business is in the lending of money, and every property that finds its way back to them as an REO is a mark of an unsuccessful deal. Therefore, these lenders are motivated sellers. Motivated sellers are what you need to make a success of the distressed property business. If the seller is not motivated, your chance of getting a good deal is reduced significantly.

BUYING FROM BANKS

Banks and savings and loan associations have special rules about the disposition (sale) of REO. For example, they almost always get an appraisal; they usually ask a broker or professional contractor to estimate the fix-up costs, and they usually attempt to sell the property themselves or to deal with a local broker.

If you plan to purchase from the bank or institution, you must know the value of the property before you contact the bank for an appointment. It is wise also to attend the sale to find out what price the institution paid to get the property back. With these two pieces of information you will know what you can pay and what openings there are for bargaining and negotiation. Sellers will always listen to proposals that either make their position better or eliminate risk of future loss.

If your initial telephone call does not reach the correct person at the bank, you will end up frustrated because the business of REO and foreclosure is usually one of the least advertised, least-known departments in the bank. Be sure you get the proper department and then talk to Mr. Big.

Even if you do get the right department, your initial telephone call may be surprising; you may be told that the bank has no REO. Of course, you've already been to the Trustee's/Sheriff's Sale and know that it does. The answer may be prompted by one of two reasons. The REO department may not have had the property turned over to it as yet, or if you are telephoning out of the blue, the bank will not know that you are not a stockholder checking to see if it has made any bad loans. Banks and savings and loan associations tend to be pretty closed about REO, justifiably, since REO depress their earnings. What you must do, having discovered the property identity, is to visit the institution yourself and talk to Mr. Big in the REO department. Your subsequent telephone discussions will be more candid.

Write all of the sources discussed in the previous section and tell them of your interest in purchasing REO. A few weeks later follow up with another letter. Send a series of at least three. Then begin to call on the REO departments regularly. Request meetings with the REO officer or officers and tell them what you can do for them. That is what they want to know, because REO generally creates a lot of extra work for their reluctant owners and, as noted, are frequently an embarrassment.

Telephone the real estate brokers and discuss your purchase intentions. Then visit the brokers and the government offices. Tell them again of your interest and desire to purchase. Local brokers usually have an inside track about how much activity is taking place in the local market. Take advantage of this information and do not overbid the property. Many local brokers have lists of foreclosed properties distributed by government agencies such as FHA/HUD and the Farmer's Home Administration, and these lists are updated regularly. With a simple request to the government agency you can receive these listings directly.

CAUTION

REO buyers are usually a little too anxious and show very little patience. They are fooled into thinking that theirs is the only deal in town at such a low price. Be patient and very cautious. Foreclosures, REO, tax sales, and the whole business of distressed real estate is very profitable, but if you buy the wrong house in the wrong location or one with structural or other problems, you won't profit. Keep in mind that the "as is" clause means just that; as the government contract reads: "it is your problem once you own it."

The author has seen properties purchased from the banks and savings and loan associations that did not meet local building codes. Local laws require that deficiencies be repaired and the property upgraded to standard before it may be occupied. If you are unable to rehabilitate the property, because of high costs or building restrictions, you will have a problem. It is very important you ascertain the costs of repairs and research local building codes and ordinances before you buy.

THE BEST DEALS IN REO

Unusual properties can be very profitable for the REO investor. From time to time, the Small Business Administration (SBA) will have a foreclosure. Such properties were originally used as security for loans to start businesses. Should the business fail, the SBA will have an REO (foreclosed home) on its hands. The properties may be located in better than average areas, so pursue this source and stay on the mailing list.

For investors who are knowledgeable about farming operations, Farmer's Home Administration has many foreclosures and REO. Find the local FHA office in the telephone book and call to request that your name be entered on the mailing list. These properties are special in that the new buyer must know either how to sell the property quickly or how to produce revenue to meet the mortgage payment. There is a tremendous amount of agricultural and forest land available to buyers of distressed property, but it is no business for a neophyte.

The best deals in the REO market can be expected on properties that are foreclosed upon by out-of-state investors. Many property owners find themselves unable to collect mortgage payments owed to them after they have moved to another state to retire or to work. These sellers are eager to sell their property or to lease it. It is difficult for the out-of-state owner to look after such an asset from a distance, and the property usually deteriorates rapidly.

Many alert REO investors make good deals quickly in their market. The out-of-state investor or owner may also be less knowledgeable about values or may just need the steady income that a new investor can provide. An additional benefit is the financing that sellers can provide. By financing the REO, the seller can assure the new buyer a quick deal with little competition.

IRS-FORCED SALES: BIG BUCKS FOR THE SAVVY INVESTOR

One profitable strategy for buying bargain properties is to purchase distressed or foreclosure property from the IRS. The property isn't necessarily distressed or damaged—however, the owner usually is. Distressed owners have liens filed against them and their assets (homes) and until their obligations are paid, they can in many cases be foreclosed upon. The statutes of the different states also apply, so you must research the rules for your state.

Who can foreclose or repossess property, you might ask? The IRS is a federal agency and has been granted a great deal of power. If a taxpayer does not pay taxes when due, the IRS will assess the delinquent tax and make a request for payment. If the taxpayer fails or refuses to pay, the IRS will then place liens on the personal and real property. The IRS will file (record) a Notice of Federal Tax Lien with the county recorder. This document will be recorded against all the assets of the individual or the corporation in the county where the real property is located.

After the lien has been recorded against the property, the IRS can seize and sell the property. The IRS will give the homeowner notice of the lien and also a notice of intent to seize. At this point, things get sticky for the homeowner/delinquent taxpayer. The revenue officer has great powers granted by the federal government to take many actions. The revenue officer will determine a quick sale price for the property. This may or may not produce enough revenue to completely clear the debt to the IRS.

When the sale takes place, the IRS will sell the property subject to the existing liens and mortgages that have priority to its attachment. The bidder at the auction should keep in mind that they are purchasing a property "as is" and subject to the liens that were recorded prior to the IRS Notice of Federal Tax Lien.

The IRS office or revenue agent is not required to advertise the sale of the property in any specific manner. This is different from the situation that applies with Sheriff's Sales and Trustee's Sales of real estate. Therefore, a relatively small group of investors follows the IRS Sales. This lack of publicity opens a window of opportunity for those who develop the knowledge of the sales process and the methods to track the sales.

The question in most investors' minds is: How do I locate these forced distressed sales? The answer lies in the Internal Revenue Code, which requires that a notice of sale be published at least once in a newspaper of general circulation published in the county where the property is located. If there is no newspaper of general circulation, the revenue officer is required to post notice at the post office and at least two other places. This notice must be posted at least 10 days before the sale. How do you find which paper is the paper of general circulation? That's a good question. If you live in a major metropolitan area, expect there to be numerous papers, perhaps as many as 10. The local library is a good place to research the newspapers. I suggest that you check with the local IRS office: Ask if they have a bidder's list or a hot line (telephone recording) to advise potential buyers of the availability of pending forced sales. At the same time, ask which newspaper they prefer to utilize for their advertising or announcements.

One owner lost his home when he failed to pay delinquent taxes by the time and date specified on a notice mailed to him. Another homeowner waited until the last day of his notice, the day of the sale. He was at the tax office at 12:00 noon, but was two hours late for the sale, which took place at 10:00 A.M.

State County Tax Sales General Information

The date and time of sales usually differ from one county to another within a state. While auction hours usually are scheduled during the course of the business day, many sales are completed before noon. As a buyer, you should expect many of the owners to pay their delinquent taxes between the time of the last published listing and the day of the sale. An up-to-date auction list of parcels for sale is published on a regular basis. Generally, the list of parcels being auctioned that day is provided a few hours prior to the sale. If you intend to bid, you should find this list well worth the price you may have to pay for it, although it is often free.

For most sales for delinquent taxes, the notice requires the auction to take place at the front door of the courthouse. Usually, however, the sales are actually held in an auditorium or an office inside the courthouse.

WHAT INFORMATION DO YOU NEED?

You need the same information that is needed by lawyers, sheriffs, county clerks, and tax collectors. This information is not a mystery, nor is it intentionally withheld from the public, but it is something most people are unaware of. This information is available to the public every working day in the public records.

It is paramount that property owners, bidders, and purchasers both search the county records and ask the county staff members to obtain information about the sale. You can bid effectively only if you know whether there is a redemption period or not, how and when a tax deed is acquired, whether the property is burdened by liens or has other legal problems. The answers to all these questions are in the public records of the county where the sale is conducted.

REDEMPTION RIGHTS AND OTHER REGULATIONS

In states that have redemption periods, tax sales are not an outright sale of the real property. They may instead take the form of a sale of the lien for the unpaid taxes and charges. A little research will tell you whether this is the case in your state. In addition, many states protect the owner's rights when the owner is serving in the armed forces.

Regulations may vary from state to state and among counties in states. For example, some states keep the excess amount of the bids. Others pass this money on to the seller or delinquent taxpayer. Laws are constantly being amended in state legislatures and other bodies. Plan on taking the time to get to know the laws in your particular state.

Lenders at auctions are high bidders the majority of the time. The cash requirements at the sale/auctions make the sale out of bounds for all but the most serious investors and bargain hunters.

There are many ways to track down lender-owned REO. Here are a few of them.

The Yellow Pages: Call every mortgage lender. Keep in mind that they won't tell you they have an inventory of foreclosure properties. Mail to lenders. Your state banking or savings and loan office will have the addresses. Be prepared to do numerous mailings in a short period of time to prove you are a serious investor/buyer.

Visit bank branches in your community and find the person who handles either foreclosures or repossessed property.

Follow the property after the Trustee's/Sheriff's Sale. Many of the properties will be owned by out-of-state lenders. This could be a benefit to you in your negotiations.

The remaining pages of this chapter represent typical examples of REO listings from banks and the FDIC, along with a newsletter *The Real Estate Exchange Reporter* that reports on the REO situation in many states along with RTC data. Additionally, the announcements for two different county tax sales are reproduced. Call your local assessor for the same type of information. The public notice for IRS tax sales is exactly what you would receive if your name was on their list of interested buyers. The IRS lien is typical of what is currently being filed.

COLORADO NATIONAL BANK OF DENVER

February 1, 1991

Mr. Ted Thomas
Box 5000, Suite 412
Dauville, CA 94521

RE: Real Estate Owned
     Property Information Report As of December 31, 1990

Dear Mr. Thomas:

Do you know someone who may be interested in 296.5 acres of land in the Del Camino area of Weld County which is zoned for mixed-use development? CROSSROADS DEL CAMINO has excellent access, good visibility, all utilities, favorable zoning, and terrific mountain views.

The above-referenced property is just a sample of the many Real Estate Owned properties offered by Colorado National Bankshares, Inc. in the enclosed Property Information Report. Please utilize . this confidential information for your purposes only.

Please feel free to call us if you have questions regarding any of the properties listed in the report. Colorado National Bankshares, Inc. welcomes any inquiries you may have regarding the listed properties.

We would like to extend to you our best wishes for a prosperous New Year!

Sincerely,

Leo H. Connell, Jr.
(303 892-4272)

James E. Obst
(303 899-4325)
OREO Administrators

LHC/JEB/pb
Enclosure

Seventeenth Street at Champa   Mailing Address:
Denver, Colorado 80202   P.O. Box 5168
(303) 893-1862   Denver, CO 80217

COLORADO NATIONAL BANKSHARES, INC.
REAL ESTATE OWNED
PROPERTY INFORMATION REPORT
AS OF 12-31-90

Type	Property Location	List Price	Comments and Description	Property Number	Contact
Com I	Commercial office building, I-70 & Kipling, Denver, CO	1,950,000	44,869 Sq Ft GLA multi-tenant office building built in 1983. Occupancy is approximately 75%.	01-104	Denver, Jim Obst, 899-4325
Com U	13th & Speer, Denver, CO	1,780,240	Part of triangular parcel of ground bordered by 13th, 14th, Speer and Fox streets. Located near the proposed convention center. Approx. 63,590 sq. ft. zoned B8.	01-007	Denver, Leo Connell, 892-4272
Com U	Hunter's Hill, Littleton, CO	1,400,000	7.14+ Acres located at the northwest corner of South Yosemite Street and East Dry Creek Road. Property is zoned for retail/restaurant development.	01-067	Denver, Leo Connell, 892-4272
Com U	Between Ohio & Kentucky Ave. Glendale, CO	1,250,000	Unimproved office/apartment, 5.39 acres planned site development district in City of Glendale.	01-048	Denver, Leo Connell, 892-4272
Mul U	Old Mill, Littleton, CO	1,000,000	15.4+ acre tract of land, Homestead in the Willows, filing #17. Property is zoned for multi-family residential development.	01-062	Denver, Leo Connell, 892-4272
Com U	Arapahoe & Holly, Littleton, CO	790,000	3.9+ acres located at the Southeast corner or East Arapahoe Road and South Holly Street. Zoned for retail and restaurant development. Under contract.	01-066	Denver, Leo Connell, 892-4272
Com I	2601 Blake St., Denver, CO	750,000	Combination of 2 multi story buildings, 22,545 sq. ft. office/showroom.	01-081	Denver, Leo Connell, 892-4272

Prepared by: OREO Administrators
Leo H. Connell, Jr. (303) 892-4272   James E. Obst (303) 899-4325

CNB COLORADO NATIONAL BANK OF DENVER

FDIC
Federal Deposit Insurance Corporation
P.O. Box 7549, Newport Beach, California 92658-7549•(714) 975-7213•OUTSIDE CALIFORNIA ONLY 1-800-327-FDIC

April 16, 1991

Dear Investor:

Thank you for your interest in the Federal Deposit Insurance Corporation Western Regional Marketing Packet. The Marketing Packet is updated bimonthly and offers a brief property description, listing price, and who to contact for more information.

Future mailings will include information regarding specific properties and/or special sales events. It is our intent to furnish you, the investor, with information about properties suitable to your investment needs.

The FDIC sells real estate in "as is" condition, and makes no warranties, either written or implied. Normally, the buyer makes his/her own arrangements for any financing necessary to complete the purchase.

Some of our properties are marketed by exclusive listing with real estate brokers, and any inquiries about these should be directed to the broker. For further information regarding properties not listed with a broker, please call the FDIC Real Estate Marketing Center at (800) 388-4607.

Please complete the enclosed form and return it to us if you would like to receive the next updated marketing packet. Your name will be removed from our list unless you respond using the attached form. Please type or print legibly on the enclosed form.

Sincerly,

Edward Kato
Department Head
Real Estate Owned/Marketing

EK:syl

Enclosures

/syl
a:invstmt-ltr

The following pages represent the reduced version of the actual document.

For Example:

Arizonz 6 of 66 properties are shown
California 6 of 80 properties are shown
Colorado 7 of 28 properties are shown
Hawaii all properties are shown
Idaho all properties are shown
Montana 6 properties are shown
Nevada 7 of 9 properties are shown
New Mexico 6 of 67 properties are shown
Oregon 5 of 42 properties are shown
Texas 6 of 15 properties are shown
Utah 5 of 63 properties are shown
Washington5 of 7 properties are shown
Wyoming all properties are shown

FDIC REAL ESTATE DEPARTMENT
Toll Free: 1-800-388-4607
LISTING OF REO PROPERTIES

APRIL 1991

<u>ARIZONA</u>
<u>BY CITY</u>

Bank/Asset #	Address Property Description	Type Property

APACHE JUNCTION
4105/000134001   <u>S/E Corner of Deleware Dr. & Round-Up St.</u>   <u>LAND</u>
10 acre parcel in Apache Junction. Multi family Resid.(CR-5)
Listed w/Prudential R.E./Paul Rizza/602-730-5200.
$225,000

COCHISE COUNTY

5986/451214001   <u>West of Hwy. 90, Huachuca City, Cochise County, AZ</u> <u>LAND</u>
Vacant land, approx. 74 acres.
$40,700

GILA BEND

4232/000191001   <u>Rural Route 796, Gila Bend, AZ</u>   <u>5</u> <u>LOTS/SFR</u>
5 single family residential lots.
$99,000

GILBERT

4105/000124001   <u>6 & 7 Palo Verde Rd., Gilbert AZ</u>   <u>COMM. SHOPPING CENTER</u>
comm. strip shopping center Palo Verde Rd. & Gilbert Rd.
20,200 sq. ft. of space.   **$660,000**

5986/351002001   <u>33 Riata, "The Groves", Gilbert, AZ</u>   <u>SFR</u>
Semi-custom 3,000 sq. ft. luxury home on 1/3 acre. 4
oversized bdrms and 3 baths, custom pool. Listed w/Prudential
Arizona/Candyce Hopwood/602-954-6888   **$189,000**

GLENDALE

4105/000118001   <u>Glendale, Lamar & 55th Ave., Glendale</u>   <u>M-1 LOTS</u>
4 M-1 lots approx. 7,000 sq. ft. each, located between
Glendale Ave. & Lamar Rd. Ready for construction.
$55,000

Date: _April 30, 1991_

Federal Deposit Insurance Corporation
P.O. Box 7549
Newport Beach, CA 92658-7549

ATTN: Real Estate Marketing

If you wish to continue receiving the marketing packet and for any changes in
mailing address, please complete the information requested below.

PLEASE PRINT CLEARLY TO GUARANTEE MAILING

(   ) Check here if change of address

NAME   Ted Thomas

FIRM   NEW GROWTH FINANCIAL

ADDRESS   P. O. Box 5000 #412

CITY   Danville, CA 94526

TELEPHONE #   (415) 837-2106

If we can be further assistance, feel free to contact the Marketing Department
at (800) 388-4607.

Thank you for your interest.

FEDERAL DEPOSIT INSURANCE CORPORATION
CONSOLIDATED OFFICE PHONE NUMBERS

DALLAS REGION

Oklahoma and Texas.

Oklahoma City, OK, Consolidated Office(405) 842-7441

Midland, TX, Consolidated Office(915) 685-6909

Addison, TX, Consolidated Office(214) 239-3317

Houston, TX, Consolidated Office(713) 270-6565

San Antonio, TX, Consolidated Office(512) 737-3100

Dallas, TX, Consolidated Office(214) 701-2402

CHICAGO REGION

Arkansas, Illinois, Iowa, Kansas, Louisiana, Minnesota, Missouri, Nebraska, North Dakota, South Dakota, and Wisconsin.

O'Hare, IL, Consolidated Office(708) 671-8800

Bossier City, LA, Consolidated Office(318) 742-3290

NEW YORK REGION

Alabama, Connecticut, Delaware, District of Columbia, Florida, Georgia, Indiana, Kentucky, Maine, Maryland, Massachusetts, Michigan, Mississippi, North Carolina, New Hampshire, New Jersey, New York, Ohio, Pennsylvania, Puerto Rico, Rhode Island, South Carolina, Tennessee, Vermont, Virginia, West Virginia and the Virgin Islands.

Knoxville, TN, Consolidated Office(615) 544-4500

Orlando, FL, Consolidated Office(407) 273-2230

South Brunswick, NJ, Consolidated Office(201) 422-9000

Atlanta, GA, Consolidated Office(404) 880-3120

SAN FRANCISCO REGION

Alaska, Arizona, California, Colorado, Guam, Hawaii, Idaho, Montana, Nevada, New Mexico, Oregon, Utah, Washington and Wyoming.

Irvine, CA, Consolidated Office(714) 975-3200

Denver, CO, Consolidated Office(303) 296-4703

Anchorage, AK, Consolidated Office(907) 786-6362

Financial Services of America

Call Toll Free 1-800-736-5263

LISTING	ADDRESS	CITY	STATE	PRICE	LENDER	CONTACT	PHONE	COMMENTS	DATE
9585712	3700 NORTH MAIN STREET #7	FALL RIVER	MA	48500	CROSSLAND SAVINGS	C21-HQ	800 321-2579	CONDO	01/18/91
9585605	3700 NORTH MAIN STREET #9	FALL RIVER	MA	51500	CROSSLAND SAVINGS	C21-HQ	800 321-2579	CONDO	01/18/91
9381419	4800 WESTHAVEN	FORT WORTH	TX	N/A	CROSSLAND SAVINGS	JAY JENKINS	817 625-9974	SFR	10/30/90
7204	536 GLEN EAGLE DRIVE WEST	FRIENDWOOD	TX	83000	CROSSLAND SAVINGS	PAT SHOLLAR	800 392-4497	SFR	01/28/91
8539678	3300 BL & HWY 441	GAINESVILLE	FL	290000	CROSSLAND SAVINGS	GARY JOHNSON	813 745-3482	SFR	10/30/90
6512	3905 SW 25TH TERRACE	GAINESVILLE	FL	N/A	CROSSLAND SAVINGS	LEE HORNE	801 321-7912	4-PLEX	03/12/91
8538720	3915 SW 26TH TERRACE	GAINESVILLE	FL	N/A	CROSSLAND SAVINGS	LEE HORNE	801 321-7912	SFA	03/12/91
	7717 SW 95TH LANE	GAINESVILLE	FL	60000	CROSSLAND SAVINGS	GARY JOHNSON	904 373-4279	SFR	03/12/91
	NW 23RD TERRACE & NW 62ND TERRACE	GAINESVILLE	FL	100000	CROSSLAND SAVINGS	GARY JOHNSON	813 745-3482	SFR	10/30/90
6924	US 441 & NW 23RD TERRACE	GAINESVILLE	FL	80000	CROSSLAND SAVINGS	LEE HORNE	801 321-7912	SFR	10/30/90
	WEST RIVER SALES	GALESVILLE	MD	N/A	CROSSLAND SAVINGS	LEE HORNE	801 321-7912	SLIPS	03/12/91
	5114 SBOREGATE	GARLAND	TX	N/A	CROSSLAND SAVINGS	REO DEPT	813 745-3482	SFR	03/12/91
6294	5417 WES PARADISE LANE	GLENDALE	AZ	110000	CROSSLAND SAVINGS	DON LEWIS	801 350-9601	SFR	01/14/91
0190199	522 AVENUE "J" EAST	GRAND PRAIRIE	TX	24000	CROSSLAND SAVINGS	LETA BOWELL	212 262-1800	CONDO	01/28/91
	3 DOBRE COURT	GREENLAWN	NY	N/A	CROSSLAND SAVINGS	DOREEN BOLY	800 638-7669	SFA	03/12/91
	S-132 MARIMERS INN	HILTON HEAD	SC	N/A	CROSSLAND SAVINGS	TOM RHOADS	803 785-8811	SF	10/30/90
8432031	3801 EAST BAY DR #104	BOLMES BEACH	FL	75900	CROSSLAND SAVINGS	RICHARD KESTIN	813 747-2045	CONDO	10/30/90
6393	11503 SUBURBAN DRIVE	HOUSTON	TX	11000	CROSSLAND SAVINGS	ERA BELTWAY PROPERTI	713 495-1300	DUPLEX	01/28/91
	401 BRIARCLIFF	HOUSTON	TX	N/A	CROSSLAND SAVINGS	BARBARA DAMIEO	713 890-7777	SFD	01/28/91
0211292	1304 GULF BOULEVARD #302	INDIAN ROCKS	FL	N/A	CROSSLAND SAVINGS	LEE HORNE	801 321-7912		03/12/91
0193854	20019 GULF BLVD #1	INDIAN SHORES	FL	98500	CROSSLAND SAVINGS	JOHN SEE	813 596-8181	CONDO	10/30/90
6253	4262 CUESTA	IRVING	TX	41900	CROSSLAND SAVINGS	SHIRLEY WALKER	214 258-8001	SFA	01/28/91
1178139	658 WINDCREST	KELLER	TX	N/A	CROSSLAND SAVINGS	LEE HORNE	801 321-7912		01/28/91
	318 SPRING BRANCH LANE	KENNEDALE	TX	29000	CROSSLAND SAVINGS	PAUL KRANTZ	813 745-3482	SFR	10/30/90
0342618	2804 CORNELL COVE	LAGO VISTA	TX	N/A	CROSSLAND SAVINGS	LEE HORNE	801 350-9601		03/12/91
0176693	12760 INDIAN ROCKS 1105	LARGO	FL	N/A	CROSSLAND SAVINGS	LEE HORNE	801 321-7912		03/12/91
1117910	9255 MCEAWK STREET	LAS VEGAS	NV	N/A	CROSSLAND SAVINGS	DON LEWIS	801 350-9601		01/28/91
0354746	6 VIA SPES NOSTRA	LEE CANYON	NV	185000	CROSSLAND SAVINGS	DON LEWIS	801 350-9601		01/28/91
8900004	627 EAST 111TH PLACE	LOS ANGELES	CA	N/A	CROSSLAND SAVINGS	CARMEN TORRES	213 585-1744		03/12/91
6952	6952 BEAVERLETT	MATHEW	VA	N/A	CROSSLAND SAVINGS	LEE HORNE	801 321-7912	LAND	01/28/91
	8350 GREENBORO DR #1-312	MCLEAN	VA	220000	CROSSLAND SAVINGS	EVA TSCMOANAS	703 971-3315	MULTI	10/30/90
1256419	148 SOUTH 54TH STREET	MESA	AZ	N/A	CROSSLAND SAVINGS	LEE HORNE	801 321-7912		03/12/91
1259219	160 SOUTH 54TH STREET	MESA	AZ	N/A	CROSSLAND SAVINGS	LEE HORNE	801 321-7912		03/12/91
1259209	202 SOUTH 54TH STREET	MESA	AZ	N/A	CROSSLAND SAVINGS	LEE HORNE	801 321-7912		03/12/91
0001693	3029 EAST CICERO STREET	MESA	AZ	N/A	CROSSLAND SAVINGS	DON LEWIS	801 350-9601		03/12/91
8305831	3817 EAST MINTON PLACE	MESA	AZ	N/A	CROSSLAND SAVINGS	DON LEWIS	801 350-9601		03/12/91
1256409	5346 EAST ARBOR CIRCLE	MESA	AZ	N/A	CROSSLAND SAVINGS	LEE HORNE	801 321-7912		01/28/91
	623 W GUADALUPE #228	MESA	AZ	N/A	CROSSLAND SAVINGS	BARB LOFITS	602-263-9696	CONDO	10/30/90
3173980	2437 RED RIVER STREET	MESQUITE	TX	N/A	CROSSLAND SAVINGS	ROBIN WILLIAMS	214 270-4411		01/28/91
0628016	129 WEST 86TH STREET #1	NEW YORK	NY	N/A	CROSSLAND SAVINGS	JAMES ROMAN	212 475-4200	CO-OP	01/28/91
0621359	140 WEST 69TH STREET	NEW YORK	NY	125000	CROSSLAND SAVINGS	SHEILA VOGEL	212 744-3516		01/28/91
0622753	167 PERRY STREET #2G	NEW YORK	NY	N/A	CROSSLAND SAVINGS	DON LEWIS	801 350-9601		01/28/91
0732438	77 BLEEKER STREET #104N	NEW YORK	NY	N/A	CROSSLAND SAVINGS	JAMES DOWAN	212 475-4200		01/28/91
	77 BLEEKER STREET #726	NEW YORK	NY	N/A	CROSSLAND SAVINGS	REO DEPT	813 745-3482	CONDO	10/30/90
2341611	10457 BIRKENHEAD ROAD	OKLAHOMA CITY	OK	N/A	CROSSLAND SAVINGS	MARILYN PYROR	800 558-2211		01/28/91
	60 DAVIS CUP DRIVE #104	PAGOSA SPRINGS	CO	35000	CROSSLAND SAVINGS	MARIETTA ARENDEL	813 758-1156	CONDO	10/30/90
	LONE PINE #106	PAGOSA SPRINGS	CO	49900	CROSSLAND SAVINGS	RANDY FEHRENBACHER	303 731-2262	CONDO	10/30/90
	LONE PINE #107B	PAGOSA SPRINGS	CO	35000	CROSSLAND SAVINGS	RANDY FEHRENBACHER	303 731-2262	CONDO	10/30/90
	LONE PINE #108	PAGOSA SPRINGS	CO	49900	CROSSLAND SAVINGS	RANDY FEHRENBACHER	303 731-2262	CONDO	10/30/90
	LONE PINE #109B	PAGOSA SPRINGS	CO	49900	CROSSLAND SAVINGS	RANDY FEHRENBACHER	303 731-2262	CONDO	10/30/90
5044408	48 PRICE STREET	PATCHOGUE	NY	N/A	CROSSLAND SAVINGS	DON LEWIS	801 350-9601		01/28/91
1085281	1449 EAST BASELINE ROAD	PHOENIX	AZ	N/A	CROSSLAND SAVINGS	STEVE WILKINS	602 831-1010	RSDTL	01/14/91
	2141 EAST RANCHO DRIVE	PHOENIX	AZ	N/A	CROSSLAND SAVINGS	BOB WHITE	602 953-4000	SFR	10/30/90
3015519	1613 GLENWICK DRIVE	PLANO	TX	270000	CROSSLAND SAVINGS	TCM VOGSEN	214 248-3409		01/28/91

The

Real Estate Exchange Reporter

Staying on Top of the Commercial Real Estate and REO Market

Editor: Terry Struthers   **Published by DataSource RE, Inc.**

736 7th Street   Boulder, Colorado 80302   Phone: **(303) 444-9194**   FAX: **(303) 447-2520**

February 27, 1991

Dear Ted,

DataSource RE, Inc. maintains a list of over 40,000 investment foreclosed properties nationwide. This includes about 20,000 Resolution Trust Corporation properties. The other 20,000 comes from approximately 4,000 financial institutions across the US.

We track all real estate with the exception of individual single family residences. Over 1/4 of the properties are in the state of Texas. The other states with large REO inventories are Florida, Louisiana, Oklahoma, Colorado and Arizona. The fastest growing lists are the states in the northeast. The midwest has weathered the current real estate storm the best.

The average price of a property on our database is about $1,000,000. There many apartments from 2 units to 600 units, office buildings, retail centers, land and many other bargains out there.

We believe that with the current real estate situation, land is a long term and riskier investment. On the other end of the safety spectrum are large apartment structures. These tend to lead a market out of a slump. The danger is getting in too late. That time has passed for many markets that were in the heart of the REO belt of the late 1980's.

Our newsletter tracks these trends in the foreclosed real estate inventory across the country. We sort through the data geographically and by property type and summarize what is happening with prices, sales, inventory level and make-up of the inventory. In addition we track the government institutions which control foreclosed real estate such as the Resolution Trust Corporation (RTC), FDIC, Freddie Mac, SBA, etc.

Currently, the government is in control of much of the investment real estate. I'm afraid the report card so far on the ability of these institutions (especially the RTC) to sell real estate is not too encouraging. A survey of our subscribers found that most were frustrated with their attempts to purchase properties. In fact, a vast majority said they would never go back to the RTC to purchase properties again. The rate of sales reflects this attitude. A study we did found that RTC properties were selling at 1/3 the rate of other foreclosed commercial real estate.

The good news is that there is value in the properties held by Uncle Sam and, with some persistence and the willingness to learn the government's new rules of the game, buyers can get to those properties. We have spoken to several investors who have said they have been successful in purchasing multiple properties once they have the system figured out. Another sign of hope is the announcement by the RTC that they plan to put much of the sales effort back into the public sector.

In any case, whether the property is in government hands or from banks, life insurance companies, savings and loans, or where ever, we are the nations most complete source of REO properties. I would remind you that we do not cover individual single family homes, townhome/condos or lots. Our focus is the investor market.

The following page exhibits how we display our information in the printed version and what data is included in the floppy diskette database for each property.

Sincerely,

Terry Struthers, President

TREND WATCH

Inventory Analysis
The numbers in () are results from 3 months ago.

ALASKA
Total # of Properties- 361
  REO-354 RTC-7
Value of Priced Properties - $41.3 Million
  (226 properties averaging $182 thousand/ppty)
Top 3 categories
1) Commercial buildings - $13.6 Million
2) Bulk Residential Land - $8.2 Million
3) Commercial Land - $3.4 Million
Top Cities/Metro Areas
Anchorage - $25.1 Million
Largest Non-RTC Properties
$2.5 million - 36,468 sq. ft. commercial bldg in Anchorage
$2.1 million - 36,351 sq. ft. retail bldg. in Anchorage

ARIZONA
Total # of Properties - 1,281 (1,257)
  REO-445 RTC-836
Value of Priced Properties - $1.42 Billion ($1.36 Bill.)
  (1,054 properties averaging $1.35 Million/ppty)
Top 3 categories
1) Bulk Residential Land - $350.9 Million (1)
2) Commercial Land - $304.2 Million (2)
3) Apartments - $165.0 Million (3)
Top Cities/Metro Areas
Phoenix - $1.2 Billion ($1.0 Bill.)
Tucson - $131.6 Million ($255.0 Mill.)
Largest Non-RTC Properties
$27.0 Million - 47,558 sq. ft. office bldg in Phoenix (New)
$22.4 Million - 1,427 acres of residential land in Scottsdale
$17.0 Million - 256,043 sq. ft. retail bldg. in Phoenix (New)

CALIFORNIA
Total # of Properties - 633 (623)
  REO-131 RTC-502
Value of Priced Properties - $604.0 Million ($518.1 Mill.)
  (368 properties averaging $1.64 Million/ppty)
Top 3 categories
1) Office Bldgs - $126.7 Million (1)
2) Apartment Bldgs - $57.2 Million (-)
3) Retail Bldgs - $47.4 Million (-)
Top Cities/Metro Areas
Los Angeles Metro - $232.3 Million ($220.0 Mill.)
Bay Area - $88.0 Million ($60.0 Mill.)
Largest Non-RTC Properties
$25.0 Million - 331,000 sq. ft. office bldg in San Mateo
$24.9 Million - 85,749 sq. ft. Mixed commercial in San
  Francisco
$17.5 Million - 146,044 sq. ft. office bldg in Santa Ana

COLORADO
Total # of Properties - 1,783 (1,747)
  REO-1,125 RTC-658
Value of Priced Properties - $1.07 Billion ($1.04 Bill.)
  (1,283 properties averaging $834 thousand/ppty)
Top 3 categories

1) Commercial Land - $181.1 Million (1)
2) Office Bldgs - $162.3 Million (3)
3) Apartment Bldgs - $143.8 Million (-)
Top Cities/Metro Areas
Denver Metro-$582.9 Million ($551.9 Mill.)
Colorado Springs - $251.8 Million ($144.1 Mill.)
Largest Non-RTC Properties
$15.0 Million - 864 acres of residential land in Colo.
  Springs
$15.0 Million - 124,551 sq. ft. office bldg. in Denver
$15.0 Million - 318 unit Apartment bldg in Westminster

FLORIDA
Total # of Properties - 1,785
  REO-983 RTC-802
Value of Priced Properties - $1.42 Billion ($1.14 Bill.)
  (1,362 properties averaging $1.04 Million/ppty)
Top 3 categories
1) Retail Bldgs - $277.9 Million (2)
2) Apartment Bldgs - $216.3 Million (1)
3) Residential land - $174.1 Million (-)
Top Cities/Metro Areas
Miami Metro-$310.1 Million ($166.0 Mill.)
Tampa/St. Pete - $248.1 Million ($176.3 Mill.)
Largest Non-RTC Properties
$16.5 Million - 600 unit apartment bldg. in Orlando
$16.5 Million - 449 unit Condos in Miami (Price Drop)
$16.0 Million - 23,959 sq. ft. retail bldg in Miami area

HAWAII
Total # of Properties - 1
  REO-1 RTC-0
$2.5 million for 6.8 acres of commercial land in Kailua
  Kona

IDAHO
Total # of Properties - 34
REO-31 RTC-3
Value of Priced Properties - $12.3 Million
  (28 properties averaging $439 thousand/ppty)
Top categories
1) Commercial land - $8.6 Million
Largest Non-RTC Properties
$6.0 Million - 3.17 acres commercial land in Coeur d'
  Alene

LOUISIANA
Total # of Properties - 2,660 (2,561)
REO-1,387 RTC-1,273
Value of Priced Properties - $406.4 Million ($379.0 Mill.)
  (1,362 properties averaging $178 thousand/ppty)
Top 3 categories
1) Apartment bldgs - $103.0 Million (1)
2) Residential land - $50.0 Million (2)
3) Office bldgs - $42.7 Million (3)
Top Cities/Metro Areas
New Orleans Metro-$173.2 Million ($167.2 Mill.)
Baton Rouge - $78.2 Million ($62.6 Mill.)
Largest Non-RTC Properties
$6.8 Million - 528 unit apartment bldg. in New Orleans
$4.66 Million - 196 unit Hotel in New Orleans area (New)
$3.9 Million - 304 unit apartment bldg in New Orleans

Please call us at 1-800-477-9194 or 303-444-9194 if you have further questions.

MONTANA
Total # of Properties - 26
REO-23 RTC-3

NEW MEXICO
Total # of Properties - 280 (275)
REO-93 RTC-187
Value of Priced Properties - $165.3 Million ($156.4 Mill.)
(238 properties averaging $695 thousand/ppty)
Top 3 categories
1) Residential land - $38.0 Million (1)
2) Office bldgs - $37.0 Million (2)
3) Apartment bldgs - $38.8 Million (3)
Top Cities/Metro Areas
Albuquerque - $113.5 Million ($104.3 Mill.)
Largest Non-RTC Properties
$9.3 Million - 158,782 sq. ft. retail bldg in Albuquerque
$7.0 Million - 40,000 sq. ft. office bldg in Santa Fe
$6.9 Million - 200 unit apartment bldg in Albuquerque

NEVADA
Total # of Properties - 92 (92)
REO-43 RTC-49
Value of Priced Properties - $83.6 Million ($74.9 Mill.)
(62 properties averaging $1.34 Million/ppty)
Top 3 categories
1) Apartment bldgs - $30.2 Million (1)
2) Retail bldgs - $13.2 Million (2)
3) Twmhm/Condo bldgs - $5.4 Million (-)
Top Cities/Metro Areas
Las Vegas - $49.0 Million ($37.5 Mill.)
Reno - $15.9 Million ($15.5 Mill.)
Largest Non-RTC Properties
$9.8 Million - 316 unit apartment bldg in Las Vegas
$6.9 Million - 230 unit apartment bldg in Sparks

OKLAHOMA
Total # of Properties - 1,052 (919)
REO-559 RTC-493
Value of Priced Properties - $232.6 Million ($226.3 Mill.)
(917 properties averaging $247 thousand/ppty)
Top 3 categories
1) Commercial land - $43.2 Million (2)
2) Apartment bldgs - $35.2 Million (3)
3) Office bldgs - $27.0 Million (-)
Top Cities/Metro Areas
Oklahoma City - $82.7 Million ($70.1 Mill.)
Tulsa - $63.0 Million ($85.4 Mill.)
Largest Non-RTC Properties
$8.0 Million - 67.3 acres of commercial land in Tulsa
$7.8 Million - 352 unit apartment bldg in Tulsa

OREGON
Total # of Properties - 101
REO-61 RTC-40
Value of Priced Properties - $18.7 Million
(47 properties averaging $398 thousand/ppty)
Top 3 categories
1) Residential land - $5.9 Million
2) Office bldgs - $3.4 Million
3) Industrial land - $1.6 Million
Top Cities/Metro Areas
Portland - $5.4 Million
Largest Non-RTC Properties
$1.6 Million - 47.1 acres of industrial land in Portland
$1.5 Million - 352 unit nursing home in Portland

TEXAS
Total # of Properties - 10,510 (9,584)
REO-5,096 RTC-5,414
Value of Priced Properties - $7.1 Billion ($6.7 Bill.)
(7,340 properties averaging $967 thousand/ppty)
Top 3 categories
1) Commercial land - $1.46 Billion (1)
2) Apartment blgs - $1.34 Billion (2)
3) Office bldgs - $1.04 Billion (3)
Top Cities/Metro Areas
Dallas/Ft. Worth - $2.28 Billion ($2.12 Bill.)
Houston - $1.12 Billion ($1.13 Bill.)
San Antonio - $.74 Billion ($.72 Bill.)
Austin - $.72 Billion ($.72 Bill.)
Largest Non-RTC Properties
$55.6 Million - 1.4 million sq. ft. of office space in Dallas
$40.0 Million - 321,488 sq. ft. office in Addison
$35.0 Million - 1,285 acres of commercial land in
           Carrollton

UTAH
Total # of Properties - 605
REO-305 RTC-300
Value of Priced Properties - $117.6 Million
(374 properties averaging $314 thousand/ppty)
Top 3 categories
1) Commercial land - $21.6 Million
2) Residential land - $21.6 Million
3) Resort land - $15.0 Million
Top Cities/Metro Areas
Salt Lake City - $27.8 Million
Largest Non-RTC Properties
$15.0 Million - resort land Park City
$6.4 Million - 5,306 acres agricultural land in
           Summit County

COUNTY OF SACRAMENTO
TREASURER–TAX COLLECTOR
COUNTY CLERK–RECORDER

George L. Thacher
ASSISTANT TREASURER
Willie H. Ross
ASSISTANT TAX COLLECTOR
Craig A. Kramer
ASSISTANT COUNTY CLERK–RECORDER
Christopher J. Ailman
CHIEF INVESTMENT OFFICER

John Dark
TREASURER–TAX COLLECTOR
COUNTY CLERK–RECORDER

January 30, 1991

New Growth Financial
P.O. Box 5000, #412
Danville, CA 94526

Dear Mr. Thomas:

In response to your inquiry, property in Sacramento County that have five
or more years delinquent taxes are offered for sale at public auction in
January of each year. Bids are accepted verbally and the opening bid is
not less than twenty five percent of the fair market value of the property.
Payment for property purchased at the sale must be made in full immediately
after the sale in the form of cash, cashier's check, money order or
traveler's check.

A list of properties subject to sale and other information pertaining to
the current sale is available in this office the first week of November
each year. No mailing list is maintained for request of this information.
The first week in January a copy of the final publication of tax-defaulted
properties subject to sale at public auction are mailed to parties who have
inquired about the auction and live outside the County of Sacramento. I
have enclosed a general information sheet for your information.

If you have further questions about the Sacramento County tax-defaulted
land auction, please contact the deputy listed below at the letterhead
address or phone (961) 440-6621.

Very truly yours,

WILLIE H. ROSS
Assistant Tax Collector

BY: Ellen Tubbs
    Deputy

700 H Street, Room 1710   Post Office Box 1703   Sacramento, CA 95812-1703   (916) 440-6744

IMPORTANT INFORMATION ON REAL PROPERTY

SOLD AT PUBLIC AUCTION

INSPECTION OF PROPERTY

CAUTION - INVESTIGATE BEFORE YOU BID - PHYSICAL INSPECTION OF THE PROPERTY IS STRONGLY RECOMMENDED. Do not attempt to purchase property at the auction unless an investigation has been made as to the exact location, desirability, and usefulness of the property. Parcels are sold on an 'AS IS' basis and the County in no way assumes any responsibility implied or otherwise, that the properties are in compliance with zoning ordinances and conform to building codes and permits. An investigation may reveal that the property is in a street or alley, in a flood control channel or landlocked. The structure that may be shown on the tax sale list may no longer exist at the time of the auction and a lien may have been or will be placed on the property for the removal of the structure. Regardless of its recorded description, the size, shape, or other characteristics may render the property useless.

Should a parcel have a mobile home, the sale is for the real property only and does not include the mobile home. Mobile homes are considered personal property, unless they are on a permanent foundation.

Vacant (unimproved) land (which accounts for most property offered at our tax sale) may not have an address, therefore, the approximate geographic location can be determined through the use of the County Assessor's Plat Maps. Exact boundary lines of property can only be determined by a survey of the property, initiated at the purchaser's expense. Parcel maps are available for inspection and/or purchase prior to the tax sale in the Assessor's Office, 700 "H" Street, Room 1650, Sacramento, CA 95814.

To determine what use can be made of the property, consult the Zoning Department of the City if the parcel is located within the city limits or Zoning Information for the County Planning Department if the parcel is located in the unincorporated areas of the County. The County Recorder's Office records may show information regarding recorded easements on a property.

BIDDING PROCESS

Anyone who wishes to bid on property offered for sale MUST FIRST REGISTER AND BE ASSIGNED A BID CARD before the auction begins. Please return the bid card to the registration table when leaving the sale.

The property will be offered in item number order. All sales are final and must be paid for immediately, unless the successful bidder wishes to continue bidding for other properties. **Should the successful bidder make a mistake and bid on the wrong property, the sale will remain final.**

No bid will be accepted for less than the minimum price as defined by Revenue and Taxation Code Section 3698.5. State law dictates that the minimum bid for a public auction tax sale parcel shall be no less than 25% of the County Assessor's fair market value, as determined within one year prior to the date of the tax sale. However, a minimum bid for a parcel can be set at a greater amount to ensure collection of the amount of delinquent taxes, penalties and costs thereon.

This is an oral public auction requiring verbal bids on the properties. Bidding will be in increments of $100.00 until the parcel is sold to the highest bidder. Higher increments are acceptable should the bidders wish to expedite the sale.

A purchase agreement is required to be signed by the successful bidder following the sale of each item offered. Payment in full of the amount bid, plus documentary stamp tax prescribed by County ordinance, is required to be paid at the time of the sale. **All sales will be for cash in lawful money of the United States, certified check, cashier's check, or travelers check.** No credit transactions are accepted. **PERSONAL CHECKS WILL NOT BE ACCEPTED.** All checks should be made payable to the purchaser and endorsed over to the Sacramento County Treasurer-Tax Collector in payment of a successful purchase. This will allow the purchaser to negotiate those checks not used. **Bidders should have proper funds on hand at the time the sale begins. No opportunity will be given for any successful bidder to leave the sale and go to the bank.** No cash refunds, other than for cash payments, will be made at the time of sale. All refunds for payments made by certified funds will be issued by County warrant within sixty (60) days following the date of sale.

Any property for which no bid is received at the time it is first offered, will be reoffered at the end of the sale.

TAX DEED

All successful bidders must complete a deed information sheet for each parcel. Since the information you provide on the deed information sheet is used to complete the recorded tax deed, it is of the utmost importance that it is correct and complete. Receipts of payment showing all deeding information will be mailed to the purchaser within seven days after the sale. These receipts should be checked carefully for any errors in deeding information so that the purchaser may notify the Treasurer-Tax Collector of corrections before the recording of the tax deeds. Approximately four weeks after the date of purchase, a tax deed will be recorded by the Treasurer-Tax Collector. After recordation, the deeds will be returned to the respective purchasers by the County Recorder. **Should title to the property you purchased be recorded incorrectly due to your failure to provide the correct information, IT WILL BE YOUR RESPONSIBILITY TO CORRECT THE TITLE.**

Example of styles of vesting:

> John Doe and Mary Doe, husband and wife as joint tenants
> John Doe and Mary Doe, husband and wife as community property
> Mary Doe, a married woman, as her sole and separate property
> John Doe, a single man, as his sole and separate property
> John Doe, a single man, as to a $1/2$ undivided interest and Mary Doe, a
>   single woman as to a $1/2$ undivided interest

TITLE INSURANCE

Title companies **MAY NOT** issue their policy of title insurance on a notice of power to sell tax-defaulted property for one year, **unless** a quiet title action has been successfully pursued in the courts, or in lieu thereof, quit claim deeds are acquired from the former owner and every lien holder.

INCUMBRANCES

Pursuant to Section 3712 of the Revenue and Taxation Code, tax deeds convey title to the purchaser free of all prior incumbrances of any kind **EXCEPT**:

A)   Any lien for installments of special assessments, which installments will become payable upon the secured roll after the time of sale.

B)   The lien for taxes or assessments or other rights of any taxing agency which does not consent to the sale under this chapter.

C)   Liens for special assessments levied upon the property conveyed which were, at the time of the sale under this chapter, not included in the amount necessary to redeem the tax-defaulted property, and, where a taxing agency which collects its own taxes has consented to the sale under this chapter, not included in the amount required to redeem from sale to the taxing agency.

D)   Easements constituting servitude upon or burdens to the property; water rights, the record title to which is held separately from the title to the property; and restrictions of record.

E)   Unaccepted, recorded, irrevocable offers of dedication of the property to the public or a public entity for a purpose, and recorded options of any taxing agency to purchase the property or any interest therein for a public purpose.

F)   Unpaid assessments under the Improvement Bond Act of 1915 (Division 10 [commencing with Section 8500] of the Streets and Highway Code) which are not satisfied as a result of the sale proceeds being applied pursuant to Chapter 1.3 (commencing with Section 4671) of Part 8.

G)   Effective July 1, 1989, any Federal Internal Revenue Service Liens pursuant to provisions of Federal Law, may not be discharged by the sale, even though the Tax Collector has provided proper notice to the Internal Revenue Service before that date.

Pursuant to Section 3725 of the California Revenue and Taxation Code, a proceeding based on alleged invalidity or irregularity of any proceeding instituted under this chapter can only be commenced within one year after the date of execution of the Tax Collector's deed. Therefore, purchasers may find it prudent to delay any improvement on the property for this one year period.

As a convenience, some bond information is provided, but its accuracy is not guaranteed. If property is encumbered with foreclosed or unforeclosed street bonds, irrigation assessments, income tax liens, etc., a notice of power to sell tax-defaulted property may or may not discharge these obligations. A notice of power to sell tax-defaulted property will not abolish easements constituting servitudes upon or burdens to the property.

ALL SALES ARE FINAL, UNLESS, the County Board of Supervisors rules them invalid. If the sale is ruled invalid, all of the purchase price will be refunded.

Any additional information concerning this sale, can be obtained by contacting the Sacramento County Treasurer-Tax Collector, Tax-Defaulted Land Unit at (916) 440-6621.

CONTRA COSTA COUNTY TAX COLLECTOR'S OFFICE
ALFRED P. LOMELI, TREASURER-TAX COLLECTOR
1991 PUBLIC AUCTION INFORMATION SHEET

The 1991 Public Auction of tax-defaulted property in Contra Costa County will be held:

WEDNESDAY, FEBRUARY 27, 1991   10:00 a.m.

Room 107, McBrien Administration Building, 651 Pine Street, Martinez, CA

****

THE TAX COLLECTOR'S OFFICE RESERVES THE RIGHT TO WITHDRAW ANY PARCEL FROM THE AUCTION LIST.

Redemptions on parcels on the list must be made by the close of business on the last business day <u>PRIOR</u> to the date the sale begins. Redemptions by mail must also be <u>received</u> on the last business day prior to the date the sale begins.

<u>MINIMUM BID</u> is one half (½) of Fair Market Value. However, minimum bid on a parcel can be set at a greater amount to assure collection of the amount of tax and penalties.

Parcel ownership CAN NOT be obtained by paying off the back taxes.

To bid at the Auction, a <u>Certified Check</u>, for $100.00 should be received by the Tax Collector's Office at least two weeks prior to the date of the sale, <u>AND NOT LATER</u> than the close of business on the last business day <u>prior</u> to the date of the sale. Checks should be made payable to either "Alfred P. Lomeli," or "Contra Costa County Tax Collector." If mailed, it should be sent to Tax Collector, P.O. Box 631, Martinez, CA 94553, Attention: Redemption.

The check can be applied toward the purchase price. If you are not a successful bidder, your deposit will be returned within fifteen days.

Purchases of property at the Auction must also pay a <u>Documentary Transfer Tax</u> on the amount of the bid. The tax is based on the rate of $ .55 for each $500.00 or <u>fractional part of each $500.00</u> when the bid exceeds $100.00. The following example shows amounts required.

Amount of Bid	Increase It By Another:	Necessary Transfer Tax
$ 0.00 to 100.00	$.00	$ .00
100.01 to 500.00	.55	.55
500.01 to 1,000.00	.55	1.10
1,000.01 to 1,500.00	.55	1.65
1,500.01 to 2,000.00 etc	.55 etc.	2.20 etc.

Puchasers of property within the City of Richmond must also pay a Richmond City Transfer Tax in addition to the Documentary Transfer Tax. The rate is $7.00 per $1,000.00 of the purchase price. For example:

Amount of Bid	Richmond Transfer Tax
$ 0.00 to 1,000.00	$ 7.00
1,000.01 to 2,000.00	14.00

Property purchased at the Auction must be <u>PAID FOR IN FULL</u> at the Auction. Cash and personal checks will be accepted. If the purchase price is $50,000.00 or greater, a credit transaction will be accepted. The purchaser must deposit $5,000.00 or ten percent (10%) of the purchase price, whichever is greater. The transaction MUST be completed within 90 days.

Map books of the parcels are available for public inspection at the Tax Collector's Office. Copies may be bought at the Assessor's Office: 834 Court St., Martinez, M-F, 8-12 & 1-4.

For further information contact the Redemption Department of the Tax Collector's Office: Room 100, 625 Court St., Martinez, CA, M-F 8-5, (415) 646-4122
Mailing Address: Tax Collector, P.O. Box 631, Martinez, CA 94553, Attn: Redemption

ITEM	PARCEL NO.	ASSESSEE	SITE	CITY/AREA	MINIMUM BID
PUBLIC AUCTION SALE					
2.	159-060-038	David & Patricia Kavert	4075 Folsom Ct	Concord	147,500
3.	430-260-014	Wayne & Evelyn Eng	N. Rancho Pl	Pinole	61,000
4.	430-260-021	Wayne & Evelyn Eng	N. Rancho Pl	Pinole	62,000
5.	430-260-027	Wayne & Evelyn Eng	N. Rancho Pl	Pinole	60,000
6.	513-162-004	Ethel Dotson	396 South St	Richmond	8,000
7.	529-180-011	Advance Mortgage Corp	2213 Burbeck Ave	Richmond	45,000
8.	534-072-017	Patricia Williams	709 Pennsylvania Ave	Richmond	3,300
9.	538-161-014	L.C. & Louise Campbell	225 MacDonald Ave	Richmond	22,500
10.	538-310-003	Mark Jr. & Jettie Mae Lowe	418 Bissell Ave	Richmond	8,000
11.	538-360-009	Frank Torres, Ronald Williams	26 2nd St	Richmond	7,000
12.	550-171-025 formerly 550-171-011	Frederick Ross	S. 3rd St	Richmond	1,750
13.	561-151-016	Buelah Mae Mason	233 Willard Ave	Richmond	3,000
14.	561-152-012	M.E. & Peggy Richards	Vernon Ave	Richmond	7,000
16.	218-420-004	E. Thomas Eck III, Tre	San Ramon Valley	San Ramon	75,000
17.	148-440-017	Robert Hooker	1346 Las Juntas Way # D	Unincorp	77,500
18.	409-021-020	Theodore Stills	Vernon Ave	Unincorp	2,000
20.	409-060-026	Alma Electric Co	1628 1st St	Unincorp	3,500
21.	409-131-013	James & Corina Ray	1733 7th St	Unincorp	2,000
22.	409-240-019	Lola Robinson	3rd St	Unincorp	2,600
23.	409-262-007	Nathaniel & Mary Evans	1926 4th St	Unincorp	4,400
24.	416-102-009	Marion & Rosemary Mc Craw	2716 Road 20	Unincorp	7,500

Additional Information:

If title is requested to be vested in other than the actual purchaser, a notarized letter stating the manner in which title shall be vested must be submitted.

ATTACHMENT TO NOTICE OF PUBLIC AUCTION SALE

John R. Doe

Description of Property Continued:

EXCEPTING THEREFROM:

That portion thereof conveyed to State of California by deed recorded February 20, 1967 in Book 5309 of Official Records, page 244.

Assessors Parcel No. 071-050-036

Site Address: 2764 Lone Tree Way
Antioch, CA 94509

Commonly known as: 200 San Joaquin Ave, 206/206A San Joaquin Ave
Antioch, CA 94509 Antioch, CA 94509

Department of the Treasury / Internal Revenue Service

Notice of

Public Auction Sale

Under the authority in Internal Revenue Code section 6331, the property described below has been seized for nonpayment of internal revenue taxes due from

John R. Doe   440 OLD HWY 4; ANTIOCH, CA   94509

The property will be sold at public auction as provided by Internal Revenue Code section 6335 and related regulations.

Date of Sale: THURSDAY MAY 9,   19 91

Time of Sale: 10:00   am - pm

Place of Sale: 2850 SHADELANDS DRIVE; WALNUT CREEK, CA   94598

Title Offered: Only the right, title, and interest of ___John R. Doe___
in and to the property will be offered for sale. If requested, the Internal Revenue Service will furnish information about possible encumbrances, which may be useful in determining the value of the interest being sold (See the back of this form for further details.)

Description of Property: The following described real property in the City of Antioch, County of Contra Costa, State of California: A portion of the Northeast one quarter of Section 25, Township 2 North, Range 1 East, Mount Diablo Base and Meridian, more particularly described as follows:

A parcel bounded on the East by a public road whose Western boundary intersects the section line on the North boundary of Section 25, Township 2 North, Range 1 East, at a point 615 feet, more or less, West of the Northeast corner of Section 25, the Western boundary of said public road extending therefrom in a direction that is approximately South $2°$ 48' East, said parcel being more particularly described as follows:

Beginning at a point on the Western boundary of a public road described above which point bears South $2°$ 48' East 8.20 feet from the intersection of said road boundary with a fence line marking the North line of Section 25, forming the line between lands of Fitzpatrick and Uren, thence from said point of beginning, South $2°$ 48' East, 100 feet; thence South $89°$ 57 West, 185.8 feet; thence North $2°$ 48' West 100 feet; North $89°$ 57' East 185.9 feet to the point of beginning.

CONTINUED ON PAGE 2

Property may be Inspected at: ___200, 206 / 206A San Joaquin Avenue, Antioch, CA   94509___
(DRIVE BY ONLY)

Payment Terms:
☐ Full payment required on acceptance of highest bid
☒ Deferred payment as follows: 20% at time of sale, balance in full no later that 12 o'clock noon Friday May 17, 1991

Form of Payment: All payments must be by cash, certified check, cashier's or treasurer's check or by a United States postal, bank, express, or telegraph money order. Make check or money order payable to the Internal Revenue Service.

Signature	Name and Title *(Typed)*	Date
Jeanne Kurtz	Jeanne Kurtz Revenue Officer	04-22-91
Address for Information About the Sale		Phone
2850 Shadelands Drive; Walnut Creek, CA 94598		946-0894

Form **2434** (Rev. 3-84)

FORM 2434-B (Rev. Sept. 1985)	Department of the Treasury — Internal Revenue Service **Notice of Encumbrances Against or Interests in Property Offered for Sale**

As of this date, the following are the encumbrances against or interests in the property (as described in the Notice of Public Auction or Notice of Sealed Bid Sale) that was seized for nonpayment of Internal Revenue taxes due from: John R. Doe

Some of these encumbrances or interests may be superior to the lien of the United States.

Type of Encumbrance or Interest	Amount of Encumbrance or Interest	Date of Instrument Creating Encumbrance or Interest	Date and Place Recorded	Name and Address of Party Holding Encumbrance or Interest	Date of Information
Deed of Trust	$ 43,056.86	11-10-82	11-16-82 Contra Costa Co. Recorders Office Martinez, CA 94553	East Bay Mortgage Inc. 250 Juana Avenue Suite 210 San Leandro, CA 94577	04-24-91
Deed of Trust	123,462.60	09-19-89	09-27-89 Contra Costa Co. Recorders Office Martinez, CA 94553	East Bay Mortgage Inc. 250 Juana Avenue Suite 210 San Leandro, CA 94577	04-24-91
Notice of Federal Tax Lien	44,226.19	02-05-90	02-08-90 Contra Costa Co. Recorders Office Martinez, CA 94553	Internal Revenue Service	04-24-91
Notice of Federal Tax Lien	20,492.84	02-05-90	02-08-90 Contra Costa Co Recorders Office Martinez, CA 94553	Internal Revenue Service	04-24-91
Deed Of Trust	8,845.84	05-03-90	05-11-90 Contra Costa Co Recorders Office Martinez, CA 94553	Founders Title Company 3000 Clayton Road Concord, CA 94519	04-29-91
Notice of Federal Tax	3,818.09	11-29-90	12-10-90 Contra Costa Co Recorders Office Martinez, CA 94553	Internal Revenue Service.	04-24-91

NOTE: The Internal Revenue Service does not warrant the correctness or completeness of the above information, and provides the information solely to help the prospective bidders determine the value of the interest being sold. Bidders should, therefore, verify for themselves the validity, priority, and amount of encumbrances against the property offered for sale. Each party listed above was mailed a notice of sale on or before 04-29-91   (date) .

Signature *Jeanne Kurtz*	Name and Title (typed) Jeanne Kurtz Revenue Officer	Date 04-29-91

FORM 2434-B
(Rev. Sept. 1985)

Department of the Treasury — Internal Revenue Service

Notice of Encumbrances Against or Interests in Property Offered for Sale

Authority and Effect of Sale

Pursuant to authority contained in sections 6331 and 6335 of the Internal Revenue Code and the regulations thereunder, and by virtue of a levy issued by authority of the District Director of Internal Revenue, the right, title, and interest [in the property described in the notice of sale] of the taxpayer [whose name appears on the reverse side of this document] will be sold.

Such interest is offered *subject* to any prior outstanding mortgages, encumbrances, or other liens in favor of third parties, which are valid against the taxpayer and are superior to the lien of the United States. The reverse of this document provides information regarding possible encumbrances or interests which may be useful in determining the value of the interest being sold. All interests of record were mailed a notice of sale.

The property will be sold "as is" and "where is" and without recourse against the United States. The Government makes no guaranty or warranty, expressed or implied, as to the validity of the title, quality, quantity, weight, size, or condition of the property, or its fitness for any use or purpose. No claim will be considered for allowance or adjustment or for rescission of the sale based upon failure of the property to conform with any representation, expressed or implied.

Notice of sale has been given in accordance with legal requirements. If the property is offered by more than one method, all bids will be considered tentative until the highest bid has been determined. The property will be sold to the highest bidder, and the sale will be final upon acceptance of the highest bid in accordance with the terms of the sale.

Payment must be made by cash, certified check, cashier's or treasurer's check or by a United States Postal, bank, express, or telegraph money order. All checks or money orders must be made payable to the Internal Revenue Service. A certificate of sale will be delivered to the successful bidder as soon as possible upon receipt of full payment of the purchase price.

Section 6339(c) of the Code states that a certificate of sale of personal property given or a deed to real property executed pursuant to section 6338 will discharge that property from all liens, encumbrances, and titles which are junior to the federal tax lien by virtue of which the levy was made. If real property is involved, section 6337 of the Code provides that the taxpayer, his or her heirs, executors, or administrators, or any person having an interest therein, or lien thereon, or any person in behalf of the taxpayer may redeem real property within 180 days from the date of its sale by the Internal Revenue Service. The redemption price to be paid to the successful bidder is the successful bid price plus 20 percent per year interest from the date of payment by the successful bidder to the date of redemption. If the property is not redeemed within the 180-day period, the District Director shall, upon receipt of the certificate of sale, issue a deed to the purchaser, or his assignee.

Form **668(Y)**

(Rev. January 1989)

Department of the Treasury - Internal Revenue Service

Notice of Federal Tax Lien Under Internal Revenue Laws

District	Serial Number	For Optional Use by Recording Office
Sacramento	53421	

As provided by sections 6321, 6322, and 6323 of the Internal Revenue Code, notice is given that taxes (including interest and penalties) have been assessed against the following-named taxpayer. Demand for payment of this liability has been made, but it remains unpaid. Therefore, there is a lien in favor of the United States on all property and rights to property belonging to this taxpayer for the amount of these taxes, and additional penalties, interest, and costs that may accrue.

RECORDED AT REQUEST OF

MAR 2 5 1991

AT _____ O'CLOCK ____ M.

CONTRA COSTA COUNTY RECORDS

STEPHEN L. WEIR COUNTY RECORDER

FEE $ ____

Name of Taxpayer

John Doe

Residence

Main Street, Harris, CA

IMPORTANT RELEASE INFORMATION: With respect to each assessment listed below, unless notice of lien is refiled by the date given in column (e), this notice shall, on the day following such date, operate as a certificate of release as defined in IRC 6325(a).

Kind of Tax (a)	Tax Period Ended (b)	Identifying Number (c)	Date of Assessment (d)	Last Day for Refiling (e)	Unpaid Balance of Assessment (f)
1120	12/31/89		11/05/80	12/05/00	$35,000

Place of Filing
County Recorder
Contra Costa County
Martinez, CA

Total $ 35,000

This notice was prepared and signed at ___ Walnut Creek, CA ___ , on this,

the __25th__ day of __March__ , 19 __91__ .

Signature	Title
	Revenue Officer

(**NOTE:** Certificate of officer authorized by law to take acknowledgments is not essential to the validity of Notice of Federal Tax lien Rev. Rul. 71-466, 1971 - 2 C.B. 409)

Form **668(Y)** (Rev. 1-89)

Part 3 - Taxpayer's Copy

Department of the Treasury
Internal Revenue Service

Notice of Federal Tax Lien Filing

This Notice of Federal Tax Lien has been filed as a matter of public record.

Penalty and Interest accrue until the liability is paid.

Excerpts From Internal Revenue Code

Sec. 6321. Lien For Taxes.

If any person liable to pay any tax neglects or refuses to pay the same after demand, the amount (including any interest, additional amount, addition to tax, or assessable penalty, together with any costs that may accrue in addition thereto) shall be a lien in favor of the United States upon all property and rights to property, whether real or personal, belonging to such person.

Sec. 6322. Period Of Lien.

Unless another date is specifically fixed by law, the lien imposed by section 6321 shall arise at the time the assessment is made and shall continue until the liability for the amount so assessed (or a judgment against the taxpayer arising out of such liability) is satisfied or becomes unenforceable by reason of lapse of time.

Sec. 6323. Validity and Priority Against Certain Persons.

(a) Purchaser's, Holders Of Security Interests, Mechanic's Lienors, And Judgment Lien Creditors. — The lien imposed by section 6321 shall not be valid as against any purchaser, holder of a security interest, mechanic's lienor, or judgment lien creditor until notice thereof which meets the requirements of subsection (f) has been filed by the Secretary.

(f) Place For Filing Notice; Form. —

(1) Place For Filing - The notice referred to in subsection (a) shall be filed -
(A) Under State Laws
(i) Real Property - In the case of real property, in one office within the State (or the county, or other governmental subdivision), as designated by the laws of such State, in which the property subject to the lien is situated; and
(ii) Personal Property - In the case of personal property, whether tangible or intangible, in one office within the State (or the county, or other governmental subdivision), as designated by the laws of such State, in which the property subject to the lien is situated; or
(B) With Clerk Of District Court - In the office of the clerk of the United States district court for the judicial district in which the property subject to lien is situated, whenever the State has not by law designated one office which meets the requirements of subparagraph (A), or
(C) With Recorder Of Deeds Of The District Of Columbia - In the office of the Recorder of Deeds of the District of Columbia, if the property subject to the lien is situated in the District of Columbia.

(2) Situs Of Property Subject To Lien - For purposes of paragraphs (1) and (4), property shall be deemed to be situated -
(A) Real Property - In the case of real property, at its physical location; or
(B) Personal Property - In the case of personal property, whether tangible or intangible, at the residence of the taxpayer at the time the notice of lien is filed.
For purposes of paragraph (2) (B), the residence of a corporation or partnership shall be deemed to be the place at which the principal executive office of the business is located, and the residence of a taxpayer whose residence is without the United States shall be deemed to be in the District of Columbia.
(3) Form - The form and content of the notice referred to in subsection (a) shall be prescribed by the Secretary. Such notice shall be valid notwithstanding any other provision of law regarding the form or content of a notice of lien.

Note: See section 6323(b) for protection for certain interests even though notice of lien imposed by section 6321 is filed with respect to:

1. Securities
2. Motor vehicles
3. Personal property purchased at retail
4. Personal property purchased in casual sale
5. Personal property subjected to possessory lien
6. Real property tax and special assessment liens
7. Residential property subject to a mechanic's lien for certain repairs and improvements
8. Attorney's liens
9. Certain insurance contracts
10. Passbook loans

(g) Refiling Of Notice. — For purposes of this section -

(1) **General Rule.** — Unless notice of lien is refiled in the manner prescribed in paragraph (2) during the required refiling period, such notice of lien shall be treated as filed on the date on which it is filed (in accordance with subsection (f)) after the expiration of such refiling period.

(2) **Place For Filing.** — A notice of lien refiled during the required refiling period shall be effective only -
(A) If -
(i) such notice of lien is refiled in the office in which the prior notice of lien was filed, and
(ii) in the case of real property, the fact of refiling is entered and recorded in a.. index to the extent required by subsection (f) (4), and
(B) in any case in which, 90 days or more prior to the date of a refiling of notice of lien under subparagraph (A), the

Secretary received written information (in the manner prescribed in regulations issued by the Secretary) concerning a change in the taxpayer's residence, if a notice of such lien is also filed in accordance with subsection (f) in the State in which such residence is located.

(3) **Required Refiling Period.** — In the case of any notice of lien, the term "required refiling period" means -
(A) the one-year period ending 30 days after the expiration of 6 years after the date of the assessment of the tax, and
(B) the one-year period ending with the expiration of 6 years after the close of the preceding required refiling period for such notice of lien.

Sec. 6325. Release Of Lien Or Discharge Of Property.

(a) Release Of Lien. — Subject to such regulations as the Secretary may prescribe, the Secretary shall issue a certificate of release of any lien imposed with respect to any internal revenue tax not later than 30 days after the day on which -

(1) Liability Satisfied or Unenforceable - The Secretary finds that the liability for the amount assessed, together with all interest in respect thereof, has been fully satisfied or has become legally unenforceable; or

(2) Bond Accepted - There is furnished to the Secretary and accepted by him a bond that is conditioned upon the payment of the amount assessed, together with all interest in respect thereof, within the time prescribed by law (including any extension of such time), and that is in accordance with such requirements relating to terms, conditions, and form of the bond and sureties thereon, as may be specified by such regulations.

Sec. 6103. Confidentiality and Disclosure of Returns and Return Information.

(k) Disclosure of Certain Returns and Return Information For Tax Administration Purposes. —

(2) Disclosure of amount of outstanding lien. - If a notice of lien has been filed pursuant to section 6323(f), the amount of the outstanding obligation secured by such lien may be disclosed to any person who furnishes satisfactory written evidence that he has a right in the property subject to such lien or intends to obtain a right in such property.

INSTRUCTIONS ON HOW TO APPLY FOR

Certificate of Discharge of Property From Federal Tax Lien

Department of the Treasury   **Internal Revenue Service**

Publication 783 (Rev. 1-84)

Submit your typewritten application and all accompanying documents in triplicate to:

District Director of Internal Revenue

(Address to District in which the property is located)

Attention of : Chief, Special Procedures Staff

Given Date of Application

Information required on application

Please give the name and address of the person applying, under section 6325 ( )( )( ) of the Internal Revenue Code, for a certificate of discharge. Give the name and address of the taxpayer, and describe the property as follows:

1. Give a detailed description, including the location of the property for which you are requesting the certificate of discharge. If real property is involved, give the description as contained in the title or deed to the property, and the complete address (street, city, state). If the certificate is requested under section 6325 (b)(1), also give a description of all the taxpayer's property remaining subject to the lien.

2. Show how, and when the taxpayer has been, or will be, divested of all rights, title and interest in and to the property for which a certificate of discharge is requested.

3. Attache a copy of each notice of Federal tax lien, or furnish the following information as it appears on each filed notice of Federal tax lien:
- the name of the Internal Revenue District;
- The name and address of the taxpayer against whom the notice was filed
- The date and place the notice was filed

4. List the encumbrances (or attach a copy of the instrument that created each encumbrance) on the property which you believe have priority over Federal tax lien. For each encumbrance show:
- The name and address of the holder;
- A description of the encumbrance;
- The date of the agreement;
- The date and place of the recording, if any;
- The amount due as of the date of the application, if known (show costs and accrued interest separately);
- Your family relationship, if any to the taxpayer and to the holder of any other encumbrances on the property.

5. Itemize all proposed or actual costs, commissions and expenses of any transfer or sale of the property.

6. Furnish information to establish the value of the property for which you are applying for a certificate of discharge. In every case furnish an estimate of the fair market value of the property which will remain subject to the lien, In addition,
- If private sale - Submit written appraisals by two disinterested people qualified to appraise the property, and a brief statement of each appraiser's qualifications.
- If public sale (auction) already held - Give the date and place the sale was held, and the amount for which the property was sold.
- If public sale (auction) to be held - Give the proposed date and place of the sale , and include a statement that the United States will be paid in its proper priority from the proceeds of the sale.

7. Give any other information that might in your opinion, have bearing upon the application.

8. Furnish any other specific information the District Director requests.

9. If you are submitting the application under the provisions of section 6325(b)(3), dealing with the substitution of proceeds of sale, attach a copy of the proposed agreement containing the following:
- Name and address of proposed escrow agent:
- Caption, type of account, name and address of depositary for the account;
- Conditions under which the escrow fund is to be held;
- Conditions under which payment will be made from escrow, including the limitation for negotiated settlement of claims against the fund;
- Estimated cost of escrow;
- Name and address of any other party you and the District Director determine to be a party to the escrow agreement;
- Your signature, and those of the escrow agent, District Director and any other party to the escrow agreement;
- Any other specific information the District Director requests.

10. Give a daytime telephone number where you may be reached.

11. Give the name, address and telephone number of your attorney or other representative, if any.

12. Make the following declaration over your signature and title: "Under penalties of perjury, I declare that I have examined this application, including any accompanying schedules, exhibits, affidavits, and statements, and to the best of my knowledge and belief it is true, correct, and complete.

ADDITIONAL INFORMATION

Please follow the instructions in this publication when applying for a Certificate of Discharge of Property From Federal Tax Lien.

The District Director has the authority to issue a certificate of discharge of a lien that is filed on any part of a taxpayer's property subject to the lien. The following sections and provisions of the Internal Revenue Code Apply:

Section 6325(b)(1), if it is determined that the property remaining subject to the lien has a fair market value of at least double the sum of the amount of the unsatisfied tax liability and the amount of all other liens and encumbrances having priority over the Government's lien.

Section 6325(b)(2)(A), if there is paid in partial satisfaction of the liability secured by the lien an amount determined to be not less than the value of the interest of the United States in the property to be discharged.

Section 6325(b)(2)(B), if it is determined that the interest of the United States in the property to be discharged has no value.

Section 6325(b)(3), if the property subject to the lien is sold and, under an agreement with the Internal Revenue Service, the proceeds from the sale are to be held as a fund subject to the liens and claims of the United States in the same manner, and with the same priority, as the liens and claims on the discharged property.

1. No payment is required for the issuance of a certificate under section 6325(b)(2)(B) of the Code. Payment is required for certificates issued under section 6325(b)(2)(A). Do not send the payment with your application, however. The District Director will notify you after determining the amount due.

2. The District Director will have your application investigated to determine whether is issue the certificate, and will let you know the outcome.

3. A certificate of discharge under section 6325(b)(2)(A) will be issued upon receipt of the amount determined to be the interest of the United States in the subject property under Federal tax lien. Make remittances in cash, or by a certified, cashier's, or treasurer's check drawn on any bank or trust company incorporated under laws of the United States, or by any State, or possession of the United States, or by order. (If you pay by uncertified personal check, issuance of certificate of discharge will be delayed until the bank honors the check.

4. If application is made under section 6325 (b)(2)(A) or 6325 (b)(2)(B) because a mortgage foreclosure is contemplated, there will be a determination of the amount required for discharge or determination of the amount required for discharge or a determination that the Federal tax lien interest in the property is valueless.

Within 30 days from the date of the application, the applicant will receive a written conditional commitment for a certificate of discharge. When the foreclosure proceeding has been concluded, a certificate of discharge will be issued in accordance with the terms of the commitment letter.

5. If applications made under the provisions of section 6325(b)(3), the District Director has the authority to approve an escrow agent selected by the applicant. Any reasonable expenses incurred in connection with the sale of the property, the holding of the fund, or the distribution of the fund shall be paid by the applicant or from the proceeds of the sale before satisfaction of any claims and liens. Submit a copy of the proposed escrow agreement as part of the application.

$$\equiv\!\!\equiv 10 \equiv\!\!\equiv$$

Not Every Property
Is a Winner

Don't Let This Happen to You

Trustee's Sales and Probate Sales offer similar opportunities for the knowledgable buyer. The homework you need to do for a Trustee's Sale or Sheriff's Auction and the research required before a Probate Sale are almost identical. The disadvantage of a Trustee's Sale or a Sheriff's Auction is that the buyer is rarely able to inspect the interior of the property or its structure. Thus, it is impossible to detect needed roof, termite, foundation, and other structural repairs. This restriction significantly increases the buyer's risk. Keep these disadvantages in mind while reading the following case study of an intended purchase at a Probate Sale. As you read this chapter you will learn:

- Where to find the appraised property values in the area you plan to purchase
- The importance of using more than one appraisal source and exhibits and illustrations of the different appraisal sources
- The importance of calculating the costs of fixing, repairing, or rehabilitating a property before committing yourself to bidding at the sale
- How to avoid the pitfalls of following the crowd and why others pay too much for property and suffer the consequences later
- To obtain free advice from the professionals and how to use it
- How to avoid the errors most commonly made
- The essential elements of any bid or offer that will make you profits before you own the property
- The major research elements that will give you the insider knowledge to buy real estate for 10 to 30 percent below market value at the auction.

A CASE STUDY

Buying at an Auction

You can learn from your successes, but you can also learn from your failures. The following account is included to show that there are some bids you do not want to win and there are some properties you lose through no fault of your own. By that I mean that there are times when all the homework in the world won't prepare you for the situation you find yourself in. *When in doubt, don't*; there are thousands of properties out there; another one will come along soon enough. In the long run, homework is never wasted; you always learn something useful from the work you have done to learn about properties.

Most metropolitan Sunday papers carry advertisements by various competing auction companies in the classified advertisement sections. They are usually large display ads. Readers who are interested in these auctions should write directly to the auctioneers and request having their names placed on the mailing list. From that point on, expect weekly advertisements for all types of auctions including estate sales, bankruptcy sales, restaurant sales, high tech firms going out of business, even automobiles.

On February 21st at 3:00 P.M., the auctioneer of the A & B Auctioneers conducted a probate auction for the Superior Court of Alameda County. This property was at 5678 Ocean View Avenue in Oakland (see Figure 10.1).

A *probate auction* is held to sell the property of a person who has died without leaving a written will. The estate must be settled and usually the government will receive a large portion of the estate. Probate sales are auctions similar to those held for the Trustee's Sales. The preparation for bidding the two types of sales are almost identical. The major difference is that before a Trustee's Sale there is rarely an opportunity to inspect the property nor to have professional home inspectors review it. Probate sales do afford an opportunity for inspection prior to the auction.

This auction was a neighborhood event with well over 100 potential bidders showing up for the auction. Only those who registered with the A & B representative and showed a cashier's check for $10,000 or more were allowed to place bids.

To advertise the sale of 5678 Ocean View Drive, the auctioneers notified all parties on their mailing list approximately 30 days before the sale. The auctioneers also placed signs in the neighborhood in conspicuous places (on telephone poles and corner posts) and had even placed a rather large sign on the home. Alert investors will be on the lookout for this type of sign since not all sales are as well attended as this one.

Before the sale, the investor should be doing the homework: Checking with local real estate people to determine the property value and possibly even checking the local Multiple Listing Service (MLS) to evaluate the neighborhood's potential for resale and rentals.

Properties sold at probate auctions are always open for inspection for a few days, so buyers may see it. This gives you time to walk through the house, look under it, and generally appraise the structure for soundness and integrity. Some auctioneers even provide termite reports. The termite report for this particular property (Figure 10.2) showed $8,635.00 in required repairs. At most auction sales, the property is sold "as is." Those are small words, but they have big

REAL ESTATE AUCTION

SUPERIOR COURT PROBATE

THE FOLLOWING TWO PROPERTIES WILL BE SOLD AT THEIR
SITES, SUNDAY, FEBRUARY 21st AT TIMES SHOWN BELOW

1:00 P.M. 7107 Arthur St. Oakland, CA
2 bedroom, 1 bath home, living room–dining room combination, fireplace, w/w carpets and drapes, hardwood floors, breakfast nook, utility room with W/D hookups, 220 v. electric service, detached garage, large fenced yard. Pest control clearance. Approx. 40'X122'. Zoned R–35. Estate of Walter Jackson, deceased, Probate No. 230279 Ala. Cnty.

INSPECTION: SAT. FEB. 13th, 12–1PM and 1/2 hour before auction.

LOCATION: Thomas Map P.12/E-5. From I–880 take Hegenberger (73rd Ave) NE direction; from I–580 take Edwards Ave/Keller Ave. to 73rd Ave. See map on reverse

----

3:00 P.M. 5678 Ocean View Dr. Oakland, CA
PRIME ROCKRIDGE AREA. Lovely 2 story stucco home, 3 spacious bedrooms w/ample closet space, full bath upstairs. Living room has built in bookcases, formal dining room with beamed ceiling, lots of natural wood, separate breakfast/bonus room adjacent to kitchen, utility area with hookups, extra 1/4 bath downstairs, large storage area, detached garage, fenced backyard. Commuters walk to BART. Close to transp. and shopping. Approx. 36'X80.72', Zoned R–35.
Estate of Edith Saunders, Conservatorship. Probate No. 232205 Ala. Cnty.

INSPECTION: SUN. FEB. 7th, 2–4PM; SAT. FEB 13TH, 2–4PM and 1/2 hour before auction

DIRECTIONS: Thomas Map P.4/D-4. Hwy 24 to College Ave. See map on reverse.

A & B
Auctioneers

Figure 10.1   Auctioneer's Announcement for Property on 5678 Ocean View (Bottom)/Map

A & B
Auctioneers

TIME AND LOCATION OF SALES: Both properties to be sold <u>ON SITE</u> Sunday, February 21st at times listed above.

FINANCING: <u>ALL CASH.</u> It is the buyer's responsibility to obtain financing at the lender of his choice.

DEPOSIT: 10% of high bid at time of auction, consisting of a cashier's check ($2,500. for Arthur St.; $10,000 for Ocean View Dr.) <u>plus</u> blank personal check for the balance of the 10%. Make cashier's check payable to your own name.

<u>BOTH</u> properties sold subject to court confirmation.

BROKER COOPERATION INVITED
WITH PRIOR REGISTRATION (24 HOURS IN ADVANCE)

THE ABOVE INFORMATION WAS SECURED FROM THE OWNER OR REPRESENTATIVE. AS ITS ACCURACY HAS NOT BEEN VERIFIED, IT IS NOT GUARANTEED.

7107 Arthur St.

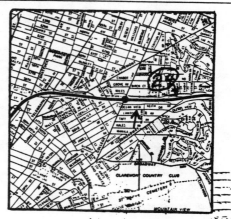

5678 Ocean View Dr.

```
NEW GROWTH ENTERPRISES
P.O. BOX 5000, STE. 412
DANVILLE, CA 94526
```

Figure 10.1 *(continued)*

STANDARD STRUCTURAL PEST CONTROL INSPECTION REPORT
(WOOD-DESTROYING PESTS OR ORGANISMS)
This is an inspection report only-not a notice of completion

ADDRESS OF	BLDG NO	STREET	CITY	DATE OF INSPECTION
PROPERTY				
INSPECTED	5678	OCEAN VIEW DRIVE	OAKLAND	12-28-87
			CO_CODE__01	

EAST BAY STRUCTURAL & TERMITE CO.
5495 CLAREMONT AVENUE
OAKLAND, CA 94618   415/652-4712

STATE OF CALIFORNIA
DEPARTMENT OF CONSUMER AFFAIRS
STRUCTURAL PEST CONTROL BOARD
REPORT OF INSPECTION   610079P

FIRM LICENSE NO. PR0417 ICO REPORT NO. _____N/A_____ ISTAMP NO. _610079P_
Inspection Ordered by(name & address) FRANCIS SAUNDERS,3518 ESMONDS AVE.,RICHMOND, 94805_
Report sent to(name & address) _____
Name & address of parties of interest _____
Owner's name & address ESTATE OF EDITH SAUNDERS C/O FRANCIS SAUNDERS._____
Original IXXI   Supplemental I I   Limited I I   Reinspection I I   # Pages __
YES|CODE see diagram   YES|CODE see diagram   YES|CODE see diagram

X	S-Subterranean Termites		FG-Faulty Grade Levels	X	CD-Cellulose Debris
	K-Dry-wood Termites		X	EC-Earth-wood Contacts		EM-Excessive Moisture Con
X	F-Fungus or Dry Rot			Z-Dampwood Termites	X	IA-Inaccessible Areas
	B-Beetles-Other Wood Pests			SL-Shower Leaks		FI-Further Inspection Rec

1. SUBSTRUCTURE AREA (soil condition, accessibility, etc.) dry accessible see below._____
2. WAS STALL SHOWER WATER TESTED? noneDID FLOOR COVERINGS INDICATE LEAKS? _see below._____
3. FOUNDATIONS (type, relation to grade, etc.)____concrete above grade.__ _____
4. PORCHES, STEPS, PATIOS_____concrete over wood;wood see below._
5. VENTILATION (amount, relation to grade, etc.)_above grade appears adequate._____
6. ABUTMENTS (stucco walls, columns, arches, etc.)__wood see below._____ _____
7. ATTIC SPACES (accessibility, insulation, etc.)_not inspected see below.
8. GARAGES (type, accessibility, etc.)__not inspected detached._____ _____
9. OTHER _____ _____

"Under the Mechanics' LEIN LAW (CALIFORNIA CIVIL CODE SECTION 3082, et seq) any
contractor, subcontractor, laborer, supplier or any other person who helps to improve your
property but is not paid for his work or supplies, has a right to enforce a claim against
your property. This means that , after a court hearing your property could be sold by a
court officer, and the proceeds of the sale used to satisfy the indebtedness.

TERMS: This contract as specified, by Owner is due and payable upon completion of work,
unless prior arrangements have been made. The Owner agrees that EAST BAY STRUCTURAL &
TERMITE CO. will be paid the contract price in full upon completion of the job. Payment
out of escrow shall be made from any funds to Owner, notwithstanding instructions from the
buyer of the property to escrow holder not to release funds held for this work. In case of
non-payment, owner agrees to pay the reasonable attorney's fees and cost of collection
whether suit is filed or not.

Our prices are subject to change after 60 days.
NOTE: Our minimum charge is $160.00.

TOTAL COST $ 8,635.00   INSPECTION FEE $ PAID
1. $ 480.00   8.$ 835.00
2.   560.00   9. 5,940.00
3.   475.00
4.   200.00
5.   25.00
6. REFER
7.   120.00

EAST BAY STRUCTURAL & TERMITE CO. IS AUTHORIZED BY THE UNDERSIGNED TO COMPLETE THE WORK
SET FORTH IN ITEM NUMBERS LISTED. _____

AT THE AGREED COST OF $ _____

SIGNATURE OF OWNER _____   TITLE CO. _____

SIGNATURE OF BUYER _____   TITLE CO. ADDRESS _____

ACCESS INFORMATION _____   _____

PROPERTY PHONE   _____   TITLE CO. PHONE # _____

OCCUPANT NAME   _____   ESCROW # _____OFFICER_____

Figure 10.2   Termite Report

meanings. If problems appear after your purchase, they are your problems. No warranty is expressed or implied—the auctioneer reads that message loud and clear into the tape recording that he makes of the actual auction. This particular property was 60 years old or more, there were water pumps in the basement, and the roof sagged. The roof didn't appear to leak, but it certainly seemed to need extensive rehabilitation in the near future.

How to Find the Value

One of the secrets of success is to know the value of what you are buying and then knowing what you can expect to get when selling it. The ability to compare various properties is a valuable talent and one common to all successful experts in distressed property. If you pay more than the house is worth, *you* will be the one in distress. The best way to ascertain the value of a property is to *ask* local real estate professionals. An appraiser would also give you a reliable report, but that would be costly if you aren't the successful bidder.

There had been numerous comparable sales in adjacent areas in the past 18 months, so our work was much easier. You should take the time to drive past each of these so-called comparables and then evaluate whether they are superior or inferior to your potential purchase. Additional data may be obtained from real estate brokers, who will have Multiple Listing Service records of comparable sales.

Title companies will also provide you with a detailed description, called a *Property Profile,* at no cost, in the hope that you will favor them in the future with your title business. Property Profile reports often show the square footage of the house, the purchase price, and other useful loan information. A successful investor should study this document carefully. It will give you a general idea of the approximate value of the property to be auctioned.

Other Appraisal Assistance

Another helpful evaluation system available to investors is the *DAMAR* system (Chapter 5). This system, known officially as the DAMAR On-Line Real Estate Information Services Report, will show data on comparable sales within a chosen grid (Thomas Brothers Map locations). This data, compiled from the assessor's records, appears to be very accurate and certainly will give you more information with which to evaluate the possible sales price.

The Ocean View Avenue area, according to the DAMAR report (Figure 10.3) showed three sales in the last five months. This data is recent enough to be considered useful. It is especially helpful to know street numbers and be able to use the square footage of the houses to compare rooms, especially bedrooms and bathrooms. Note that prices per square foot are listed with a range from high and low, which is another variable for the investor to consider.

Reviewing the Neighborhood

By referring to the second page of the report, we are able to formulate a more accurate appraisal of neighboring properties. Three recent sales are listed, all on the same street. In addition to the date of sale, we are given information on the

```
                    D A M A R   C O R P O R A T I O N
                     Real Estate Information Systems
Username: 88jan503
Password: ▓▓▓▓▓▓▓▓▓▓▓▓▓▓▓▓▓▓▓▓▓▓▓▓▓▓▓▓▓▓▓▓▓▓▓▓▓XXXXX

**********************************************************************************
                    D A M A R   C O R P O R A T I O N
                   On-Line Real Estate Information Services
                      < Copyrights 1988 DAMAR Corp. >

          Please call toll-free (800)873-2627 for customer assistance.

          >> Reported data believed reliable but accuracy is not guaranteed <<
**********************************************************************************

08-Feb-88                                                            10:04 AM

Please enter one of the following numbers or 'E' to logoff.

     1. SFR Sales Database (CA)
     2. SFR Area Sales Analysis Profile
     3. Real Property Files (CA Counties)
     4. California Statewide Owner Search
     E. Logoff from Incomnet

Enter option: 1

    ** CMDC SFR Database updated with new sales on 26-January-1988.

Your initial defaults are:

Database        : SFR Sales Database (CA)
Print Format    : 80
Sort Sequence   : Searchable Date descending
Type Ownership  : SFR

*** New Search ***                                        10:04 AM  08-Feb-88
```

Figure 10.3   DAMAR Corporation Printout

```
                    *** Summary of Selected Features ***
          1  City                  ALAMEDA
          2  City                  OAKLAND
          3  County                ALAMEDA CA
          4  Page-Grid             11-(B4)
          5  Page-Grid             4-(D4)
          6  Street Name           FAIR OAKS
          7  Street Name           OCEAN VIEW

   Most restrictive filtering parameter is Page-Grid
   Scanning 336.. 3.
   +++
   3 records found.


   Command/Feature: pri

   No. Page/Grd     Address      Date    Price     Area    $/SF  Rm Br Ba YB Sty P S
      1 4-D4      6062 OCEAN VIEW  87/12  $249,500V  1,530 163.07  5  2  2  49 1
      2 4-D4      5659 OCEAN VIEW  87/08  $288,000V  2,467 116.74  8  3 1H  30 2
      3 4-D4      5617 OCEAN VIEW  87/07  $189,500V  1,432 132.33  6  2  1  27 1

   Command/Feature: opt
```

Figure 10.3   *(continued)*

```
             ---------------------------------------------------------
                              A S A P    Report
                           Area Sales Analysis Profile

County: ALAMEDA CA                    Page/Grid: 4-D4

          Total Sales                         89
          Total Resales                        7
          Total New Home Sales (sold within one
            year of construction)

          Average Living Area Size          1953
          Average Year Built                1928
          Average Lot Area                  5361
          Average Number of Rooms           6.97
          Average Number of Bedrooms        3.06
          Average Number of Baths           1.65

          Pool= 1%   View=21%  Central Air=      Waterfront= 1%   Floodzone= 5%


Price Range (1986 only)  $95,000 to  $327,500  Predominant Value    $188,500
Age Range (entire sample)  15 yrs to  82 yrs   Predominant Age        57 yrs

% Distribution of Sales (in Thousands of $) for 1986:
  21- 30   31- 40   41- 50   51- 60   61- 70   71- 80   81-100  101-125  126-150
                                                           5%       5%       5%

 151-175  176-200  201-225  226-250  251-275  276-300  301-350  351-400  401-450
    5%      27%      16%       5%       5%      16%       5%
 451-500  501-600  601-700  701-800  801-900  901-1000   >1000


Type Loan for 1986:
Conventional            FHA           VA     Assumable     Creative          Other
      50%                                                     44%

Living Area in Square Feet (entire sample):
  200- 400  401- 600  601- 800  801-1000  1001-1200  1201-1500  1501-1750
                                    1%        2%        22%        14%

 1751-2000  2001-2500  2501-3000  3001-3500  3501-4000  4001-5000  over 5000
    16%        22%        14%         5%

Year built: Pre-1900  01-20  21-30  31-40  41-50  51-60  61-70  71-80  81-90
                        20%    47%    24%    3%     2%             1%
```

Figure 10.3 *(continued)*

```
        A V E R A G E   S A L E S   D A T A   ( B y   Y e a r )
Year  Total    Average     Average     Average    Living   $ Per    Median
      Sales    Price       Cashdown    Loan       Area     Sq Ft    Price
1986  13       $225,669    11%         $157,650   2,152    $104.86  $220,000
1985  5        $176,400    25%         $121,600   1,986    $88.79   $184,000
1984  9        $180,888    19%         $131,780   1,915    $94.44   $183,000
1983  6        $169,666    41%         $116,830   2,087    $81.29   $159,500
1982  6        $137,083    28%         $73,910    1,680    $81.55   $130,000
1981  2        $130,568    13%         $56,500    1,556    $83.91   $174,136
1980  8        $148,875    25%         $116,042   1,739    $85.60   $140,000
1979  12       $121,608    21%         $96,218    1,987    $61.18   $117,000
1978  10       $103,450    24%         $78,760    2,017    $51.28   $112,500
1977  18       $72,661     20%         $55,912    1,946    $37.32   $75,000

   DAMAR Corporation (c)1988    Real Estate Information Systems    (800)873-2627
   -------------------------------------------------------------------

Please enter one of the following:
  <NEW>      To generate a new ASAP report
  <OPTION>   To select another database
  <LOG>      To log-off
:
        A V E R A G E   S A L E S   D A T A   ( B y   Y e a r )
Year  Total    Average     Average     Average    Living   $ Per    Median
      Sales    Price       Cashdown    Loan       Area     Sq Ft    Price
1986  13       $225,669    11%         $157,650   2,152    $104.86  $220,000
1985  5        $176,400    25%         $121,600   1,986    $88.79   $184,000
1984  9        $180,888    19%         $131,780   1,915    $94.44   $183,000
1983  6        $169,666    41%         $116,830   2,087    $81.29   $159,500
1982  6        $137,083    28%         $73,910    1,680    $81.55   $130,000
1981  2        $130,568    13%         $56,500    1,556    $83.91   $174,136
1980  8        $148,875    25%         $116,042   1,739    $85.60   $140,000
1979  12       $121,608    21%         $96,218    1,987    $61.18   $117,000
1978  10       $103,450    24%         $78,760    2,017    $51.28   $112,500
```

Figure 10.3 *(continued)*

size of the houses, the price per square foot, the number of rooms and the number of bedrooms and bathrooms—all very useful information for comparison purposes. For example, the home referred to as 5617 Ocean View Avenue appeared to be comparable to the one we were interested in at 5678 Ocean View in terms of repair, size, and the characteristics of the adjacent homes on either side. The second nearby property that had recently been on the market, at 5659 Ocean View, was considerably larger—by almost 1,000 square feet—much younger and significantly more stately, in addition to being in an excellent state of repair. The third recently sold property shown on the report was 6062 Ocean Avenue, only a few blocks away. However, the neighborhood changed dramatically in the few blocks from 5600 to 6000. The homes in the 6000 block and beyond were superior in terms of condition and exterior improvements.

The third page of the report shows other sales within the particular Thomas Brothers Map grid for the last 14 months.

The final pages of the report show an Area Sales Analysis Profile for the same grid with data such as total sales, total resales, new homes, average living area size, average year built, average lot area, average number of rooms, average number of bedrooms, and average number of bathrooms.

The last page gives the predominant value for the area and the predominant price. The average sales data by year is the last item given in the report.

Determining What to Bid

The objective of purchasing at the Trustee's Sale or Probate Auction is to buy the property below market so that it can be sold at market or, if rehabilitated, sold at a price that is above market, and thereby return the rehabilitation costs and generous profits.

The first step is to decide what a fair profit margin would be for an undertaking of this nature. After all, Trustee's Sales and Probate Sales require cash to the auctioneer and then more cash is needed to rehabilitate the project.

Assuming that a fair profit after expenses is 8 percent of the selling price, the author set the profit at $15,000. If the property requires extensive rehabilitation, you may want to increase this percentage dramatically, because you will need extra money to compensate yourself for the effort, time, and resources required to accomplish the rehabilitation.

No one can predict exactly what a house will sell for, but averages are pretty useful. With the information gleaned from the assessor's records, local real estate agents, property profile reports from the title company, and computer report databases such as DAMAR you should be able to decide the market value of the house and from that estimate a reasonable bid—*reasonable* in this case meaning one giving you a profit.

After reviewing all of the appraisal sources available, the assessors records, brokers comparables, DAMAR, and property profiles, it was concluded that we should be able to re-sell the property for $195,000. With that figure in place and an estimated profit figure in mind it was a simple matter of subtracting the expected rehabilitation expenses and the expected carrying costs.

- Brokerage commissions were calculated on a straight percentage of the selling price; in the Oakland area, that is 6 percent. Our estimate for

repair of termite damage was taken from the report shown in Figure 10.2;
20 percent was added for probable cost overruns.

- We obtained a bid for a new roof from a local roofing company.
- Carrying costs include payment and taxes and we estimated that it would
take four months to sell the house because the average selling time in the
county was 100 days.
- Bids for exterior paint and stucco repairs and for the interior painting
were obtained from a local handyman.
- The Home Warranty was included because most buyers expect some warranties.
- The closing costs were estimated at 1 percent.

The estimate of the value of the property and costs to repair were as follows:

Ultimate selling price	$195,000
Less (the following are planned expenses):	
Real estate brokerage commissions @ 6%	11,700
Termite repair ($8,600 + 20%)	10,300
New roof	9,000
Carrying costs ($2,000/mo. × 4)	8,000
Exterior paint & stucco repair	3,500
Interior paint	1,000
Home warranty & closing costs	1,500
Expenses	45,000
Project profit	15,000

To estimate a reasonable purchase (bid) price, one must deduct expenses of
selling, repairing and holding the property from the selling price.

Ultimate selling price	$195,000
Less: Total costs	60,000
Top bid	$135,000

From that calculation, I decided that a good starting bid would be $120,000.
Not only is it important that you calculate these figures, but also that you
remember them. Auctions can be heated affairs and it is very easy to get caught up
in the excitement of the atmosphere which keeps the price going up, up, up.

At the Auction

The first bid of the auction was $200,000. There was a gasp from the audience.
Here was an opportunity to make money, and this buyer in haste and greed
passed up a legal bargain. He could have saved himself thousands of dollars.
Poor tactics, poor strategy, and poor market knowledge. That first bidder ultimately bid $212,000 for a property that was worth at most $195,000 *after* repairs.
Those repairs would bring the price of the house to over $220,000. This buyer
would pray for inflation!

Knowledge of the market is vital if you are going to be successful. Knowledge of the costs of selling and repairing are essential if you plan to make profits.

The lesson is: Do your homework. Know the value and expect to review many properties to get those few that will bring in the big dollars. The success stories all use the same formula.

TEN COMMON MISTAKES MADE BY PURCHASERS AT THE TRUSTEE'S SALE

Following is a list of pitfalls. If you don't see them (or choose to ignore them), you may find yourself in trouble. The list is also, if you look at it positively, a checklist. Pay attention to these items as you do your homework and you'll find you're walking on steadier ground.

- Prepayment Penalties: Read the Deed of Trust for the requirements; these can really hurt.
- Other Trust Deeds on the property: Check the files at the County Recorder's office.
- Liens: Ask the Title Company to help; the most common are tax liens for unpaid taxes (back taxes), federal, state, and county; also possible are mechanic's liens and other claims against the property.
- Judgments against the previous owner: Check the county records.
- Ownership: Review the Grant Deed to find out whether the occupant actually does own the property.
- Appraisal: Have one done to make sure that the value is higher than the mortgage.
- Property damage: Be aware that the seller might destroy the property before leaving; do not, under any circumstances, pay out or, indeed, give the seller any money, until the property is vacated.
- Underestimating of the cost of repairs: The key to determining repair costs is to ask professionals to bid and then compare the bids. When you get the reports—termite, roof, and foundation and structure (the professionals will do this for you if you don't feel qualified yourself)—review all the clauses; most investors don't. Keep records and use the checklist and forms.

The successes have been very profitable, but I've discovered that I've learned more from the failures than from the successes.

=== 11 ===

Negotiations

Win without Losing Your Shirt

At every stage in the purchase and resale of property, you will be negotiating something. People do not make decisions easily. Once a decision is made, they have to convince themselves that it is a good one. Having gone through the effort of negotiating, making up their minds, and proving to themselves that the decision is sound, they are reluctant to re-open the matter. In the process of deciding, they have further committed themselves by telling others that the deal is reasonable, so it becomes even harder to resist escalation. The difference between what they thought they were going to get and what they actually get becomes relatively less important.

Make it difficult to get! People put greater value on things that are hard to get. Sellers and buyers don't appreciate easy victories as much as they should. If you really want to make them feel good, make them work hard for everything they get. Don't be in a big hurry to make concessions, to offer extra money or service.

PATIENCE

Foreclosure buyers must learn to exercise patience in all negotiations. By using patience, you will give the seller time to understand your viewpoint before he or she settles on the price. It takes time to understand the issues, weigh the risks, and determine one's expectations. Patience gives the seller and the family time to get used to the idea that what they wish for must be reconciled with the realities of what they can get. In a quick negotiation, this is not possible.

Patience therefore is a major component of negotiations. Patience gives the buyer and seller a chance to find how best to benefit each other before a negotiation begins. It is not possible for either side to know the best way to resolve the problems, issues, and risks. New alternatives are discovered as information is brought to light. Both sides can benefit as a result of patient bargaining.

Patience works. This is what it can accomplish for you; it:

- Divides the seller's family. The anxious members of the family tire quickly of waiting and begin to pressure the procrastinator.

247

- Can lower the other party's expectations. If members of the other party are anxious and concerned about making a deal, they will lower their aspirations if you are patient and wait them out.

- Leads to concession after concession. Patience and the fact that you don't *need* to deal could easily create doubt in the opposition's mind. To relieve that anxiety the opposition will make concessions in the hope of concluding the negotiations.

- Forces a new look at priorities. The members of the other party know their own motivation better than you do and your patience will cause them to review their best alternative and, if they have no other alternatives, they will mentally begin to re-evaluate their priorities, which could mean cash today or nothing at the Trustee's Sale tomorrow.

- Separates wishes from realities, forcing the opposition to lower unrealistic expectations to consummate a real world negotiation.

- Brings new problems and issues to the surface. Maybe the opposition is under time pressure. Possibly it is the money that's important or it is the terms. Maybe a balloon payment is due. Try to ferret out any new problems that patience itself or delay will cause.

- Gets other people involved. The possibility that the deal won't close right away will cause anxiety and doubt on the part of the opposition. Expect the opposition to bring more fire-power to the table: different family members, co-workers, senior officers, each trying to finish, to draw the negotiations to a close.

- Can cause a change in leadership from husband to wife. Your negotiations may have been with the less motivated or the procrastinator of the family. The party that feels the most threatened may step forward and make the concessions needed to complete the deal.

- Allows third parties to mediate. Patience will create the opportunity of bringing in an independent third party to help the two sides resolve their differences.

START WITH THE EASY ISSUES

It is better to start talks with those issues that are easy to settle rather than with the highly controversial ones. Agreement on controversial issues is easier to reach if the issues are tied to other issues discussed earlier in the procedures on which agreement was more easily reached. Among the easy issues, you might include: When will they move to a new location? Who will be responsible for the house cleaning upon departure? Among the difficult issues would be the questions of how much and when the selling party gets the money.

In discussing issues, of whatever kind, keep in mind:

- It is more effective to present both sides of the issue than one side.

- When the pros and cons of an issue are being discussed it is better to present the viewpoint you favor last.

- Listeners remember the beginning and end of a presentation better than they remember the middle.
- Listeners remember the end better than the beginning, particularly when they are unfamiliar with the arguments.
- Conclusions should be clearly reviewed rather than left for the seller to decide what he thinks was decided.
- Repetition of a message will help the other party to understand the issues and accept them.

Questions and answers can be regarded as negotiations in their own right. Every question has the character of a demand. Every answer is a concession. Those who demand better answers in the right way are more likely to get them. Negotiators who have the guts to be skeptical and to demand evidence get more information.

THE DON'TS

- Don't pick just any time to ask a question; wait for the right time.
- Don't interrupt if the other person is talking. Write your question down and wait.
- Don't think you are a Perry Mason. A negotiation is not a courtroom trial.
- Don't ask antagonistic questions unless you want to fight.
- Don't ask questions that cast doubt on the honesty of the other party. They won't make him honest.
- Don't talk; listen. Explain the benefits and the gains.
- Don't assume that the opponent knows what he has to gain from a settlement.

THE DO'S

- Do write out your questions in advance. Few of us are bright enough to think on our feet.
- Do use every early contact as a fact-finding opportunity. A telephone response questionnaire is a valuable asset for getting fact about the seller.
- Do ask questions like a "country boy," down to earth, not like a sophisticated negotiator. This attitude encourages more informative answers.
- Do shut up after you raise a question.
- Do ask some questions for which you already have the answers. It can help you gauge the credibility of the other man.
- Do have the courage to ask questions that pry into the seller's affairs. Most of us don't like to.
- Do have the courage to ask what may appear to be dumb questions.

- Do have the courage to ask questions that may be evaded. Evasion in itself tells a story.
- Do be persistent in following up your questions if the answer is evasive or inadequate.
- Do ask questions of the seller's wife, children, relatives, and neighbors. They'll give you better answers than the seller will.

PLAN AHEAD

Do not go into a negotiation without listing every issue beforehand. Determine the price you will pay (this is your aspiration level) and the minimum and maximum initial price for each issue.

Do not be tempted to play it by ear. Nobody is smart enough to know all the answers unless he or she has thought about the issue beforehand. Never let an issue be discussed unless you are prepared for it. If you are unprepared to handle an issue when it is raised, ask for a recess to think it over or delay the decision until another day.

DEADLOCK

Deadlock is one of the most important tactics in negotiations. There is almost nothing that tests the strength and resolve of an opponent like deadlock. Most people are afraid of it. Alienation and deadlock have a traumatic effect on people. Having gone into a negotiation desiring agreement, we are left at the impasse with a sense of failure. We tend to lose confidence and question our own judgment. Was there something different we could have said or done? Should we have accepted the last offer?

For you, the power of deadlock lies in your understanding what it does to both parties. It is a test of resolve and strength. The buyer and the seller become more flexible after a deadlock. Both are more willing to compromise, especially if an escape in good faith is possible (face saving). If you are willing to reach a deadlock, you are in a position to get better results.

KNOW WHAT YOU WANT

Chester Karrass, in his book *Give and Take* (Thomas T. Crowell, New York) said again and again: "People who had higher aspiration levels got high settlements. Those who expected less were willing to accept less." According to Karrass, an individual's level of aspiration represents his intended performance goal. It is a reflection of how much he wants. It is a standard he sets for himself. It is not a wish, but a firm intention to perform and it involves his self-image. Failure to perform results in loss of self-respect. Karrass further elaborated that aspiration levels, risk taking, and success are related. In choosing goals, men are like gamblers placing a bet. They balance a need for success with its tangible and intangible rewards against the probability of failure and its possible costs. He went on to say: "People who know where they are going and why make better negotiators."

The outcome of successful negotiation depends on the power you have and your skill at using your power. There is no specific rule that states what is fair and what is not fair. Negotiation usually determines the outcome of who gets paid the most.

WHAT IS THE LOWEST PRICE YOU CAN BUY IT FOR?

One of the best reasons for making an offer a person can't accept is to help zero in or focus on what he will accept. When people believe that no deal is likely, they talk candidly with one another. It is then that the real motivation and goals are revealed. There is no good reason why a man cannot then follow up with bargaining in good faith. So make an offer he or she must refuse.

PROBLEMS AS OPPORTUNITIES

Concentrate on your opponent's problems. They are your opportunities. Don't forget that you are at the negotiation because you believe you have something to gain by being there.

OFFERS AND DEMANDS

Don't set the initial demand too close to your final objective—leave some room for negotiation.

There is insufficient evidence to conclude that it pays to start low. Don't be shy about asking for everything you might want and more. Don't set your initial offer too close to your expected final objective. Leave some room to negotiate. Otherwise you will be too rigid and the other party will not have the satisfaction of negotiating with you. If you stop negotiations too soon and make very few concessions of any kind, the other party will feel that you are not flexible and have little interest in the consummation of the agreement. The negotiation must be win-win-win and satisfactory to both parties.

- Do not assume you know what your opponent wants.
- Do not assume your aspiration level is high enough. It is possible your demands are too modest.
- Never accept the first offer. First, your opponent is probably willing to make additional concessions. Second, your opponent will be left with the feeling that perhaps he was a bit foolish for starting at the wrong price.
- Don't be intimidated by the "last and final" offer.
- Don't be afraid to admit you have made an error in coming to an agreement.

- Do not make your own "last and final" offer until you have evaluated precisely how the statement will be made and how discussions will be continued if it is not accepted.

CONCESSIONS

Never give a concession without obtaining one in return. A concession granted too easily does not contribute to the opponent's sense of satisfaction as much as one he struggles to obtain.

Do not agree with an opponent who claims that an issue is beyond compromise.

When the opponent makes a concession, don't feel guilty or shy about accepting it. Be matter-of-fact and resist the impulse to tell the opponent how wise he is to give the concession.

Don't make the first concession. Concessions that are easily made can serve to separate the parties rather than bring them together.

Keep track of how many concessions you make. The final number is an important matter that can provide bargaining leverage. Keep a record.

Do not signal your concessions too clearly. Be careful of setting up predictable patterns. Each concession should point to a possible settlement. However, your opponent should not be confident that he can foresee where it will be made or whether it will be made.

Don't worry if they don't like you. In the final phase of negotiations, you will not succeed in winning your objectives if you also try to be popular.

IT MUST BE WIN-WIN

Negotiation is not a contest. With a little effort a better deal can be found for both parties. Never fear to negotiate, no matter how great the differences are.

To put you on the right track from the seller's viewpoint, ask yourself three simple questions:

1. What decision do I want the seller to make?
2. Why has he not already made that decision?
3. What action can I take that would make it easier for the seller to make the decision to sell?

=====12=====

Financing and Managing a Small Business

How to Find Money and Markets

For any business, the bottom line never varies: Those who become successful had planned for it. They have done their homework thoroughly, with diligence and a high degree of motivation. Success is achieved through persistence and planning. Those who are aware of these facts and willing to take the trouble will succeed. In this chapter, you will learn:

- To build a long-term relationship with your banker
- To structure your loan applications so that they get attention
- To reduce the banker's risk
- To work out a business plan
- To raise money from zero, using hidden assets, credit sources, nonbank borrowing, and vendors
- To manage the purchase and resale of distressed property as a successful small business.

The reasons banks turn down loans are varied and numerous. Lack of patience is one of the most common faults of new business people. Sooner or later, if you decide to do business in the foreclosed property market, you will need the services of a bank because that is where the money is. Banks are in business to lend money, but they always want their money back, with interest. A good banking relationship will take time. Don't assume that you will walk into the bank, shake a few hands, and then be on your way with a briefcase full of money.

It doesn't happen that way. It doesn't even make sense. Would you, as a trained businessperson, lend money quickly to an unknown person or entity? Never! You would spend time getting to know the person and the business and find out what the money was going to be used for.

What you are going to do is to educate your banker and make him or her your friend. But for now let us get back to this matter of patience. The bank does want your business but it wants it on terms that will enable it to make money, not lose it. Your job will be to educate and build confidence that you know what you are doing and to demonstrate how you will pay the bank back.

Remember that you are trying to cultivate a long-term relationship. You plan to purchase more than one distressed property, don't you? If yours is a one-shot deal, the banker probably won't waste time with you. After all, he only has so much time and he understands that building this relationship will take time and lots of effort on his part. The time you take to educate the loan officer is time he spends being educated. The bank expects its loan officers to make productive, profitable loans with the minimum amount of risk, in a short time, and efficiently. Patience is a virtue that is respected by the loan officers. If you have patience, you are demonstrating your ability to plan for a long-term relationship.

Lack of patience usually indicates that you have a crisis pending. Remember, bankers love to lend you money when you *don't* need it. By demonstrating your patience, you indicate your confidence in yourself and your business proposal. Thinking for the short-term, lack of planning, lack of knowledge, and lack of confidence in yourself will kill any deal. Slow down and do your homework. You must know what you want the money for; how much you will want—to the penny; how much you will be needing as a reserve—to the dollar; how long the money will be out of the bank; how you will pay the bank its interest and principal; when and from what source you will pay. *Be prepared.* One of the most common errors committed by people new to business is to visit the bank to request a loan, but have no business plan.

TEN REASONS FOR TURNING DOWN A LOAN

When bankers review loan applications, they are looking for elements in the deal that will give them security—the assurance that the money they lend will be returned to them at a profit and within a reasonable time. They turn down loans when they have doubts. Reasons for rejecting loan applications vary from bank to bank, but they are likely to include the following. If the prospective borrower has:

- Inadequate collateral
- Little management experience
- Little business experience
- No other sources of repayment except the purposes for which the loan is being sought
- No track record
- A poor credit rating
- Insufficient income
- Too much debt (referred to as "being overleveraged")
- Provided little information—a formal loan request or a written business plan are essential
- Too speculative a purpose for requiring money.

A smart borrower will review this list and, if possible, make sure that each of these concerns of the loan officer is addressed within his business or personal loan request.

BE PREPARED—AND BEAT THE COMPETITION

Look at things from the banker's perspective. First review in depth, that is, really study the reasons loans are turned down and find any that would apply to you. If you prepare an answer for the banker that will eliminate his concerns, you are miles ahead of your competition. Don't forget you are not selling your deal at this point. You are solving the banker's problems and answering his questions. He wants to lend the money—that's what he is in business for. The key to the vault is in resolving his apprehensions and anxieties. Be prepared.

Build up your banker's confidence by demonstrating your planning ability and your overall business acumen. This preparation will raise you to the rank of good customer, but it won't be accomplished without patience and planning on your part.

Obtaining and maintaining a good relationship with a bank is a major rung in the ladder to success. Without the banker, your success and progress toward financial independence will be slowed considerably. The long-term relationship will develop only if you are honest and reliable. Your credibility will be demonstrated each time you perform as you agreed to in your loan contract.

Remember the five questions the banker will ask, no matter who wants the loan. He will ask:

- What is the purpose of the loan?
- How much money do you want?
- How long do you want the money for?
- How are you going to repay?
- If the deal does not work out as planned, where will you get the money to repay?

Make sure that you can answer these questions in detail.

Remember, bankers want to lend you the money. However, they like to lend money with the least amount of risk. if you can show more than one method of repayment, the banker will know you understand the problem. Eliminate the bank's risk as much as possible. For example, you plan to borrow to buy the house, fix it up, and sell it again. If the market is slow and you can't sell to repay the bank, what will you do? If you don't know, it is best to figure out a solution *before* you apply for the loan. Preparation is the key to the vault. It is a simple formula. Make the banker's work less risky and you're building friendships and credibility.

QUESTIONS TO ASK YOURSELF

- How can you prepare a business plan that will have the greatest appeal to bankers and investors?
- What the bankers and investors look for and look out for in any business plan?

- What should you emphasize?
- What should you play down?
- How should you package the plan for greatest effect?

THE COVER LETTER

Start with a cover letter. In it explain your request, briefly. Be sure to include a current financial statement.

Write a narrative explanation of what you are trying to accomplish. This written report should both clarify your thinking and be easily understandable to the banker.

A business plan can be a tremendously complicated document or it can be a mental sketch inside the entrepreneur's head. The latter is more likely. Attempt to commit your business plan to writing, especially if you foresee the need for future funding. Once you put your thoughts on paper, the plan will begin to materialize. First of all, it must be perceived as being market driven rather than real estate driven.

The process of assembling a business plan is really a matter of evaluating the market, and making forecasts and projections based on where you are today and where you intend to go.

Here are a few steps and requirements that you should be thinking about as you begin to plan your distressed property business.

What do you expect to accomplish three to seven years into the future? Try to explain in narrative form, in simple and understandable terms, the benefits you can offer to your clients. In this business, you have two groups of clients: Those from whom you buy (you help them by giving them something for their property) and those to whom you sell (you supply a commodity they want at an affordable price). In deciding which category of the distressed property market to tap, you need to know whether you can best solve the problems of owners whose lenders are foreclosing on them; or the bankers who have had to take back the property because the loan has been foreclosed and nobody picked up the property at the Trustee's Sale.

ADVERTISING

Try to justify in your own mind how best to sell your products. Will it be by newspaper ads, fliers, or brokers? Reduce your thoughts to a narrative explanation. It will make you rethink your plan and approach to the market place.

MANAGEMENT

Try to review the details of management. Ask yourself:

- If you purchase a ten-unit property, who will manage it?
- Is that the best use of your time?
- Who will handle the rehabilitation to fix the property up?

Think about partners or investors, ask:

- Will they be part-owners or stockholders?
- Who will vote and who will manage?
- Is there a potential for conflict?
- How will you handle the conflicts?
- Do you need a written contract between the parties or is every one a member of your family?
- Is the business going to be run as a corporation or would partnership be better?

If this is to be a team effort, who is the leader or will decisions be made by consensus only? What is the experience level of the other team members? What skills will they bring to the venture?

Will the partners who provide money actually work? Or will they just wait for your reports and expect performance statements? Will you have a manager?

Are your skills complementary or do you have the skill and the others the money?

Do you all have the same goals? Is the investment group committed to move in the same direction in unison? Have you discussed the group's ultimate objective?

FINANCIAL PROJECTIONS

When it comes to financial projections, be aware that they will be estimates only, but make them credible. Is it possible for you to explain in narrative form what the projections mean and what is meant by each item?

Don't balloon the values of properties, automobiles, and other assets. Include appraisals, if available. Pictures, diagrams, and maps are helpful. Prices taken from the Multiple Listing Service (MLS) of comparable properties will enhance your credibility and allow the banker to compare your project with similar real estate values.

The section on financial data will show what funds are needed from banks, investors, and yourself. It should show how you intend to raise the money and how you intend to use it. How you plan to pay it back. Keep in mind that lenders and investors will have different objectives and that their objectives will be different again from yours.

DON'T FORGET YOUR EXIT PLAN

Do you have an exit plan? How will you cash out of this business? How will you cash out of each property? Will you become a lender? Is the plan agreed to by everyone? How will you sell the business?

FOCUS ON THE OBJECTIVES

Make sure your plan has a focus: Is there a customer to buy your real estate? Do the investors get a good return? Have you found a market niche? Have you decided on the location of or the type of distressed property you intend to purchase? What will make you unique? Will it be your financial savvy? What funds do you need?

New businesses seeking loans (funding) must always submit a business plan. The plan will help you crystallize your thinking by clarifying your objectives. A good business plan will keep all the company personnel focused on the company's major objectives.

Convincing business plans are what the bankers and investors are searching for. The skill required to write a business plan will be used again and again in your business future. No matter who prepares the plan, the incentives you are offering the bankers and the investors must be thought out and understood and appreciated.

Try to answer the questions about how much up-front investment in time, money, and effort is required. The questions about risk will be answered if you will take the time to evaluate and plan.

Evaluating what you do best should be part of your planning process. Concentrate on the one or two things you do best which maximize your strengths.

Don't spend all your time in the business plan evaluating the real estate. Try to spend a significant amount of time on your planning skills and how you will market and sell the products. No one makes any money till you sell something.

Decide how fast you will grow. Is it a realistic projection? Will you do just one property at a time? Will you branch out and take over other companies or do you want to run this business from your home and keep it small? Where will you get the money? If your projections are too spectacular no one will believe them. You'll lose your credibility! Do your homework, be conservative, and then outperform your projections.

CONFLICTS

Even the most optimistic plan will have some drawbacks. Positives and negatives must be confronted head on. Don't discount the caution flags and don't ignore the red flags. It is easier to confront them in the plan and make allowances for them than to be completely surprised later.

EMPHASIS

The importance of the market research is second to no other part of the business plan. If there is no market, you have no business. Describe your market and why you will be successful within that market. Show hard evidence of your market knowledge, state clearly who will buy your real estate and why. Describe in detail how you will locate and then sell your distressed property purchases.

BORROW YOUR WAY TO WEALTH

To build a real estate empire starting from zero is difficult but not impossible. It requires that you become resourceful, very flexible, and creative. Don't spend all your earnings on consumer goodies—cars, TV, eating out. Save those hard-earned dollars to build a real estate empire. If you spend only on essentials, you soon will have a cash hoard to get you started or to help you to continue to grow financially. Real estate that appreciates is like money in the bank: It continues to grow and produce profits year after year.

PARTNERSHIPS

If you have little or no money available to purchase your next property, then you will need to think about partnerships, joint ventures, and properties that do not need a down payment. Let's think things through together. The following paragraphs contain a few suggestions that you may find helpful.

Start making a list of people you know who might need some extra income from an investment that they don't have to work at. How about a fifty-fifty partnership? You could purchase a distressed property with their money. Your experience and labor could contribute the other half of the investment.

How about forming a small group of investors, a syndicate? Assuming you need $5,000 to buy a property before the Trustee's Sale, could you find ten friends, relatives or co-workers each prepared to put up $500.00? I don't suggest that you put them all on the deed as co-owners. This could create a cumbersome situation when you sell. Consider instead an informal written agreement or a partnership agreement. They put up the money; you do the work. On their behalf you purchase, manage, fix up, and sell the property. Both sides of the partnership benefit.

NEED A DOWN PAYMENT?

Most property purchases need down payments. You have no money for the down payment? Do you own life insurance? Most whole-life policies allow you to borrow against them. The interest rate on such loans is normally substantially below market rates. Check your policy. You will be surprised at how cheap it is to borrow.

If borrowing is impracticable, remember that term insurance is cheap. You can probably cash in your old whole-life policy and purchase good term insurance for a much smaller annual payment. You will then have a lump sum in cash to buy and rehabilitate one or more distressed properties.

ADVERTISE FOR THE CASH

You can advertise for the cash you need. Place the advertisement in your local newspaper under *Money Wanted*. Don't be surprised if the newspaper asks you to pay in advance.

To succeed with an advertisement for money, you need a unique selling proposition (USP). You need to offer, for example, a short-term or a high yield, or some security for the money partner. After all, who are you? That is the question you must answer before the investor calls. Plan your presentation, otherwise you will ramble. Give information on the facts and benefits for the investor right away. Be sure your incentives are adequate to attract people who have the money.

Everyone can get between 5 and 7 percent interest in any bank. You must offer 25 percent or even 50 percent to attract good investors.

CREDIT CARDS

Some very creative investors in real estate actually use the cash provisions of their credit cards to start building their wealth. The rate of interest on the borrowed money is high but certainly no higher than the rate you would pay a joint-venture partner.

GOOD JOB, GOOD CREDIT

Many small finance companies will lend you money if you have a good job and your credit rating is good. If you have a short-term real estate deal such as a foreclosure or pre-Trustee's Sale purchase, the transaction will probably have more than enough actual return to pay the high interest of a finance company loan and still leave you with substantial profits and your credit rating enhanced. If your credit rating is less than desirable, even disastrous, you had better start looking for a co-signer for the note. Sometimes small finance companies will take the co-signer's property as security or collateral.

WHAT ABOUT YOUR BOSS?

Many employers will advance funds for education, new cars or trucks, sometimes even down payments for the first home. Your employer might be prepared to provide the down payment and take title to the house while you do the work. You would then split the profits. As an added incentive, the employer might receive all the tax benefits.

CREDIT UNIONS

Does your firm have a credit union? Does a member of your family work for a firm that has a credit union? This could be a great source of cash. Credit unions sometimes request payment on the loan be deducted from your paycheck, so keep that in mind. Credit unions may lend money to you and your new-found partner if you both have existing savings accounts, which will provide the needed security.

HYPOTHECATION

You need also to be aware that most lenders require some sort of security and will accept hypothecated securities. By hypothecation, you are pledging assets but are not required to deliver to the lender either title to those assets, or the assets themselves. Thus, you might have the ability to pledge your car, your tools, your other property, or even your skills (barter).

HOME IMPROVEMENT LOAN INSURANCE (TITLE I)

There are a number of other sources of money, especially for fixing up property for re-sale. Uncle Sam, for one, has various loan programs that will advance money for property rehabilitation. The Department of Housing and Urban Development (HUD) allows credit unions and other qualified lenders to make home improvement loans from their own funds and, in exchange for a premium, insures the lender against a possible loss.

These loans may be used for any improvements that make the home more livable and useful. They cannot be used for luxury items or to pay for work already done. The Housing and Community Development Act of 1974 provided that the loans may also be used to finance improvements to conserve energy or to install solar energy systems.

The loan may be for up to $17,500, bear interest up to no set limit, and be paid back within 15 years. Lenders determine eligibility for and process these loans, generally as unsecured personal loans. Loans in excess of $2,500, excluding finance charges, must be secured with a lien (a mortgage or Deed of Trust) against the improved property. Loans in excess of $17,500 excluding finance charges, require prior approval from HUD. Loan limits are applied only to one particular property. Individual borrowers are not subject to the limits.

Eligibility Requirements

1. Borrower(s) must have at least a one-third interest in the improved property and must hold:
   (a) a fee title
   (b) a life estate
   (c) either (a) or (b) above, subject to a mortgage, Deed of Trust etc., and hold an installment land contract or a lease that has a fixed term expiring not less than six months after the maturity of the note (unless the improvement is a built-in kitchen or carpeting, which require a 99-year renewable lease)
2. Borrower(s) must have a satisfactory credit rating
3. Borrower(s) must have enough income to repay the loan over its term
4. To the lender's knowledge, the borrower must not be past due more than fifteen days on any obligation owing to or insured by the federal government.

The advantages of the FHA Title I Home Improvement Loan program are numerous. First of all, it is easy to qualify and that can be important if you are starting out with no money. Even the requirement that you own the home is fairly easily met. You could own as a partnership, or as a joint tenant, or as a tenant-in-common. The amount loaned can be up to 120 percent of the purchase price of the house. This loan will give you the money to fix up the property and make it salable. Often the loan may be regarded as free money from the government because you yourself don't have to pay it back. Title I loans are usually fully assumable by the purchasing party. Most purchasers are happy to assume this loan for it means they will be required to provide a smaller down payment in the transaction. Figure 12.1 shows a letter from a participating savings and loan association soliciting borrowers for Title I funds; Figure 12.2 shows a newspaper advertisement placed for the same purpose. Reproduced as Figure 12.3 is the complete Title I loan application package.

PROMISSORY NOTES

Sellers of distressed property need cash, but they might be prepared to take a promissory note with either monthly or even weekly payments. This type of financing would give you the time to fix up and re-sell the property.

WHAT ABOUT THOSE VENDORS?

If you plan to use the same vendors for the paint, carpeting, appliances, and so on, or the same craftsmen, carpenters, and roofers, they may lend you money in return for the business *and* a good return on their money.

YOU MIGHT EXPECT

Whenever you borrow money, you should be aware that you will be expected to meet certain conditions:

- That you will need a co-signer
- That you will need parents, friends, and acquaintances to help
- That you will pay higher-than-market interest rates
- That your monthly payments will be higher
- That your loan terms will be shorter
- That you might be required to share your profits with the lender
- That you will need to establish a win-win-win attitude—first the seller wins, then the investor wins, and finally you win.

MANAGING A SMALL BUSINESS

This book is based on proven methods. The information has been tested and is working today. The examples are taken from actual transactions. If you apply the rules and procedures given here, you will consistently make money buying and selling foreclosure and distressed property.

Citizens
Thrift & Loan Association
Member of FDIC

Hi, let me introduce myself, my name is Kevin S. Parker Manager for **CITIZENS THRIFT AND LOAN ASSOCIATION OF CONCORD.**

We are proud to be a part of the community in this area, and are looking forward to helping your company grow and for filling all your customers needs. Let me take a few moments of your time, and out line one of the special exclusive programs we offer in this area.

YES, IT IS CALLED THE FHA-TITLE ONE HOME IMPROVEMENT LOAN this loan is a fixed rate program at 13.95% owner occupied, (non-owner occupied may be slightly higher), where equity is not a requirement, no appraisal necessary, no points, 48 hour approval, 7 day funding, up to 15 year term, fully amortized with no balloon payment or prepayment penalty.

Loans up-to $17,500 for single family residence and $43,750, for apartments,(3 units or more). The only fees involved are a processing, acquisition fee, which cannot be financed. This fee must either be paid by the customer or the Contractor/ Dealer upon funding.

Loan Amount	% Rate	Fees
$2500.00–$4999.99	15.25%	Case By Case
$5000.00–$9999.99	13.95%	$595.00
$10,000.00–$17,500.00	13.95%	$695.00
$17,501.00–$43,750.00	14.25%	$1,750.00
(Apartments only)		

By being approved by CITIZENS to offer this exclusive program, the fees are less.

Not all improvements are eligible, here is a list of a few, Kennels, Barbecue pits, Bathhouses, Burglar alarms, Burglar protection bars, Dumbwaiters, Fire alarms or fire detecting devices, Flower boxes, Green houses, Airplane hangers, Kitchen appliances which are designed and manufactured to be freestanding and are not built in and permanently affixed as an integral part of the kitchen in a residential structure, Outdoor fireplaces or hearths Steam cleaning of exterior surfaces, Swimming pools, Television antennae, Tennis courts, Tree surgery.

If you have any other questions give our office a call and one of the staff will be able to help, if I'am unavailable.
Thanks,

Kevin S. Parker
Manager Citizens Thrift and Loan Association

1390 Willow Pass ● Suite 120
Concord, California 94520 ● 415/674-1125

Figure 12.1   Citizens' Thrift and Loan Association Letter

Figure 12.2   Newspaper Advertisement for Borrowers

It won't be easy . . . are you motivated? I'm not advocating a get-rich-overnight scheme. There's really no such thing in business. I am writing about building a respectable, enduring business in foreclosure and distressed property that is based on sound and innovative business practice. What I am writing is a guide to success. Allow the book to help you and you'll be surprised how well you will do.

Success is not magic. Here are some of the reasons that small businesses were successful and some hints about managing growth. To be successful in a small business, you must wear many hats and perform numerous duties. You must be first of all an entrepreneur, then a technician, and a manager. Although it is sometimes difficult, you must know your competition and your field of expertise inside out.

To stay ahead, constantly evaluate your business so that you can incorporate innovative ideas; take the time to know your market thoroughly and be familiar with the products it values. For example, everyone wants fixer-uppers. If you know your market, you won't be purchasing the wrong property at the Trustee's Sale. Homes in the country club areas might be nice, but can you sell them easily?

Understand your weaknesses and your strengths and those of your products. Take pride in your business—after all it's an extension of you. Provide the customers with the products they want. Be sensitive, know their needs, be aware of how to reach them and, most important, what will convince them to buy your properties.

 **Citizens**
Thrift & Loan Association
Member of FDIC

Thank you for your inquiry regarding our Home Improvement Loan Program. As we discussed, this package includes the necessary forms which need to be completed. In addition to these forms please provide us with the following items which are required to fully process your application.

1. ONE MONTH'S RECENT paystub(s) for each applicant, including any part-time employment.

2. Last two years TAX RETURNS, with original signatures on the second page. Be certain to include all schedules ("A", itemized deductions, "C", self-employed profit and loss, "E", rental or partnership income). Include W-2's and 1099's if available.

3. If self-employed, provide a current year signed Profit and Loss Statement on your business.

4. If you are requesting the loan for improvements on a rental property (non-owner occupied), provide current rental agreement(s) and a current income and expense statement.

5. If more than one property is owned, complete a list of all properties owned, indicating year purchased, purchase price, mortgage holders, payments, balances, rental income and expenses and indicate the current market value.

6. Copy of any unpaid note(s) (1st, 2nd, etc.) on the subject property.

7. Copy of declaration page of current fire insurance policy showing company name, agent, address, phone number and policy number.

8. We will need your mortgage payment information on the property to be improved. A month-end or year-end statement showing loan balance, loan number, payment amount, and lender's name, address and phone number for ALL LIENS. (1st, 2nd, etc.)

9. Copy of the contract, bid, or a detailed estimate on all desired improvements, signed by you or the contractor.

STOCKTON	**CONCORD**	**SUNNYVALE**	**CITRUS HEIGHTS**
4555 N. Pershing Ave., #31	1390 Willow Pass, S-120	753-1 E. El Camino Real	8031-A Greenback Ln.
Stockton, CA 95207	Concord, CA 94520	Sunnyvale, CA 94087	Citrus Heights, CA 95610
209/952-6016	415/674-1125	408/732-5083	916/722-7566
TUSTIN	**ANAHEIM HILLS**	**IRVINE**	**SAN CLEMENTE**
17291 Irvine Blvd., S-150	5556 East Santa Ana Canyon	14252-G Culver Dr.	61 Calle De Industrias
Tustin, CA 92680	Anaheim Hills, CA 92807	Irvine, CA 92714	San Clemente, CA 92672
714/731-1803	714/921-1000	714/559-4000	714/498-7101

Figure 12.3   Citizens' Loan Application Package with Introduction Letter

INSTRUCTIONS FOR COMPLETING THE ATTACHED FORMS:

1. Be sure both applicant and co-applicant sign all forms as needed.

2. Notice to Borrower - Sign where indicated by ✓

3. FHA Application - Complete each item requested and sign the last page where indicated by ✓

4. Statement of Information - Complete and sign where indicated by ✓

5. Verification of Employment - Applicant to sign one form and co-applicant to sign the second form where indicated by ✓

6. Verification of Deposit - Both applicants to sign where indicated by ✓

7. Mortgage Rating Letter - Both applicants to sign where indicated by ✓

8. Information Disclosure Authorization - Both applicants to sign where indicated by ✓

9. Fair Lending Notice - Both to sign where indicated by ✓ and keep copy marked "Customer Copy" for your records.

We realize this is a lot of paperwork, however, to comply with the various regulations governing lending, all of this information is required. Thank you for your cooperation.

If you have any questions, please call our office. Your prompt completion and return of this package will expedite your request.

Thank you,

Figure 12.3   *(continued)*

FHA TITLE ONE
HOME IMPROVEMENT PROGRAM

UNIQUE FEATURES OF THIS PROGRAM

1. No equity required

2. May be in 2nd, 3rd, 4th lien position

3. No appraisal required

4. No costly title insurance required

5. Fixed rate for the full term, up to 15 years

6. Fully amortized, no balloon payment

7. No prepayment penalty

8. Assumable subject to approval

9. May be able to subordinate to new financing or refinancing, subject to approval

10. Financing available for most improvements such as, landscaping, fencing, room additions, roofing, patios, built-in appliances, painting

    Exclusions include luxury items such as pools, spas and drapes.

11. Loans up to $17,500.00 on a single family residence, and $43,750.00 on multi-family dwellings. Also available for retail, commercial and industrial properties, up to $17,500.00

12. Properties may be owner or non-owner occupied

13. Proceeds of your loan funded directly to you

We pledge to you a quick response to your request and will make every effort to give you an answer within one day of receiving the complete information required.

Figure 12.3 *(continued)*

Advertising is a must, but test each ad. Is it pulling in the calls? If not, drop the ad and write a new one. An ad that is met with silence is not offering your customers what they are looking for. You need an ad that will serve the customer.

Managing Your Time

Be willing to work day and night but don't do it all yourself. Prepare your helpers to handle the routine day-to-day work. If necessary, hire a consultant to help you tap the full resources of your business. Staff is the nucleus of your business. They face the customer, so select them carefully. Everyone of your employees is a different individual. Each has a different personality. Expect to treat each one differently.

Keep up with what is happening around you. Read at least one newspaper daily and know and be familiar with the financial pages. Keep up to date so that you understand the big picture.

The way to become an expert is to read. First of all, set aside time every day to read and prepare yourself for the future. If you can find only twenty minutes every day, you will have made available more than two hours a week; approximately ten hours every month. In ten hours you can easily read at least two books on real estate, finance, sales, home inspections, banking, and all the related subjects that will make you an expert. The average person reads five books each year; most read fewer. You will be way ahead of your competition if you spend 20 minutes a day reading about your business. By the time you have read 120 books about real estate and distressed properties, the world will consider you an expert!

Creating a Market Plan—Some Ideas

Effective and detailed business plans are sometimes difficult to produce. But a written business plan will cause you to crystallize your thinking. It will be your blueprint to success. Keep it flexible, so that you can adjust to market changes. Be aware that high interest rates mean more foreclosures; low interest rates mean that defaults will probably be refinanced and the properties will not appear at Trustee's Sales tomorrow. Adapt to changing circumstances. Working capital will be the critical issue. Line up investors when you have spare time. Plan your cash flow.

Define Your Business

Define your product or products. Will you be a specialist in buying the real estate owned by the banks or institutions (REO), or do you see yourself as the auction specialist, buying the Trustee's Sales? Possibly your strength lies in dealing with the homeowner before the Trustee's Sale and purchasing the property in the default period.

Define the geographical area in which you will specialize; which region— or are you prepared to work all over the United States? Describe your competition. Name names. Describe how the competition works. Describe how you are different from the competition. Describe the way you will promote your properties.

Define Your Customers

- Who are your customers?
- Who needs the kinds of property you intend to deal with?
- Give details of income, sex, age, etc.
- Describe their patterns or habits. Where do they go, what do they do, what do they read?
- What do they buy from you?
- What is it that they value and you can supply?

Define Your Advertising

How will you communicate? How do your customers find you? Decide whether you will use direct marketing, newspapers, fliers, or other means of advertising your business. What works; what doesn't? What does it cost? What about different methods? How do you test the market? What can you improve in the future?

Where Can You Get Help for a Small Business?

The Small Business Administration (SBA) sponsors SCORE, the Service Corps of Retired Executives. This organization was established in 1964 as a volunteer program staffed by retired businessmen and women. These volunteers offer their skills, knowledge and experience without cost to the owners and managers of small businesses who experience management difficulties and to people who have never been in business and want to start a business. In the United States, there are over 250 chapters of SCORE, and a membership of more than 12,000 executives.

SCORE chapters sponsor and conduct business workshops and seminars for the small business community. The members share their diverse business backgrounds and skills in such areas as management, retailing, wholesaling, accounting, marketing, manufacturing, sales promotions and advertising. What they offer is free counseling.

Staying Out of Trouble

Purchasing real property can be a risky proposition. Most new investors in foreclosure property have little experience with purchasing, repairing, and selling real property. Hundreds of experts are available to assist you with the purchase: brokers, attorneys, relatives, friends, and so on. There are experts who will help you with your inspections and repairs or you can do them yourself to save money. The big questions are always: What work needs to be completed? and What will it cost? Home inspection companies will perform detailed surveys to familiarize you with the good and bad features of what you are buying. Termite and roof companies will provide formal report within days to allow you to make up your mind about the condition of your prospective purchase. Develop reliable sources of information and your property purchases will be less eventful and you won't be confronted with surprising extra costs. If you buy a property with hidden defects, if the foundation is deteriorating, the house is infested by termites or if the roof is damaged and leaking you need to know beforehand. If you are aware of the problems you can deduct the cost of such repairs from the purchase price.

Index